THE SUGAR RUSH

THE
SUGAR
RUSH

A MEMOIR OF WILD DREAMS, BUDDING BROMANCE, AND MAKING MAPLE SYRUP

PETER GREGG

PEGASUS BOOKS
NEW YORK LONDON

From the author:
I have done my best to tell this story as close to how I remember
the 2022 maple season. I have changed many names and identifying
details, and some characters are composites of real people.

———

THE SUGAR RUSH

Pegasus Books, Ltd.
148 West 37th Street, 13th Floor
New York, NY 10018

Copyright © 2024 by Peter Gregg

First Pegasus Books cloth edition July 2024

Interior design by Maria Fernandez

Illustrations by Sarah Letteney

Library of Congress Cataloging-in-Publication Data is available.

ISBN: 978-1-63936-681-1

10 9 8 7 6 5 4 3 2 1

Printed in the United States of America
Distributed by Simon & Schuster
www.pegasusbooks.com

To

Annabel and Bruce

CONTENTS

Map   xi

Prologue   1

PART I: PRELUDE TO A SUGAR SEASON   5

EARLY DECEMBER 2021   7

1. Blossom Road   9
2. Bert   16
3. Five Pounders!   20

EARLY JANUARY 2022   27

4. The Tanks I Get   29

LATE JANUARY 2022   41

5. A Trip to Bascom's   43
6. The Maple Mecca   48
7. The Country Girl   54
8. This is Why We Can't Have Nice Things   58
9. The Pull-Out Method   61

EARLY FEBRUARY 2022   65

10. Opening Day   67
11. Enter the Maplex   74
12. Firehouse Breakfast   82
13. Call of the Wild   90
14. Hurry Up and Wait   97
15. New Saddles and a Nut Driver   105
16. I'd Tap That   110

SAMARA: SEEDS OF A LIFE IN MAPLE   117

17. My Maple Hazing   119
18. The O.G. of Sugarhouse Builders   126

PART II: THE FLOW BEGINS   131
LATE FEBRUARY 2022   133

19. Tapping the Light Fantastic   135
20. Every Great Flood Begins with a Single First Drop   140
21. First Days Always Suck   146
22. The Phenomenon of the Scorch   154
23. The Juice is Worth the Squeeze   161
24. Kinking the Loyne   168

EARLY MARCH 2022   173

25. Tapping with the Governor   175
26. The Mysterious Case of the Missing Maple   181
27. Quinlan Storms In   185
28. This Is What It All Boils Down To   190
29. To Redrill or Not Redrill?   199

MID-MARCH 2022   205

30. Vermont on a Sunny Day   207

LATE MARCH 2022   217

31. The Neighborhood Watch   219
32. Alpenglow and Moonglow   234

THE FIRST WEEK OF APRIL 2022   245

33. The Grind   247
Epilogue: Off-Season 2022   259

Acknowledgments   265

"Either you decide to stay in the shallow end of the pool, or you go out in the ocean."
—Christopher Reeve

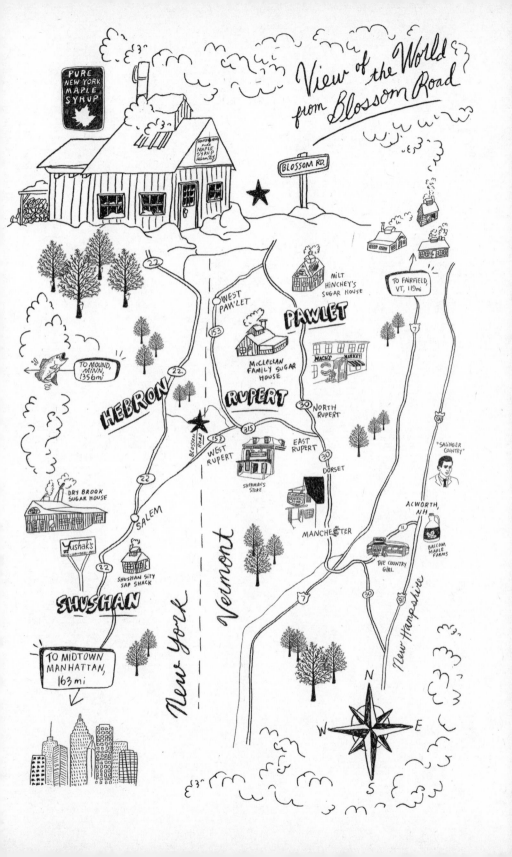

PROLOGUE

Everything was dripping everywhere. The snow was melting fast off the eaves of the sugarhouse—*ping, ping, ping*—making little wet divots in the drifts underneath. On this, the third day of February, the temperature was 55°F with blunting sunshine. That meant up on Blossom Hill, our maple trees were ready to burst like water balloons filling on a firehose.

This was it, sugaring season, the time of year when winter buckles, red stripes on thermometers dance above the freezing mark, and startled maples send sweetened sap up their trunks. Then we race to drill 'em with holes, suck out the sap by the tankerload, and furiously boil it into syrup.

This bizarre warm-up was coming a full three weeks earlier than we'd ever made syrup before. That's global warming for you, messing with your rhythms. Three weeks early or not, it was time to hike my ass up the hill, unholster the DeWalt, and start drilling those holes.

The melting snow would make the terrain slick up there, warranting crampons. Mine are the cheap kind—bought off Amazon for eighteen bucks—with an orange rubber skin that stretches over the boot and chains with sharp triangles that run along the soles. They gripped surprisingly well as I scrambled up the steepest section of Blossom Hill.

By steep, I mean it probably would have been easier to crawl up it than walk—about a 40° slope, as sheer as any double black diamond ski run in New England. When I got to the top, I paused and drew a ragged breath, let it out, watched it dissipate in the air, turned to look back down the mountain, and thought, *Maybe I should've taken up pickle farming.*

I approached the first maple on my line. Snow was heaped in the crotches of the branches and, higher up in the air, a big limb had broken off. Sap was weeping from the wound and leaching down the trunk, making it look a little bit like the tree had wet its pants. A nice juicy maple. I slapped the bark like a pat on the back. "Looking forward to working with you this season, ol' buddy," I said. If I hadn't been in a hurry, I'd've given it a hug. Reverence. I secured myself to the incline by upturning my boot perpendicular to the hill. My left arm clung to the tree, and my other hand triggered the DeWalt. With the bit rotating at maximum RPMs, I plunged it into the wood. As it gorged, a gust of vapor released. Trees are full of gases which, today, were warmer than the air. With sleight of hand, I swapped my drill for a mallet and knocked a polycarbonate spigot-like thingy called a *spout* into the hole. On each swing, oozing liquid from the punctured tree spattered back at me. A splash landed on my lips, and I swabbed it with my tongue. *Daaaamn, that's some sweet sap all right.*

Then, just like that, I took a tumble. A chunk of snow avalanched from underneath me. When falls happen up here, they happen fast. So astonishingly fast that when you're lying on your goddamned keister, you're still thinking about how great you were doing just a nanosecond before. I happen to be genetically blessed with good balance and tend to stay upright with remarkable consistency. But a dude could have the balance instincts of The Flying Wallendas and be no match for a double-crossing hillside with the gradient and integrity of a scoop of ice cream. I crash-landed line-parallel with the ground, my full weight absorbed by my vertebra. I felt a tease of the full-on body ache that was sure to come later that night or tomorrow morning.

But I got up, brushed the snow off my pants, and kept moving. *Suck it up, buttercup*, I told myself. *On to the next one.* I traversed to tree number two, drilled another hole, and pounded in another spout.

Whirrrrrurrrert—thwack, thwack, thwack.

I lingered for a moment and admired saline-clear globules of sap percolating through the head of the spout and dripping down an attached length of tubing, as it began a zig-zagging chute run through our herringbone pipeline back to a giant collection tank at the bottom of the hill.

PART I
PRELUDE TO
A SUGAR SEASON

EARLY DECEMBER 2021

1

BLOSSOM ROAD

It might be hard to believe there are dirt roads in New York, but around here you'll find quite a few. Most people think the whole state is paved. Man, if only that were true. Our commute to the sugarhouse would be so much easier. We're located about one mile up on Blossom Road, a winding canopied lane with a bare earth surface and the last left turn off NY Route 153 before you hit the Vermont state line. In the spring, when the frost gives way, the mud ruts on Blossom Road get so deep we can barely pass through in our high-clearance four-wheel drive pickup trucks. Sometimes the town highway crew will take pity on us and spread gravel over the worst sections of the pudding, but even then the lane is still very treacherous, especially in the dog days of sugaring season when we're on it the most.

No homes exist on Blossom Road. Just a few hunting cabins, a summer retreat for a software mogul from Texas, another one for a cellist from New Orleans, a small horse farm, and two sugarhouses, mine and Truman Dunn's. And we got trees. Lots and lots of trees.

In a fifteen-mile radius of Blossom Road, there are probably 200,000 tapped maple trees and two dozen sugarmakers. This includes a private equity millionaire who bought the maple-rich backside of Mount Equinox over in Sandgate a few years ago and hired a crew to install 120,000 taps.

The rest of us are farmers. And even though we're technically competitors, we go out of our way to help each other out, which is what farmers do.

I require the most help because I'm a *flatlander*, which is what you're called when you come from pretty much anywhere else but here—I'm from Minnesota, as flat as they come. Meanwhile, my neighbors have been sugaring here all their lives, tending these forests, tapping these trees, and learning maple trade secrets passed down through the generations.

Me? I grew up on a cul-de-sac.

My twenty-five-acre farm is bisected by the long linear border of New York and Vermont. The state line runs right through our woods. I tend to orient the mapling part of my life equally to the sugaring communities of both states like I have a split personality.

During the messy transition time between winter and spring, we gather sap from the besotted maple trees on the side of our mountain and boil it, evaporating out much of the water to condense its natural tree sugars into a rich amber syrup for you to pour on a pancake.

When I say syrup, I don't mean Mrs. Butterworth's or Log Cabin or any of that stuff. That's *corn* syrup with maple flavoring and aromatic compounds, agriculturally appropriated to taste like what we make. We make *maple* syrup concentrated from the sap of two species of maple tree—the sugar maple (*Acer saccharum*) and the red maple (*Acer rubrum*), producing it the same way Indigenous peoples did two hundred years ago but with modern technology.

Let me paint a picture of where all this maple madness takes place. Looking east from the top of my mountain—known as Blossom Hill—lies Rupert Valley, where the hayfields and sugarbush lots intersect and overlap like a wafer of Chex. This is West Rupert, Vermont, we're looking at. Beyond that is Rupert proper, where I take my mail. North of there is North Rupert, and east of there is, well, East Rupert. (There's no South Rupert for some reason.) Presiding over all the Ruperts is Rupert Mountain, the highest peak in this part of Vermont. Over from Rupert Mountain is Egg Mountain and after that comes Fan Mountain and then a few no-name peaks fade to the south.

Back atop Blossom Hill, spinning around and looking west now toward Hebron, New York, you'll see another broad valley of hay meadows and rows of field corn, edged on the far side by the northernmost reach of the Taconic Mountain Range—a ridge, dip, ridge, dip progression, lying across the horizon like the spine of a Stegosaurus.

At the base of the hill is the sugarhouse, a board and batten barn shack with a steep pitched roof covered by sheets of rusty corrugated tin. The entire building is framed and sided with rough-cut lumber of hemlock and pine, which means it isn't smooth surfaced but has the texture of a wet cashmere sweater. Rows of three-pane wavy glass windows sequence the sides of the sugarhouse. Running the length of the roof ridge is something called a *ventilator cupola*, which has flaps we flop open to evacuate the steam when we're boiling the sap. A rope of ivy crawls up the front of the building, and when it leafs out in the summer, it garnishes the square yellow sign hanging in the gable that advertises PURE MAPLE SYRUP in bold Doric font.

Inside the sugarhouse, one sees a hunk of mirror-quality stainless steel dominates the room. This is the evaporator, which, in rudimentary terms, is a stove with a firebox underneath called an *arch* and long, deep-sided cooking pans sitting on top, which we flood with sap.

Attached to the side of our evaporator is a sworl of pipes and valves. These route raw sap to the three different pans stacked adjacent to one another that perform different functions in the various stages of boiling our sap into syrup.

Our evaporator is exactly two feet wide and eight feet long—a *two-by-eight*, which falls in the midsized class of evaporators in the maple world. Bigger sugarmakers have six-by-sixteens, four-by-fourteens, or three-by-tens. Smaller producers on the sugarmaking totem pole might have a two-by-six, a two-by-four, or even a spritely two-by-two evaporator, a model that becomes somewhat emasculating when referred to by its trade name: a Half Pint.

Making maple syrup—we call it *sugaring*—is one of the most accessible ways to participate in agriculture, which is one of the reasons I got into it

in the first place. For low patience/quick reward–seekers like me, you can
go from zero to maple in no time flat.

Have a maple tree or two in your backyard? Drill a hole into it, pound
in a spout, let the sap drip into a pail, then gather it up and steam it in a
spaghetti pot on your kitchen stove. After twelve hours and a lot of peeled
wallpaper, you'll have a tincture of delicious maple syrup.

Look at that, you're a farmer.

What happens to a lot of dudes, and certainly what happened to me,
is they become *addicted* to making maple syrup. We call it *The Bug*.
Instead of the two trees in your backyard, you'll find yourself knocking
on your neighbor's door and asking to tap *their* maple trees. Next, you're
driving all over town looking to buy land with a bunch of maples on it.
Once you do that, you'll have to invest in an evaporator to boil all the
sap and many tanks to hold all that sap, and maybe you'll even decide
to lay out some big bucks for a reverse osmosis machine, which will
squeeze 75 percent of the water out of the sap ahead of time, so you
won't have to boil it as much.

Maybe you'll start off old school, using antique galvanized sap buckets
that you bought off eBay to collect from the tree. Quaint at first, but then
you might find that hefting pails of sap through the woods in a foot or
two of snow is a lot of frigging work. So you upgrade to a plastic tubing
system, where the sap moves through an arterial pipeline to a central
gathering point convenient to the road. For a year or two you might rely
on gravity to circulate the sap through all that tubing, until your patience
wears thin again and you return to the bank to finance a high vacuum
system that sucks sap out of the trees with enough force of pressure to
dislodge a brick.

Keep that checkbook handy, because you're going to need to buy thousands of plastic fittings to traffic all that sap through the pipeline. You'll
need to purchase lots of pumps, too. Pumps for that vacuum system. Pumps
to move sap from one tank to another. And pumps to shove your finished
syrup through a filter press to distill it clear as a mountain stream.

And don't forget all the little things. You'll need gauges for monitoring temperatures, sugar refraction, vacuum pressures, and syrup density. Pails and more buckets and scrub brushes better be on your list. Then there's the nagging little necessities like syrup scoops, tapping hammers, tools for splicing and repairing the vacuum tubing. It can seem like a never-ending progression of stuff to buy, but this is what happens when you're afflicted with The Bug.

You'll eventually graduate to bigger, faster, improved versions of each of these things. I'm now on my third evaporator. The first two cost as much as a motorcycle. My current one, as much as a car.

In the end, you might earn a little money selling your sweet nectar—either by peddling it to your friends and neighbors or by selling it to a wholesaler in a forty-gallon drum like we do.

But if *profit* is your goal, you might be better off panning for gold or fishing for tuna. Maybe buy yourself a racehorse. Better yet just play the lottery. You'll probably have better odds.

Besides having mechanical intuition, a hard work ethic, and a required sense of taste—the sap instincts—sugarmakers are typically innovative, funny, forward-thinking, optimistic, and very curious. Sure, we kvetch about the varying conditions of the maple market or the frustrations inherent to coaxing sap out of a tree in the dead of winter, but for the most part we sugarmakers happily keep tapping away with abandon. Perhaps more than any other type of farming, sugaring is something one can improve upon with practice, skill development, and embracing modern technology. It's a little like golf, but maybe not as pointless.

It's high good times to be in the sugar game. Pure maple syrup is winning the pancake wars. In the past ten years the US maple industry has doubled in scale. It's expected to double again, maybe even triple, in the decade to come, just to keep up with the demand for an authentic product like ours.

The rush became starkly evident after the 2021 season, a *very* short crop in both the United States and Canada, when demand so exceeded supply that the industry held a valid concern it would literally run out of syrup. You might've had to eat your pancakes dry.

The season was cut short because spring came too fast. When day-to-day temperatures warm up for good, and there's no more freezing nights, the trees begin the budding process and that's when maple season is over.

Thanks to climate change, spring comes quicker and quicker these days.

⧢

"Farming is a combination of humility and tenacity," a sage old dairy farmer told me once. True dat. On a farm, equipment is always breaking, or not working. Pieces and parts never fit. It's an inch and a quarter when you need an inch and a half. It's torqued too tight, mismeasured, not found. At a maple farm, or at least at mine, everything is always leaking, or about to boil over, or *is* boiling over, or, worse yet, scorching.

We've accidentally ignited a few grassfires with the embers spitting out of our evaporator, including one along the hedgerow one March afternoon. By chance, a rare passerby on Blossom Road spotted the fire and hollered at us to stomp it out. It could've easily spread to the sugarhouse and conflagrated it—which will probably happen at some point anyway since we're burning tinder-dry firewood at 1,200 goddamned degrees.

Maple is a lifelong pursuit. I know many sugarmakers who are still tapping trees well into their eighties. They just never quit. Last summer, a neighbor of mine, Ken Potter, who's seventy-nine and sugars up the road in Poultney, Vermont, watched the sugarhouse he built with his own hands burn to the ground. (Sugarhouses burn down a lot in this business.) It was zapped by a lightning strike. A bolt from Zeus decimated a fifty-year endeavor. At three o'clock in the morning, Kenny was jolted out of bed by hose-wielding firefighters pounding on his door. All he could salvage from the blaze were six barrels of syrup from the previous season (thank God, we needed every drop in '21). Everything else burned or fused into the ground.

I stopped by a couple weeks later and, lo and behold, there was Kenny, full of smiles, already busy constructing a new sugarhouse he vowed to make bigger and better. He was wearing bib overalls, a duck canvas Carhartt jacket torn at the elbows, and a snug, sweat-stained ballcap, as he and his grandson edged some planks of lumber with a chainsaw.

"A lot of folks almost eighty who just lost everything in a fire would probably give up, Kenny," I said. "They'd call it a career and find a sandy beach in Florida to look for shark's teeth."

He laughed but kept working. "Oh yeah, the guys at the coffee shop say, 'What the heck's wrong with you?'"

In great health, handsome and trim, Kenny attributed his stamina to clean living.

"I don't drink or smoke, and I eat cornflakes piled with blackberries and bananas every morning. As long as I'm healthy, I'm gonna keep sugaring. I still got lots of syrup to make yet."

Like I said, it's an addiction.

2

BERT

My partner in this whole operation is a fellow named Bert Jones. We live a few towns apart, each about a twenty-minute drive away from the sugarhouse. He and I were part of a extended friend group that used to play poker once or twice a month. One beery night, it came up during a card shuffle that all of us played instruments. "Let's start a band, man!" someone shouted. So, we ended up forming a seven-piece dad band that jammed every Tuesday night in the bass player's barn. We played a lot of Neil Young, Rolling Stones, and Velvet Underground covers—loudly, and usually not well. But once in a while we'd hit a nice groove. I was on rhythm guitar (Gibson Les Paul with P-90s and a 30-watt Orange amp; a Tele tuned to open G for the Stones songs). Bert played keys.

He and I relate well partly because we grew up in similar, single-syllabled towns in the mid-to-late eighties. Me in Mound, Minnesota, and he in Yoe, Pennsylvania. We both had mullets in those days, although his was much more severe, according to the Polaroid evidence. We like to swap glory-day stories about high school parties and ditching cops and trying and failing to interest girls, but occasionally succeeding—he more often than me, a mullet apparently a bigger draw with the females of Yoe than the beauties of Mound.

Bert has a disarming smile, and a sincere and genuine disposition. He's as big as a mixer wagon. He's always crashing his head into crossbeams, low-hanging pipes, tree branches, and pretty much anything below six-feet-two-and-a-half-inches from the ground. When called upon, Bert can conjure the raw brute strength of a gorilla, which comes in handy on a farm.

Bert tends to move at the velocity of plate tectonics. There's time, and then there's *Bert Time*. Bert Time is about twenty to twenty-five minutes slower than the time the rest of us observe. Sometimes forty-five minutes slower. Sometimes an hour and fifteen minutes slower. Variable, but always slower. Meanwhile, my sense of time is frantic; I get frustrated more easily and have no patience whatsoever, like a horsefly. He and I are a classic tortoise and hare. I'm a hard-charging, ready-fire-aim type of person. Left to my own devices, I'll swoop into something too quickly, leading to mistakes requiring a do-over, while Bert will sometimes contemplate incessantly and never move forward. I'll give you a good example:

For years, let's call it *three* years, Bert's wife, Faith, an absolute peach of a woman and his childhood sweetheart (who swooned over the mullet, I'm told) had been making a modest request for a new couch. So, Bert and Faith made a regular routine of going couch shopping on Saturday nights, almost like a date. I ran into them once at the Big Lots, one of those mid-tier box stores common in the suburbs and now popping up in small towns like ours. They had already been there two hours. By then, they had narrowed their sofa choices down to *four*. The salesman looked like he wanted to jam a pen in his eye, while Bert and Faith were having a great time bouncing from couch to couch. The next day, I asked Bert which one they picked.

"None of them," he said.

I face-palmed. "None of them? After two hours? After *three years*?"

He shrugged. "Faith had a clear favorite," Bert said, "but I just couldn't decide."

Bert and Faith are among the happiest couples I know, but Bert acknowledges Faith puts up with a lot. Most notably his buying of tools (in favor of a couch). When it comes to tools, Bert has no problem quickly reaching for his wallet. The guy has every single tool ever made, which besides his overall camaraderie and an uncanny mechanical intellect, is an essential contribution to this thing of ours. If there's been a one-time use for any job or project in his life, Bert has gone and bought the tool for it. He owns at least four floor jacks, two air compressors, and multiple nail guns and torque wrenches. He is ordained in all things DeWalt. He has every drill and every saw in the DeWalt saw family—table saw, chop saw, jigsaw, circular saw, reciprocating saw. Plus, a muster of 20v batteries to power them all.

As you might imagine, Bert's garage is hyper-organized—pristine and hallowed as a Catholic tabernacle. Each tool has a designated shelf or corner; each hose or cord hangs neatly coiled. Standing like a pulpit in the nave of the garage, he has a towering mechanic's tool chest for fixing anything with a motor, plus all the essentials for electrical work—voltage meters, nut drivers, wire strippers, etc.—and plumbing work—pipe cutters, deburring tools, crimpers, etc. Arranged on the shelves in places only he knows exactly where, he has all the proper tools for grouting tile, forming concrete, and roofing a house.

Our maple partnership began one wintry Sunday afternoon in Bert's man cave watching an NFL divisional playoff game between the Broncos and Ravens (won 38–35 by Baltimore on a Justin Tucker field goal in double overtime; Manning choked). Between the two overtimes, and as I reached for the last slice of pizza, I mentioned that, after much study and advice gathering, I wanted to build a sugarhouse on the twenty-five acres of land I owned on Blossom Road.

"Damn, that sounds like fun," Bert said, smushing his beer can. "Can I help? I got tools."

And that was that. Instant partners in maple.

From the band, we recruited our drummer and the bongo man and broke ground the following week, chopping boards and popping nail guns. Sort of like an Amish barn raising but with a crew of office-worker types with not great backs. By the middle of February, the sugarhouse was raised, equipped, and ready for boiling. Its basic structure has gone through many iterations and improvements since then. And Bert and I have evolved as equal partners. I have a day job as a magazine editor, and Bert is a compliance officer with a company down in Schenectady. But we've made maple a major part of our lives, and it's become the footing of our friendship. We split the crop of syrup we make each year fifty-fifty. We have yet to formalize our partnership or give it a proper name. (We just call it "the Sugarhouse" or "Blossom Road.") I've suggested really going for it, maybe incorporating as an LLC. I even tossed out the name idea of "Two Old Saps Maple Farm" or something corny like that. But that was three or four years ago.

Typical Bert, he's still thinking it over.

3

FIVE POUNDERS!

When people ask the size of our sugaring operation, I always say "about a thousand taps." A nice round number. But like fishermen, sugarmakers tend to exaggerate. The truth is, at last count, our maple farm had exactly 856.

A "tap" is shorthand for the tricky hole we drill into a maple's trunk every season to draw sap out of it. That 856 number ranks us solidly in the hobbyist classification of the maple-syrup hierarchy—guys assumed to be making syrup for fun rather than for a living.

It didn't used to be that way. Fifteen or twenty years ago, having a "thousand taps" meant you weren't messing around. It was a reputable enough number that other sugarmakers would take you seriously when you shot the bull at the farm show or the county fair. But there's been a veritable arms race in our industry—yes, over that stuff you pour over waffles and flan—and sugarmakers new and old have been drilling trees like crazy. In Vermont, the statewide tap count has tripled to about four million, and that's a conservative estimate. Maple might comprise a tiny segment of US agriculture, but it could be the most thriving. Leap-and-bound advancements in high-vacuum systems and reverse osmosis technology means that syrup can now be made with a flip of a switch (well, not really, but sort of),

21

fostering huge economies of scale. Tap counts keep going up and up and up. Ten thousand- and twenty thousand-tap operations are the norm now, and one hundred thousand-tap operations don't shock anyone.

A few years ago, a group reportedly venture-financed by the Connecticut State Teachers' Retirement Board developed a half-*million*-tap operation in the thickly mapled Northeast Kingdom of Vermont, that regal-sounding swath of land pushing into Canada and Maine, containing Orleans, Essex, and Caledonia counties. I hear they're adding even more taps up there, so it's possible that operation could become the world's first to top a million. If they don't do it, someone else will.

Why all this expansion and why now? Consumer demand for pure all-natural maple syrup has gone through the roof, driven largely by the hipster foodie movement and farm-to-table eating trends, and boosted yet again by pandemic cooking-at-home crazes: families quarantined in their kitchens making big breakfasts with their bored-hungry virus shut-ins. And once you've had the real stuff, you ain't never going back to the corn-syrup imitation.

The serious sugarmakers in Vermont do a lot of math to measure their output and compare themselves to one another. They do this by calculating their per-tap average—in other words, how much syrup do they get, on average, from each tap in the sugarbush. They measure this in pounds, since wholesale syrup is priced by weight, not volume.

The hard-core Vermonters strive for an average production tally of five pounds of syrup produced per tap (which equates to roughly half a gallon). That's considered the Vermont benchmark to be taken seriously as a real-deal sugarmaker.

A *Five Pounder* is what they call you if you hit that.

Meanwhile, the most syrup Bert and I ever made in a single season was exactly 201 gallons—not even a *three-pound* year.

But twenty years ago, that would have been a respectable production total. With that size of a harvest, back then, it would've meant Bert and I had done something right. Now, three pounds per tap means we've been doing something wrong.

For the 2022 sugaring season, I made up my mind to change that up, to be able to finally hold my head up high at the urinal, so to speak.

Also, circumstances in my life had changed dramatically since the season before. My primary job of raising my two kids had come to an end—one moved three hours south to New York City to get her master's degree, subway commuting to class in Greenwich Village, and the other tossed his sneakers and a sleeping bag into an '08 Prius and left for Hollywood to chase a dream.

Suddenly it was just me, my cat, and the trees. And Bert.

The day-to-day source of joy, purpose, and fulfillment in my life, parenting, was gone and I wasn't adjusting well. Making a shit-ton more syrup might make me feel better, I reckoned.

What the hell, I didn't have anything better to do.

I don't own enough land to tap more trees; every single maple on the property is spoken for. But I figured that with an insane amount of hard work, risk, and strategy, and with some luck and cooperation from Mother Nature, we could certainly do a better job of extracting every ounce of sap from each of those trees. That way, even if our tap count was low, our per-tap production average would measure up with all the big guys in Vermont.

But I had to convince Bert.

I said to him one morning, "Man, I'm tired of being kicked around by these trees."

It was early December, and we were out for breakfast at a diner on a little frozen lake a few miles from the sugarhouse.

He crossed his arms over his chest and leaned back. "Whaddya talking about?"

I looked at him with fire in the eyes. "I want more sap," I said.

He looked back at me warily. "Well, that's kinda up to the weather, isn't it?"

A waitress dropped an oval plate of eggs Benedict in front of him with flanking piles of corned beef hash. For me, a stack of puffy pancakes and a double side order of grease-lathered bacon. Then she plunked down four or five pleated paper ketchup cups filled with syrup.

I tapped a finger on the table. "We're not *maximizing* the trees."

Bert sat forward and began ladling excess hollandaise sauce onto the hash with a spoon. "What the hell are you talking about?" he said.

"Sure, the weather's a big part of it, but we're not pulling our weight," I said, cutting into the pancake mound. "This season we need to keep the vacuum super high. That means the pipeline needs to be frigging tight tight tight. No leaks! That should get us way more sap. We need to be super aggressive if we want to be Five Pounders."

Gauntlet thrown.

He looked at me funny. "What the hell is a Five Pounder?" he asked through a mouthful of egg, so it sounded a little like he said "Pfive Flounder."

I laughed. "It's what the Vermonters say. Guys who make five pounds of syrup per tap."

Bert pressed his lips together and did the conversion math in his head. "That comes out to us making about 400 gallons of syrup, buddy."

I nodded. "Yeah, that sounds about right," I said.

He lifted his chin. "Are you kidding? We've barely made more than 200 before."

"I think we can do it."

He gave me the *talk to the hand* gesture with one mitt while he scooped up more breakfast with the other. "Ugh. I'm exhausted already," he said, looking back down at his plate. "Anyone bother to ask the trees their opinion on this idea? How they gonna feel about getting milked of all that extra sap? My guess is they won't like it much."

I smiled and pointed a finger in the air. *"Au contraire mon frère."*

I told him that the PhD'ed plant scientists who research maples have found that we sugarmakers are only taking a tiny fraction of the sap trees are juicing through their trunks.

"We can suck out as much as we want," I said. "The trees don't care. Scientifically proven."

Maples are remarkable in so many ways. No one can definitively say why there's sugar in the sap of a maple tree during a six-week window every winter and spring. It's an amazing phenomenon. Currents of sap flush through the trees on days when temperatures are below freezing at night and then in the forties or fifties during the day. Some researchers have estimated that at most, we're taking only 10 percent of the sap, maybe less. There are some families in Vermont that have been tapping the same trees for 150 years or more. Maples are the true giving tree.

Bert tore a piece of toast in two, buttered and jellied the halves, then closed them into a sandwich.

I went on. "Here's the thing: everyone who makes syrup comes to a crossroads—are we just gonna do this thing as a hobby and fart around, or are we gonna try and go for the big time?"

He pondered for a moment, chewing quietly. "A 'Five Pounder,' huh?"

I nodded. "That's what they call 'em. That's what we'd be."

"Is there some sort of certifying agency?"

I dunked a divot of pancake into a syrup cup. "Naw, it's just the honor system."

"Would we get a patch or a lapel pin maybe?" he said.

"Nope. Only glory."

Bert put a fist to his stomach and tried to hold in a belch. "Sounds kinda arbitrary."

"Yeah, but it's still a cool-ass goal," I said. "Like joining the mile-high club or breaking par or something."

Bert considered this.

"Lemme tell you a story," I said, continuing my sales pitch. "Last summer the kids and I went to the Coney Island hot dog eating contest. It was insane. The winner ate *seventy-six* hot dogs."

"That's a lotta wieners."

"—and *buns*—the whole event they kept reminding everyone that these jokers were eating the buns, too."

Bert excavated a heap of hash onto his fork.

"Dude broke the record of seventy-five hot dogs and buns," I said. "Know who held the old record? Same dude. Know what the prize was? A mustard-colored belt."

Bert grinned. "Bet I could eat at least forty-five," he said.

"It was maybe the most exciting sporting event I'd ever been to. When he downed number seventy-six, the crowd went nuts. He was a hero. For eating a giant pile of hot dogs—"

"—and buns," he said.

I smiled. "You see? That's way more arbitrary than anything we're doing. I'm tired of everyone laughing at us, thinking we're a couple pudknockers."

My voice was distressed, and I was getting overanimated with my fork.

"Put Faith on notice she's not gonna see you much the next three months," I said. "You're gonna be with me in the goddamned woods and in the sugarhouse filling barrels. It's us against the sap, man. *Five Pounders*. Let's frigging do this. Whaddya say?"

I could almost see the ellipses of a coming response in Bert Time as he chomped on his hash. The man gulped hard and then answered.

"Okay, okay, you got me," he said. "I'm in."

EARLY JANUARY 2022

4
THE TANKS I GET

After Bert and I made what came to be known as our Five Pound Pact, we immediately determined we'd need more holding tanks if we were going to try and collect double the amount of sap this season. In the maple business, one can never have enough tanks since there's massive amounts of liquid to store. "Right now, we got the holding capacity of a specimen cup," Bert reminded me.

I scoured the classified ads of the local pennyshopper for sap tanks, which often come up for sale in late fall or early winter when everyone's getting ready for a new maple season. I especially kept a keen eye out for sap tanks made by the G.H. Grimm Evaporator Company of Rutland, Vermont. Grimm tanks are my favorite because they're so damn cool—and old.

I've always been attracted to old things. Old houses, old cars, old books, old Cushman chairs, old Formica tables, old towns, old fishing lures, old 45 RPM records, old table lamps, old mopeds, old Realistic stereo receivers, old rotary telephones, old Bally pinball machines, old brands of shampoo, old webbed lawn chairs, old Schwinn bicycles, old pop machines, old boat motors. You get the idea. And I especially love old Grimm sap tanks.

Grimms, as the manufacturer was colloquially known, was quartered in a four-story wooden factory on the industrial side of Rutland near the railroad yard. The building was filled with sheet-metal brakes, drill presses, and welding-gas cylinders arranged across a vast wood-slatted floor. In the front of the factory, there was a showroom where they'd line up sparkling new evaporators in a slanted row like a car dealership. It closed during the pandemic.

Grimm tanks were made of mottled-gray galvanized steel. On the side, Grimm would stencil the volume capacity of the tank measured in barrels, which they abbreviated as bbl. (In agriculture, a "barrel" is equivalent to forty-two gallons.) They'd also stamp MAPLE SYRUP UTENSILS with the same blocky black lettering.

I already owned a round three-bbl Grimm tank I bought at a barn sale a few years ago over in Ira, Vermont, when I was getting started in maple. It's my favorite tank, a cylinder variety that was designed to be carried on the back of a pickup truck for sap collecting.

In the "Agricultural Equipment" section of the classifieds, I found a promising listing for a Grimm tank at a farm a couple of towns away near Castleton, Vermont.

I drove over one morning and was greeted in the driveway by a grouchy retired sugarmaker with a bristly walrus mustache and a shock of white hair that looked like someone glued a bunch of cotton balls to his head and tried to run a comb through it.

"It's out in the woods still," he said. "Hope you like walking."

He hadn't listed a price for the tank, so I asked how much he wanted for it.

He scowled. "You're gonna wanna see the damn thing first—then we'll talk."

We must've walked half a klick into his woods. He had a gaunt frame and moved along briskly for an old man. Even though it was January, there was no snow. The rug of leaves on the path was mushy with frost. After a bit, we came upon an abandoned sugarhouse, where, he told me, his family had sugared since the 1940s. "This was my home away from home every March." It was in rough shape. The roof of the shack was caved in, most of the windows were smashed, and the door had separated from its top hinge. It tottered on the bottom one. I asked him if it was ok to peek inside. "Not much worth looking at," he said, dismissively. I poked my head through the window opening. Vines of honeysuckle tendriled through a rusted evaporator arch. Along the walls there were rows of tapered galvanized sap buckets, stacked upside down like Slurpee cups and listing leeward.

I pulled my head back out. "You miss sugaring much?" I asked.

He crossed an arm under his elbow and propped his chin with his palm.

"Oh yeah. I loved makin' syrup more than anything," he said through his fingers.

"Why'd you give it up?" I asked.

He lifted his shoulder in a half shrug. "Too many heart attacks."

"Whoa. Jesus. How many is too many?"

He rolled his eyes back and counted on his fingers. "Up until I quit sugaring, four. But now I think I'm up to seven. Can't remember."

"Seven?"

"I know I've lost count of the stents," he said.

I was wide-eyed. "I got here in the nick of time, I guess."

He patted his pants pocket. "Got the nitro tabs right here," he said. "The docs said no more sugaring. Too much lifting and moving heavy shit around. Although I always thought croaking at the evaporator during a nice rolling boil wouldn't be a bad way to go out."

I nodded in agreement.

He led me behind the sugarhouse, and we found the tank lying upside down in a patch of weeds. It was a rectangular five-bbl jobber, sharp-cornered and sturdy-looking. There wasn't any rust, at least on the inside. (For sap collecting, a clean inside is what counts.) I shoved it over and a bunch of pill bugs scattered on the pale dirt beneath. The basin was remarkably spotless.

I instantly knew I wanted it. It was a beauty. Classic Grimm.

"What do you think?" the old grouch asked.

I kicked a rock, pretending I wasn't too eager. "Does it leak?" (Note to all you tank buyers out there, that's the first question to ask.)

"How the hell do I know?" he snapped. "It's been laying here twenty years."

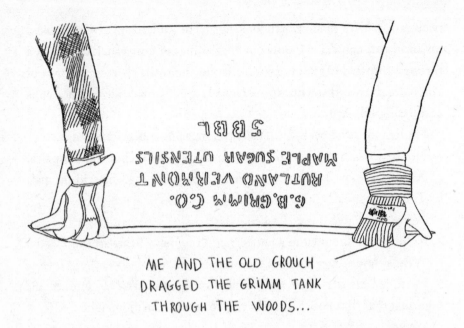

ME AND THE OLD GROUCH
DRAGGED THE GRIMM TANK
THROUGH THE WOODS...

I slipped my hands into the kangaroo pocket of my hoodie. "Well, you and I both know the going rate for old sap tanks is buck-a-gallon," I said, meaning one dollar paid for each gallon of capacity. "How much you want for this one?"

He drummed at his brushlip like he was tapping Morse code. "Oh hell, I don't know," he said. "Since I can't tell you for sure if it leaks or not, and I don't want you trying to bring it the hell back here and dumping it on my goddamn lawn if it does, I'll give you a deal," he said. "Hundred bucks, how 'bout? You look like you can swing that."

I would've paid twice as much, easily. "A hundred's not too far off from what I was thinking," I lied. "Sold."

We shook on it. "You're not gonna write me a goddamned *check*, are you?" he said.

I peeled off five twenties, folded the bills, and stuck them in his hand, and he unfolded and recounted them before tucking them into the breast pocket of his checkered field coat.

"Grab an end," he said.

Then me, the grouch, and his mustache dragged the Grimm back through the woods to my truck. It wasn't so heavy to drag, but it was awkwardly shaped and hard to get a good grip. We had to stop quite a few times to adjust. It was mostly me who did the stopping, and it annoyed the old grouch. "C'mon, Jesus. We're never gonna get this thing out of here if you keep stopping like a damned dog lifting his hind leg every five minutes," he said.

It wasn't just the awkward angle of the grip that made me want to stop. I also didn't want the guy to have grabber number eight halfway through the woods and to have to fish around in his pants for the goddamn angina tabs. Each time we stopped he took the opportunity to hike up his trousers, and I swear, each time he did I thought he was going to reach for his nitroglycerine.

But we made it out of the woods without incident, thank God. Then we hefted the Grimm onto my truck and secured it with a ratchet strap. "Now I better not be seeing either of you again," he said, and then he heel-turned and walked back to his house without saying goodbye.

When I got home, I dropped the tank outside the sugarhouse and Bert frowned.

"You got us the Charlie Brown Christmas tree of tanks, blockhead," he said.

I raised my palms. "C'mon man, it's cool as shit, ain't it? It's an old Grimm."

Bert unenthusiastically flicked at it with his finger and shook his head.

"It's all very quaint and charming you got us an antique tank but we're gonna need a lot bigger one than this if you're really serious about the Five Pounder thing," he said.

He was right. Which he usually is. Then he thought of something I should've thought of in the goddamned first place.

"Listen, why don't we call Shakey?" he said.

Timmy Dwyer is a veteran sugarmaker whom everyone around here calls "Shakey." Over the years, Shakey has become our primary consiglieri in maple, someone we turn to often for advice and support. Shakey is a swarthy, barrel-torsoed guy of indeterminate age who typically wears a cable-knit sweater in winter and a tie dye T-shirt in summer. He has a thick white beard and a chop of white hair, and he wears square wire-rimmed glasses, giving him a slight resemblance to Jerry Garcia. He definitely has Jerry's carefree spirit. Shakey's sugarhouse is in Shushan just a few miles from us. He calls it Shushan Sity Sap Shack (misspelling intentional, I'm pretty sure). He prides himself on the quality of his syrup but takes just as much pride, if not more, in being the social center of Shushan during maple season. At Shushan Sity, every day is Saint Patrick's Day. Shakey's famous for his sap-boiling parties, and he invites everyone he knows in town. His bashes tend to represent our area demographics. Half the crowd are rednecks with whom you might end up conversing about diesel tractors, logging skidders, or the performance advantages of 2-stroke snowmobile engines. The other half are New York and Boston transplants—retired college professors and such, with whom you might try to talk smartly about the lyrical stylings of William Butler Yeats or share your theoretical perspectives on international diplomacy while the sap boils and beer spills.

One of the things we love about Shakey is he talks about maple as if we're all in on a big conspiracy together. He's always showing me a clever new trick he thinks has outsmarted everyone. One night, I was hanging out at Shushan Sity during a boil, and he gave me a furtive look. "Come 'ere, you gotta see this," he said and pointed to a red lightbulb over his evaporator set to a timer. "Every five minutes the bulb flashes to let me know it's time to throw more firewood into the arch. Everyone should have one of these goddamned things."

I gave it proper reverence, agreeing it was pretty clever.

"Nifty gadget," I said. "I want one."

Shakey angled the back of his hand to his mouth, leaned to me, and whispered.

"You got it buddy. I got a line on another one. I'll hook you up."

The best part about Shakey is he never lets us forget that making maple syrup is fun.

"If it's not any fun then why do it? Sugaring is just a lot of goddamned work otherwise." He's said that to me and Bert over and over.

I texted Shakey that we were on the lookout for a sap holding tank and asked if he had a line on any decent non-leakers. Shakey claims his thumbs are too fat to text, so he's big on leaving voicemails instead, and he left me a long rambling one: "Hey Peter, yeah, got a nice tank right here for you if you want it. I know it don't leak because we used it as a clam steamer last year and it worked great"—he stopped and audibly blew his nose, foghorn-like—"Shit, sorry. I got a goddamned cold. Anyway, let me know if you want the tank. We might've also used it as a hot tub at one of our parties. I'll take two fifty for it. Call me back."

Among his many signature traits, just when you think he's finished talking, Shakey loves to sign off with a PG-13 joke and a mic drop. "By the way, please keep my family in your prayers. My uncle has become addicted to Viagra. My aunt is taking it hard. Bye-bye."

I asked Bert what he thought.

"Moving it will be a bitch and a half," he said. "Did he really use it as a hot tub?"

We drove over to Shushan the next morning with Bert's utility trailer. Shakey was waiting for us in the driveway, sitting on the lid of the tank clipping his fingernails. He had built makeshift skis for it out of some planks, so it resembled a sleigh. "I'll be sorry to see this old girl go," he said, patting it, demonstrating a lot more tank nostalgia than the grouch had.

Shakey's tank was way bigger and heavier than the Grimm. This tank was a bulk milk tank off a defunct dairy farm—600-gallon capacity, a 15-bbl. Most sugarmakers use old bulk tanks from the dairy industry to hold sap. The dairy industry and the maple industry have long been kissing cousins. Since both maple and dairy move large quantities of liquid around, much of the equipment is interchangeable. Maple mostly developed as a bonus crop for the legacy New England dairy farmers since many of them had a sugarbush adjacent to their farmland. Come March they'd tap the trees and boil some sap, and once maple season was over, they'd slide right into planting silage corn or alfalfa. Over the years, the small-scale dairy

industry mostly collapsed around here, and as the farms went out of business, in swooped the sugarmakers like scavenger crows to pick off their bulk
tanks. Milk tanks are usually shaped like submarines: oblong, stainless-steel
tubes with ports on the top, so it's easy to reach in and clean them. They
work just as well for holding sap as milk, keeping it cold and sanitary. Bulk
milk tanks are also seriously heavy, made of stainless steel and cast-iron
framing. They're typically insulated with some sort of material (jacketed
asbestos, I think) that makes them weigh even more. It was so heavy that
after the three of us skidded it onto the trailer it flattened one of the tires.

"Oh shit," Shakey said. "Hold tight, I'll be right back."

He ran and fetched a neighbor who had an "air pig," a gas-can looking
thing filled with compressed air used to inflate flat tires in emergencies.
He plugged it onto the tire's valve stem and squeezed a trigger on the pig.
Pfffffffftsssssssssst.

"Back in business," he said and shuffled his feet in a way that looked a
little like a jig.

Once we got it home, it didn't take long for us to figure out that Shakey's
hot tub wasn't going to help us much, either. Including it, the two tanks
already in our fleet, and the new tank from the grouch, we now had four
tanks scattered around the yard of the sugarhouse. The problem was that
none would be voluminous enough by itself to hold all the sap we'd typically gather on our biggest flow days, especially now with our aggressive
five-pound goal and the exponential increase in sap we were expecting to
collect. Then the smart one in our operation got an idea.

"Duh," Bert said, a lightbulb flashing over his head, "let's connect all
the tanks together." Out of thin air, Bert built a clever thing we called the
"Centipede." It was basically a long piece of PVC pipe with four connecting
legs of hose that would marry them all with Banjo quick couplers.

We decided to test it with water one morning, and it was a good thing we
did. The Centipede wasn't going to work. The problem was, the tanks were
various heights. They'd fill up simultaneously for a while, but then when
the shortest tank filled to the top, all the subsequent water spilled over its
brim instead of filling the other tanks. If that had been actual sap instead

of water, we'd've been ruined—nothing kills the soul of a sugarmaker more than sap spilling to the ground. Plus, we weren't entirely comfortable with Shakey's tank anyway—especially the idea we'd be sloshing our sap over the same surface that might have once sloshed Shakey's bare ass.

We had to find a better way.

What we really needed was one tank that would never overflow—a huge mother. I knew just where to go to source such a piece of equipment—a place called Bascoms.

⚛

Bascom Maple Farms in Alstead, New Hampshire, is a supercenter for sugarmaking supplies and considered the county seat of maple in the Northeast. After the Centipede flop, I scoured Bascom's equipment catalog and found a tank five times the size of the one we bought from Shakey—sixteen feet long, five feet wide, sixty one inches tall, with an oceanic 3,100-gallon capacity. With a tank like that, we'd be able to just sit back and let it fill all day long and never worry. Around Christmastime, I called over to Bascom's and put down a deposit.

"Guess what Santa's getting us this year," I announced to Bert.

Now, how to get it to Blossom Road? I stressed over the logistics of transporting the new tank all through the holidays. Bascom's doesn't deliver and there ain't no Uber Eats for sap tanks. Hauling this new monster was going to be a damn big job, and for it we were going to need a damn big trailer. The trailer we'd been using to haul the other tanks, the one whose tire squished under the weight of Shakey's hot tub, was Bert's Tractor Supply special, a utility trailer about eight feet long. For the Bascom's job, we would need one at least sixteen feet, preferably twenty.

After putting out word all over town, I managed to find a sixteen-foot tandem axle from a farmhand who worked on Chambers Valley Farms over in Salem and rented out big-ass trailers as a side hustle. He told me his rate for renting the trailer for the day was seventy-five bucks and he'd throw in a couple heavy duty ratchet straps to tie the tank down. "I just changed the wheel bearings on 'er so she should roll real nice for ya." I reached for my wallet. "Deal," I said.

Once we had the trailer lined up, Bert and I had another thing to figure out—whose truck to take to Bascom's. Bert was lobbying hard to take his brand-new bright red Ford F-150, which we'd dubbed "Red Beauty." By some miracle, Bert went and bought a new pickup after test-driving dozens of trucks over the past couple of years (sometimes on the same nights as the couch shopping excursions with Faith). Shockingly, he picked one, justifying it as a fiftieth birthday present for himself (even though he'd just turned fifty-two. Bert Time). He cares for Red Beauty like it was made of porcelain. A speck doesn't stand a chance against his sharp eye and will get polished away as soon as it lands. At any given moment it looks like it's ready for a parade. It's a full-package pickup with all the luxury. Heated seats, sunroof, inflatable lumbar support.

My truck, on the other hand, is a Toyota Tundra, also red. My whole life I've been a Toyota guy. I learned to drive on my mom's manual '81 Corolla, and in my twenties I owned an '83 Corolla stick shift until it got stolen when I was living in South Boston for a short while after college. I've since owned two Toyota Highlanders, a kick-ass Supra, a Tacoma, and now the Tundra. It's been my experience that Toyotas take a beating and rarely break down. They almost *like it* when they are abused. My Highlander has 220,000 miles on it and drives like brand-new. As for the Tundra, I smashed it into a light pole once. Still runs. Bashed it over the ruts on Blossom Road thousands of times. Doesn't care. I never wash it because it looks cooler when it's filthy. The Tundra has power, too, more torque than the Ford, which I mention to Bert often.

Allow me a quick anecdote about the Tundra: Last fall, I got a wild hair to move a giant rock lying at the edge of a grassy slope near our barn. Now when I say rock, I mean a huge, solid boulder, a monolith about the size of a lawn tractor. Bert didn't like the idea.

"Let's go do something else," he said. "The rock is fine where it is."

I was in a squirrely mood that morning and thought it would be fun to test the mettle of the Toyota. Bert could tell by my lopsided smirk I thought so.

"Let's chain 'er up," I said.

Bert twisted his lips. "There's no way that rock is going to budge," he insisted.

"Well, it's been budged before. Something got it where it is now," I said.

"Yeah, a glacier. Leave it alone."

Now a word about the rock. The weight of a rock is rated by units of "man"—which is an official measurement apparently devised by the boulder industry to calculate how many men it might take to move a sedentary stone, similar to how horse height is measured in "hands." A one-man rock is about the size of a basketball. I estimated my rock to be probably an eight-man one, which would put it in the neighborhood of *eight or nine thousand pounds* or so.

I put the Tundra in reverse and lined it up behind the rock, then jumped out, turned my cap backward and fished out a long, rusty farm chain jumbled in a corner of the truck bed.

Bert crossed his arms and watched me. "Are we really going to attempt this folly?"

Now a word about the chain. Chains come in different grades, rated by strength. A Grade 30 chain, for example, is one you might use to lock your bicycle to a Manhattan stoop railing. With a Grade 120 chain you could tug a container ship into the Port of New Jersey. Mine is in the middle, a Grade 80 chain, and we've used it plenty of times for towing heavy crap around the yard, such as eight-foot logs to the woodshed after we've felled a tree.

I hooked an end of the chain to the trailer hitch then lassoed the other end around the base of the rock. "C'mon dawg, let's give this rock a ride!" I climbed back in the Tundra and revved it a couple of times. I adjusted the rearview mirror and looked back. Bert had a funeral expression. He was getting genuinely nervous, which he doesn't tend to get. Usually when we're about to do something stupid and dangerous, he's raring to go.

"I don't think you're thinking enough about how much this damned rock actually weighs," he shouted. (This was before I looked up the "man" measurement thing.) "You're pretendin' like that rock is made of cork. It's made of granite! Granite weighs a lot."

He just couldn't picture the boulder moving, but in my gut, I had a good feeling. I levered the shifter arm into low gear and pressed the "tow/haul" button on the dashboard.

"You're going to melt your damn transmission," Bert said, shaking his head as he jogged out of the way. "Or you're going to bend the *hell* outta your chassis. Something bad is going to happen with this one."

I waved a hand at him. "Nahhh," I shouted. I hit the gas, slowly gave it the beans, and felt the torque kick in. Now a word about torque. I'm a big fan of torque. Torque is how the power of a vehicle makes you *feel*—that moment when you ask the machine to do something, and it does. That jolt when the wheels engage, that's torque.

Sure enough, the rock slid across the field like I was dragging a dead fish.

Bert walked behind tentatively, holding his breath, with his hands clasped together over the top of his head. The Tundra barely broke a sweat.

"Yee-Haw!" I hollered.

I brought the rock to rest next to a pine tree, positioning it nicely as a bench for sitting in the shade. I climbed out of the truck, plopped down Buddha-like on the great stone, and gloated. "Look at that now, will ya? I bet it took a million years of geological phenomena for this monster to get where it was before, and in five minutes I figured out a way to move it to this perfect spot."

"Congratulations," Bert said, "you outsmarted a rock."

As for which of the two red trucks we'd take to Bascom's, we just flipped a coin and Red Beauty won, which was fine. Bert's far more steady behind the wheel than I am anyway. Yanking rocks across a yard is one thing. Towing a two-ton sap tank is another. More on that in a minute.

LATE JANUARY 2022

5

A TRIP TO BASCOM'S

I have an unusual way of waking up in the morning. My cat has this thing where she'll sit at the edge of my pillow, and just as dawn is about to break, she taps her paw on my forehead. *Pad. Pad, Pad. Get up. Get up. Get up.* Usually, it annoys the crap out of me, and I'll shovel her off the bed. But this morning I had to get up early anyway to head to Bascom's with the big-ass trailer to get the big-ass tank. So I just gave her a head scratch and quickly got dressed. Bert must have recognized the magnitude of the occasion, too, because for the first time ever he was prompt. He pulled into my driveway at exactly seven o'clock and tooted the horn.

I walked out the door and into the day. Cloudy, with moisture in the air. We saluted each other through the windshield then I climbed in the truck.

"Fair warning, I had Taco Bell for dinner last night," I said, sinking into Red Beauty's plush seat. Bert's hair was combed and sharply parted, his chin polished from a fresh shave. He wore an ironed, tucked-in plaid shirt and a crisp white tee exposed at the collar. It looked like he'd buffed all the dirt off his boots, too. As spiffy as I'd ever seen him, like school picture day.

He noticed me noticing him and beamed. "Bascom's. Special occasion," he said.

The ride to Bascom Maple Farms would be about sixty miles cross-lots over the state of Vermont and into New Hampshire, with many mountains and snaky roads along the way. I'd checked the "Vermont Road Conditions" Facebook group, and it sounded like we were going to have clement weather for the ride over in the morning, but that things could get dicey on the return.

Meanwhile, Bert had been studying the F-150's owner manual like it was the menu at the Cheesecake Factory and was convinced Red Beauty could handle our trailer-tank's combined weight, which we estimated would be about 10,000+ pounds, a ten-man load at least.

We got underway, climbing up and out of Rupert on VT Route 315, and my ears popped. A few minutes later, we descended into the tiny ski town of Manchester via Malfunction Junction, a notorious traffic circle usually clogged with flatlanders from Jersey and Boston heading to the froufrou fashion outlets or Stratton resort. But this early morning it was empty.

"I guess we beat the ski traffic," I said. "Not many Land Rovers up with us farmers."

We ascended east out of Manchester on Vermont Route 11 and plateaued into the center of this skinny state. One of the things that sucks about driving on a rural road in southern Vermont is there's no room to pass. Two-lane (barely) with no straightaways. So when you're stuck behind a slow fucker (Subaru drivers, mostly) you're stuck for a long time. And so it was, just like clockwork, we got behind a dude driving about ten miles an hour in a Ford Ranger who had an avocado-green '70s-era double-door refrigerator upright in the back.

We watched him for a moment. "Bet the guy's gonna put that in his garage," Bert said.

I nodded. "Garage fridge for sure," I said. "Every man needs a space to call his own."

The guy wasn't using any kind of straps to secure the fridge, just what looked like some packaging twine looped through the door handle and tied off to the side of the truck bed.

I turned to Bert. "How's it possible either of us have gone this long without a garage fridge?"

He chuckled. "I'd just plug 'er in and fill it with meat."

The dude kept swerving, which made me think he was either drunk or focusing out the back window to see if the thing had fallen out yet.

"A whole shelf of Genny Lights, too," Bert added. "Cans, though. Not bottles of Genny. *Cans.*"

I nodded. "And of course, every good garage fridge has a lawn chair and patch of Astroturf carpet in front of it."

"Hell yeah," Bert said.

"And a transistor radio—"

"—with a telescoping antenna—"

"—and the ballgame on."

We both smiled at the same time.

"Yup. That's livin'," I said.

After a while we came into the Connecticut River Valley, which bisects Vermont and New Hampshire, flanked on both sides by steep uprises. Many writers and artists are scattered here on the hillsides and dales. The area has similar topography to Blossom Road, but with more of a literary vibe. My favorite example of this is the local repair shop along Vermont Route 5, just outside Bellows Falls. It's called Cheever Tire Service.

We crossed over the Connecticut River on the Church Street Bridge, where the state border for New Hampshire is marked with a red perforation line. Right then, I undid my seat belt, and Red Beauty's warning chime went nuts.

Bert flashed me a look. "What the hell are you doing?"

I threw my hands in the air. "Taking off my seat belt. We're in New Hampshire, man."

"So?"

I bounced in my seat from side to side. "Forty-nine other states, they lock you up for not wearing one," I said. "But not New Hampshire. We're in the 'Live Free or Die' state, baby!"

Bert glowered. "Well put it back on, the beeping is gonna drive me nuts."

"It'll stop in a minute," I said.

But a minute passed, and it didn't.

"C'mon, seriously. Put the stupid belt back on," Bert said.

I pouted and clicked myself back in. "That's weird. In my Tundra the beep stops after about twenty seconds. I never wear a seatbelt in New Hampshire"—a liberating feeling, like riding a motorcycle without a helmet, which, by the way, you can also do legally in New Hampshire. Home of the head splat.

Bert and I next rolled into a part of southwest New Hampshire I call "Salinger Country."

I pointed out the window. "J. D. Salinger used to hole up around here."

"*Catcher in the Rye* guy," Bert said.

"Yeah. You ever read it?"

Bert nodded his head yes. "Of course. In high school. Required reading, even in Yoe."

It was my favorite book in college. My thumbed copy was the maroon Ballantine paperback edition with the gold-serifed font. It lived in the pouch of my JanSport. I hero-worshiped Salinger as a writer. His descriptions of smoking were so sensual it made me take up cigarettes.

I craned my head to look into the hills. "You know the whole story about how Salinger fled New York after his book became a big hit? Well, he exiled himself to a little town called Cornish, which is right up the road from here. The reason why I know that is because in college I spent half a spring break driving around Cornish trying to meet the damn guy."

Bert snickered. "Really? Geez. What'ja think was gonna come from that?"

A faraway smile emerged across my face. *"Answers,"* I said.

"Or a restraining order," he said.

Bert dropped Red Beauty out of overdrive into a low gear as we climbed through the cat's cradle of New Hampshire state highways—5, 12, 123, 12A, 123A—that circumnavigate the region.

"So didja just go around knocking on people's doors asking if J. D. Salinger lived there?" Bert asked.

I recalled that I had found a *Life* magazine article from the early sixties, and in it were some photos of his house and an inlay of a red jumbo mailbox that said SALINGER on it.

"I tootled the length and breadth of Cornish for *hours* in my Corolla looking for that damn mailbox, rehearsing the cannily brilliant literary questions I was gonna impress him with so he'd invite me inside to critique a secret manuscript he'd been working on all those years."

Bert laughed. "And . . . I take it you never found him?"

I shook my head. "Nope, he must've taken the mailbox down."

"He was probably tired of being stalked by English majors," Bert said.

We kept driving, getting closer to Bascom's.

6

THE MAPLE MECCA

The entrance to Bascom Maple Farms off Crane Brook Road makes you feel like you're arriving at a grand country estate. Old dry-stacked walls of stone line Bascom's sharp driveway. Inside the compound, there are several field cobble houses with colonial brick fireplaces and leaded glass windows, where various Bascoms live. Beyond there are three or four metal-sided pole-barn warehouses, and stainless-steel forty-gallon syrup barrels are pyramided everywhere you look.

Bascom's is perched atop a vista point with a hundred-mile view back into Vermont on a clear day. Down below, in a slim valley, lie the dairy barns that were the origin of the farm before the cows were sold, back in the eighties, and the Bascom family went gung-ho into sugaring. Throughout the surrounding hectares of Bascom-owned forest is an embroidery of sap lines that connect the farm's 100,000 or so taps, making this one of the biggest maple sugaring operations in the United States, in addition to being the biggest equipment dealership in New England.

Bert carefully tooled Red Beauty into Bascom's tight, slopy parking lot. I jumped out and went to go find a Bascom inside the store. Many of them work there. I'm not sure how they're all related. Cousins and uncles and nephews, some wives, and nieces.

Inside, the store is like the Walmart of maple, stuffed with evaporators, reverse osmosis machines, bottling equipment, tubing, spouts, tools, pumps, candy molds, and tanks of many sizes. I ran into a few other sugarmakers I knew who were stocking up on preseason supplies like plastic jugs, glass bottles, defoamer, hydrometers, filter papers, and grading kits.

I walked to the back of the store and found young Sam Bascom helping a sugarmaker who was kicking the tires on a new evaporator. I tapped my foot impatiently while I waited for him to wrap up with the guy. Sam is a quiet man with a vigorous beard outcropping. He'd been holding my tank for a couple of weeks while I arranged to get the big-ass trailer to haul it home.

He finally finished with his customer and then turned to shake my hand.

"Hey Sam, is my tank ready?" I asked.

He said it was and he walked me up to the sales counter.

"Man, it's like Black Friday in here today," I said.

"Yeah, the season's almost on us, everyone's stocking up," Sam said as we excused ourselves past a bunch of sugarmakers with shopping lists in their hands.

I recalled the super tanker we were there to pick up on this day being listed in their catalog last year for $500 less than it was selling for now. When we reached the counter, I smiled at Sam and attempted a last minute haggle.

"Are you going to sell me the tank for the price I saw it for last year?" I asked.

Sam positioned himself in front of a cash register and tilted his head to the side. "Well, eh, that tank had to sit on my lot for a year," he said.

"So I take it that's a no?" I held up my palms. "But it's the same exact tank, isn't it?"

He grinned through his whiskers. "Maybe you should've bought it then."

I reached for my wallet and rolled my eyes at Bert, who by this time had found his way inside to join me. "Right." The transaction just about maxed out my Capital One Venture card.

After the register finished *ca-chinging* and spewing out receipt tape, Sam waved a hand. "Follow me," he said, and the three of us walked out of the bustling retail area, through a couple of high-ceilinged warehouses, and then entered into another big building, and there sat our tank.

We went slack jawed. Wow.

It was parked with a navy of other enormous tanks that were at rest on little caster carts, like ocean liners in port.

Sam said, "You're gonna have to help push."

It was a monster all right, as big as a dirigible.

The tank had a long black steel cage supporting welded sheets of stainless steel bent into a *U* shape. It dwarfed us. Its rim was over my head and almost over Bert's.

"No way this sucker is gonna overflow," I said to Bert, taking it in, awestruck.

Sam clasped his arms behind his back. "Exactly 3,106 gallons of capacity," he said.

I turned to him. "We mere mortals are just gonna be able to move this thing? Don't we need a backhoe or bulldozer or something?"

Sam tugged his ear. "Nah, it should move right along on the casters. I'll steer."

He was right. Even though the tank weighed at least a ton or two, on the casters we could shove it along practically with our pinky fingers. The three of us weaved it through the warehouse to a loading ramp, where Bert had docked Red Beauty and the big-ass trailer.

Getting the tank onto the trailer is what I thought was going to be the tricky part. But, apparently, I was the only one worried about it. Sam summoned a couple cousins, and Bert and I stepped aside. They hooked the tank to a small crane on the edge of the platform, and with a handheld remote controller, Sam hoisted the enormous vessel high in the air and then gently lowered the front end onto our trailer. Then, another Bascom scurried over and slid a dolly cart under it, grabbed the side rails, and heaved the Goliath forward. Next, Sam gently lowered the back end onto the trailer, and presto, the whole thing fit like a glove.

I let the air out of my lungs and offered Sam a high five. "Holy crap," I said.

"Yeah, we've done this a time or two," he said, with a wink.

We ratchet strapped it, exchanged handshakes with the crew, and climbed back into Red Beauty.

Sam patted the side of the truck. "Now going home, just take it slow and easy and you should be fine," he said, maybe noticing Bert's fingers tense at 10:00 and 2:00 on the wheel.

"Don't worry, slow's his specialty," I said, and Bert shot me an annoyed look.

Then, just as we were pulling out, we saw the man himself making his way across the parking lot toward us and waving us down—Bruce Bascom, the chief Bascom of the farm.

Bruce is a sugaring celebrity in our industry, but he never puts on airs, and he's always up for talking maple with any sugarmaker, big or small. Even us.

When someone is described as an "old Yankee farmer," Bruce Bascom is who they mean, the shrewdest man in all of maple. He was sporting a floppy ball cap and hiking boots, and even though it was only 30°F, he wore a short-sleeved pinstriped Sta-Prest shirt with his name stitched over the breast pocket.

We pulled up alongside him, and Bruce glanced back and forth between Bert and me and the trailered tank, as though he wondered where it had come from.

"We just bought this baby from you," I said through the window.

"Ha-ha, okay, okay," he said, a little vaguely.

Bruce is maybe one of the few guys in sugaring who's figured out how to make a lot of money at it. In fact, some folks like to joke that he's made *all* the money and the rest of us none of it. A lot of sugarmakers refer to him as "Uncle Bruce."

Uncle Bruce will buy all the syrup you make, guaranteed. Besides being a big equipment dealer, he's also what's known as a bulk buyer (or a "packer"), a guy who buys syrup wholesale from sugarmakers then rebottles it and sells it to the grocery store chains under his own label.

There are two kinds of sugarmakers: those who make syrup, jug it up, and sell it to their friends and neighbors, and those who squeeze all the syrup they make into forty-gallon barrels and haul it to a packer like Bascom. What's great about Bruce is he pays on the barrelhead for it, sending you home with a tax-free New Hampshire check in your pocket.

Bert and I usually bring most of our syrup in drums to Uncle Bruce. Somewhere along the line, he and I decided to just let Bruce deal with the bottling headaches. We've tried our hand at jugging syrup ourselves and peddling it around town, but it's a huge pain in the ass.

For starters, it's messy. To bottle syrup, we use something called a *canner*, which is a ten-gallon stainless steel box with a spigot in front, rigged underneath with propane burners. Before filling the bottles, we must first heat the syrup to 185°F. Scalding temperature. Inevitably I will overfill a bottle and the boiling-hot syrup will spill over my hands.

The other problem is maintaining a consistent 185°F temperature. If we get it too hot, say 195°F or more, the sugar can crystallize, and chunks of mineralized syrup that look like kidney stones will float around in the bottle. Not exactly appetizing. Pack it too cold, say below 175°F, and over time the syrup can become moldy and little wormy strands will swim around in it.

Bascom's has mastered these problems, and their syrup is always gorgeous.

Bruce propped himself with a hand outstretched against the hood of the truck. Wherever he goes, gaggles of sugarmakers crowd Bruce to pick his brain for what he'll be paying for bulk syrup at the end of a coming season. And today that was my question for him, too.

"Are we gonna get a raise this year, Bruce?"

He swatted at a mosquito in the air before answering. "Bulk prices will be up some," he said, a touch reluctantly, trying to make it seem like he wasn't the one in control of them. "But I can't tell you how much just yet. We'll have to wait and see."

This was news.

The bulk price Bruce pays to us farmers has been relatively low the last couple years. The expansion and improvements in technology means there's been a *sea* of syrup made lately, creating a buyer's market and seemingly putting Bruce in the catbird seat. "I always seem to get an infinite supply," he told me once. Some sugarmakers gripe about the price Bruce is paying them. Many producers owe a big nut to the banks for all their gilded equipment, and they count on Bruce's benevolence.

But the tables turned on Bruce after the 2021 crop, one of the worst in fifty years, with the pandemic driving demand for real syrup through the roof at the same time. The shortage was forcing Bruce to consider raising his prices to lure more syrup out of the field. If ever there was a year for us to try and hit the five-pound mark, this would be it. If Bruce were to indeed capitulate and raise his bulk price, we'd maybe make a decent profit.

A voice on a loudspeaker cut across the parking lot: "Bruce, a call for you on line two."

He didn't acknowledge it. "So, you fellers planning on making a lot of syrup, huh?"

I pointed at the tank. "Yeah, we're gonna fill this behemoth over and over this season."

He grinned. "Heh, heh, we'll see," he said, a little skeptically.

Bruce then drew in a long breath and launched into a layered soliloquy on international market conditions, the Quebec syrup cartels, and Canadian exchange rates. He has a Rain Man–like knowledge of maple macroeconomics that I usually find fascinating, even though much of it goes over my head. But I cut him off after a few minutes, telling him we were in a hurry.

"Sorry Bruce. We gotta beat the daylight back to Blossom Road."

Bruce said he understood and stepped away from the truck. "You know how it goes in maple, won't be long before you want another one of those tanks," he said and tipped his cap. "We'll be here when you do."

We got moving for home.

But first—lunch.

I turned to Bert, "Step on it, will ya?"

That's really what I was in the hurry for.

7

THE COUNTRY GIRL

The clouds were darkening and threatening snow when we left Bascom's. Red Beauty was handling the payload of the new tank without protest. She was the right truck to take. "I'm not feeling any drag or wag at all," Bert said, relief in his voice, but I couldn't help but check the sideview mirror every few minutes to make sure the tank wasn't about to capsize.

After a bit, we came into the postcard village of Chester, Vermont, and we swerved into the Country Girl Diner, which is possibly the best place to eat in the entire state. We stop here every time we make a trip to Bascom's. We could see folks in the window turning their heads in curiosity as we rolled past the restaurant to the far edge of the parking lot. I'm sure we were quite a sight. The tank was practically the same size as the diner. We got out and I plucked at the tie-down straps to make sure they were still taut and secure. "C'mon. That's not going anywhere," Bert said.

I'd been looking forward to eating here all morning. The Country Girl is one of those steel-sided railroad-dining-car-type diners, but with a funky flair. There's usually hippie music on the speakers, and the owner and staff, for some reason, have a particular obsession with G. Love & Special Sauce, a blue-eyed hip-hop group out of Philadelphia that had a hit in the nineties called "Cold Beverage." The Country Girl hosts a music festival every summer featuring a lineup of jam bands, and a few years ago they had G. Love himself on the bill.

The lunchtime crowd was thinner than usual. "Just grab a seat anywhere," said one of the waitresses. She was leaning one hand on the counter and pouring coffee for one of the patrons with the other. Bert and I slid into a two-top right at the front window. A song by the Tedeschi Trucks Band was ambient on the sound system, which had a nice bass low end.

I squinted at a whiteboard hanging on the wall. Today's special was a Reuben plate with fries. At diners like this, it's been my experience to always order the special, because when you order a special, it's just that—usually prepared with a little more love and thoughtfulness than the rest of the fare. Reubens happen to be my favorite sandwich anyway.

I waved over the waitress, who was muraled with tattoos.

"Do you use rye bread on the Reubens?" I asked.

Her eyes narrowed. "I'm pretty sure it's pumpernickel," she said and swung her head back toward the kitchen. "Jessica, what kind of bread do we use on the Reubens?" she hollered. "Pumpernickel!" a voice called back.

Bert looked at me strangely. "What the hell else kind of bread would you put on a Reuben, raisin bread?"

I raised my shoulders. "I just want to make sure I get rye bread for my sandwich."

"Pumpernickel *is* rye," he said, his voice rising.

I scrunched my face. "It is? I don't think so."

Bert turned to the waitress. "Help me out here?"

The waitress shrugged and tapped a pen on her order pad.

He looked back at me. "Pumpernickel is rye. Rye is pumpernickel. Get it?"

I put my hand up. "Okay, Poindexter. Didn't know you had a PhD in *yeast*."

The waitress snapped her chewing gum. "You two should maybe look into couples therapy."

We both ordered the special, and ten minutes later the waitress set high-piled Reubens in front of us: fresh rye/pumpernickel bread, fresh corned beef, fresh sauerkraut, just the right slather of Russian dressing. Next to each Reuben, a giant pile of slender fries and dill spears.

We dug in and munched unhurriedly, enjoying the food and the music. Van Morrison.

After a bit, Bert looked at me. "I was thinking about what you said about Salinger."

I opened wide to take huge bite. "What about him?"

He stopped chewing. "I was thinking I want to be a recluse."

I laughed. "Dropping out, huh?"

He swirled a bouquet of fries in a pool of Heinz 57. "What I had in mind is I'd like to buy an old school bus and drive it into the woods as far as it will go, and where it stops is where I'll live."

"Hmmm. What about Faith? She down with this idea?"

He shrugged. "She puts up with a lot."

"You got that right. What about food? How will you feed yourself?"

"I'll eat what I kill," he said.

I wiped my mouth with my sleeve. "Lots of woodchuck stew, huh? What about heat?"

"I'll put a stove in it."

I laughed again. "The stop sign arm is gonna swing out every time you leave the house to take a leak."

The waitress returned with a stack of napkins. "How those going down, fellas?" she said. Both our mouths were ballooned with Reuben, so we just nodded frantically, and she smiled. "That good huh?" We both gave her a thumbs-up and resumed annihilating the sandwiches.

"Well, buddy, lots of people check out from society," I said. "The Unabomber comes to mind."

He pointed a fry at me. "Yeah, except I wouldn't blow people up."

"Good to know. Never can tell with you recluses."

Bert harvested some lingering stubs and went quiet. Probably thinking to himself, "Yeah, I'd do *just fine* living in a goddamned school bus." I could easily see him pulling it off. He's the kind of guy who likes to beat the system and stick it to the man, doing things for himself. He changes his own brake pads, refuses to let an accountant do his taxes, pickles vegetables in his basement. That kind of thing.

I pinched at stray crumbles of corned beef on my plate. "Didn't the guy from *Into the Wild* live in an old bus? Then there's the Partridge Family of course. Hey man, I say go for it. Live in a bus. I'll miss the crap out of you and Faith being a part of society, but I understand. The woods are better. I'll stop by for squirrel kebabs sometime."

The waitress cleared our dishes but left the utensils.

"You two strike me as dessert people," she said.

Bert and I both ordered the pie special, which happened to be key lime, also my absolute favorite. Sometimes a day just goes your way.

Within seconds, she slid two wedges across the table. I applied a fork to my slice and took a bite. "Oh my," I said. It was transcendent. A deep-cut Bob Marley song came over the hi-fi: "Don't Rock My Boat." I gazed out the window at our new tank sitting snug and cozy on the trailer—a tank that would give us a puncher's chance of becoming Five Pounders this season and all the respect that comes with it. And right then I had what could be considered a moment of Zen. It was fleeting, but for a flash, everything seemed right in my world. The pie, the music, Bert's good company. Joie de vivre. Unfortunately, life has taught me that when I enjoy something too much, down the road there's always a steep price to pay. As quickly as the Zen moment came, it was replaced with a far more familiar feeling: dread.

Bert snapped his fingers close to my face. "You okay, buddy?"

A reality postponed by the key lime slice, the Reuben, and the Country Girl ambience regained my thoughts. Before the day was over, when we returned to Blossom Road, we'd have to somehow get that monstrosity *off* the trailer. Just me and Bert.

And there'd be no cranes or Bascoms to help.

8

THIS IS WHY WE CAN'T HAVE NICE THINGS

I had a plan. Really, I did.

The get-the-tank-off-the-trailer plan was to have Bert ease the trailer alongside the sugarhouse—which sits on an incline—and then we'd hook my farm chain between the back of the tank and the Tundra, which I had dropped off at the sugarhouse the night before. The idea was that while Bert and Red Beauty and trailer pulled in one direction, me and the Tundra with the chained-up tank and I would pull the opposite way, and the tank would just slide right off.

"And it'll land exactly where we want it," I said to Bert, clapping my hands.

But in my head, I couldn't stop reminding myself of that Mike Tyson line that goes something like, *all plans are great until you take that first punch in the mouth.*

There had been a light snow falling all afternoon, and by the time we got back to the sugarhouse, a veneer of fluff smeared the surface. To give us a good running start into the driveway, Bert hit the gas hard coming off Blossom Road, but the instant Red Beauty's tires hit the slippery snow, the force combination of extreme weight and accelerating speed sent the truck and trailer careening sideways and over a culvert ditch.

"Oh shiiiiiiit!" we shouted in unison, like Bo and Luke Duke.

We landed with a thud and puff of snow.

Then, stunned silence, interrupted only by the metronome click of Bert's right turn blinker and the low frequency of the dethrottled engine. A flurry of talcy snow settled to the ground around us. I undid my stupid seatbelt, which had flossed into my midsection.

"Pretty sure we caught air," I said.

We crawled out of the truck and stood on opposite sides of the wreck. What lay before us resembled a train derailment. We looked back at each other with bulging eyes.

"Donkey balls!" Bert shouted.

The F-150 had mostly cleared the culvert, but the trailer not so much.

Bert clambered back into the cab and floored the gas, in a futile attempt to pull it out, but the trailer had anchored the truck to the ditch, so Red Beauty's wheels just spun over the layer of fluff. The truck slid and swayed from side to side like a pendulum.

I waved at him through the windshield. "Give it a rest, it's not gonna work," I shouted.

Bert threw his hands in the air. "Holy fuckannoli," he said. "Whatta we do now, call Triple-A?"

"Or the suicide prevention hotline," I said under my breath.

Bert got out and offered to drive back to town to grab his "come-along," a ratcheting leverage tool with slip hooks on both ends. He thought we could hand-winch the trailer out of the spill. "We'll tie the other end to that tree," he said, pointing to a lone birch on the edge of the yard. But I vetoed the idea. "Dude, a come-along will move the trailer maybe a half-inch on each crank of the tool," I said. "That plan might *work*, MacGyver, but it'd take the rest of the weekend."

Bert frowned and nodded in agreement.

I turned to him. "We're out of options," I said. "I'm calling Archie McClellan."

He brightened. "You're calling Archie McClellan? Shit, man, that's all you had to say," he said, like Samuel L. Jackson in *Pulp Fiction* when they told him they were sending the Wolf.

Archibald McClellan belongs to a sprawling farm family in West Rupert who operate a 400-cow dairy and a sistering 16,000-tap maple operation.

Archie McClellan is the third brother in succession on the dairy farm, but his primary winter business is "caretaking." A lot of rich people from Manhattan and North Jersey own second homes in the Ruperts, and most of them hire Archie to maintain their properties, plow driveways, and check for frozen pipes on subzero days.

I speed-dialed Archie's house and got his wife, Jill, on the horn. I explained our predicament.

She understood immediately. "Don't worry, Archie'll be right there," she said. "Sit tight."

Point of information, Archie does not own a cell phone, but he does have a shortwave radio. All the farmers in town have them, too. What I found out later was that Jill had broadcast an all-points bulletin. Jill's mayday, "Pete Gregg dumped a trailer in a ditch on Blossom Road. Stranded. Request aid. Over," was heard by everyone on the same frequency. Everyone, that is, except Archie. He was inside Sherman's General Store over in West Rupert picking up a six-pack. Luckily, one of the guys who drives a manure spreader for the Holstein farm came in and asked Archie why he wasn't on his way to the "emergency."

At the time, we were oblivious to the behind-the-scenes scrambling to get Archie to our farm. We were just taking a gamble that Archie would show; we didn't know for sure.

"We might want to start formulating a plan C," Bert said.

It was turning bitter cold and starting to snow again. Daylight was fading fast.

"I wonder if this is how it feels for those poor bastards who have to go to the ER with things stuck in their butts," I said.

We got back in the truck to get warm, checked our watches, and waited.

9

THE PULL-OUT METHOD

When Archie McClellan turned in to the driveway in his big maroon GMC Sierra 2500, Bert and I exchanged looks of relief like trapped miners in a cave rescue. Archie stepped out of the truck and packed a dip of chew between his cheek and gums. Then he slipped his hands into his pockets, eyeballed the situation, and whistled.

"You boys got yourselves in quite a *mess* right here, din't ya?" he said and sent a brown loogie splotching into the white snow.

The chilled air had flushed his face radish red. He wore a seed-corn cap and navy-blue coveralls with a spiral notepad and pen tucked in the breast pocket.

We walked over to shake his hand. "We thought about trying Dial-a-Prayer," I said. "Instead, we called you."

The minute he arrived I could see we called the right man. Archie was equipped with three things that would be essential to saving our bacon. First, he had a snowplow mounted on the front of the heavy-duty GMC. Second, he had a hopper strapped to the bed with a flywheel that would toss sand like a lawn sprinkler. Third, the Sierra was set with studded snow tires, which Red Beauty wasn't. She only had radials, which Archie pointed out with emphasis.

"That's your problem right there, see," he said. "It's your *tires*."

Archie went around to the back of his truck and yanked a lever on the hopper spreader.

"Tell you what," he bellowed back to us. "I'm gonna toss down two or three layers of sand, see, and then you should be able to *grip* it with that pretty truck of yours."

I made a fingers-crossed gesture to Bert.

Archie got back into his cab, he pressed a button, and the hydraulics wailed, lowering the plow.

He spat out the window and revved the Sierra. "You boys stand back," he shouted.

With his studded tires gripping like crazy, he made short work of clearing a path for Bert's truck. Then he spread three thick courses of sand across the sugarhouse driveway.

"That oughta do it," he said. "That's more sand than Cocoa Beach."

Now it was Bert's turn. He climbed into Red Beauty.

Archie motioned his hand toward the ground. "Just *ease* it up out of there," he shouted to Bert.

Bert gave him a thumbs-up then tippled the gas petal—

"Remember, nice and easy till you feel it *grip*," Archie said. "Then thump 'er."

—and when the tires seized the sand, Bert vroomed the V8, tilting the truck forward. "That's it, give it a little more," Archie shouted, and Bert pressed the pedal further, then a little bit more, tension building, and then with a lurch, *Vrrrrump!*, the trailer popped out of the hole.

He pulled it up into the yard, and I chased behind doing a raise-the-roof gesture. "Woot! Woot!" I hollered.

Bert stopped and got out, admired his performance, then did a fist pump.

Archie dangled his arm out the window and slapped a hand against the door. "Attaboy!" he said, grinning. "You're a fast learner."

We weren't out of the woods. We still needed to get the tank to its final destination, up another stretch of incline beside the sugarhouse. Now, no proper farmer—certainly not one with the last name of McClellan—was going to just up and leave before a job was complete.

He gear-shifted his Sierra. "Now let's see to that tank," Archie said.

He plowed another path toward the landing spot for the tank then spun down more sand. "Okay, try tugging it up there," he yelled.

Bert got back in Red Beauty, gave me a here-goes-nothing look, and gunned it.

Once more the radials performed surprisingly well over the sand, and he towed the trailer right where we wanted it, parallel to the sugarhouse.

"You're on a hot streak," Archie shouted.

Now for the finale. Getting the tank off the trailer and onto the ground.

Archie looked over to me. "How were you fellas fixin' to get that thing off there?"

I explained my trucks-pulling-in-the-opposite-direction strategy.

He crinkled his face. "Hmmm," he said, a little doubtful.

While Bert idled in his truck, I hopped in the Tundra, let it warm up for a minute, and backed it up to the trailer. Then I dragged out the farm chain, and hooked an end to the tank and the other to my hitch.

I smirked at Bert. "This is gonna work like the ol' tablecloth trick," I said.

Archie shook his head and scrammed out of the way.

I got back in my truck, stretched my head out my window, and shouted, "Ready, Bert?"

He wristed into low gear and floored his gas; I stomped mine. Clouds of exhaust from the straining motors congested the air, and the chain grew taut as a fiddle string. In my side-view mirror I could see the leviathan tank slowly begin to creak forward. "It's working!" I shouted.

It inched a little bit more . . . a little bit more . . . *Twank!* It landed hard off the trailer. The vibration of the sheet metal made a sound like a bowling ball dropping into a dumpster.

After the smoke cleared, the three of us got out of our respective vehicles and gathered around the tank.

I tugged at my shirt collar. "Well at least nobody died," I said. "Except my stomach lining."

Bert exhaled. "I'm gonna go home, get under my weighted blanket, and eat some comfort food," he said.

Archie wagged a finger at us. "Lemme give you boys a little advice," he said. "Next time, rent a helicopter."

I pulled every bill I had out of my wallet and handed it to Archie.

"Not sure your fee for saving a couple idiots, but it's all I got," I said.

He tried to wave me off, but I stuck the wad in his palm, and he smiled. "I'm late for dinner," he said, and then he climbed back into the Sierra and headed back home to Jill.

EARLY FEBRUARY 2022

10

OPENING DAY

On the first day of February, I got up early and was raring to go. I threw on some long johns, found my heavy snow boots in the back of the closet, and fed the cat.

In the run-up to when the sap starts flowing in the trees, there's much to do to prepare. Right after New Year's we start making regular trips to the sugarhouse, and it's tick, tick, tick against nature's clock. If we don't get our maples tapped and equipment hooked up in time, we'll miss production and that's not what Five Pounders do.

Bert wouldn't be ready until mystery o'clock, that I knew.

Bert Time.

Our predawn text exchange went something like this:

Me: "*Yo, you rolling yet?*"

Bert:

Twenty minutes later.

Me: "*Yo buddy. Any signs of life over there?*"

Bert:

Me, thimble-deep patience: "*Yo, let's roll!*"

Another twenty minutes.

Bert, finally: "*I'm up. Give me 20 minutes.*"

That meant it was going to take Bert twenty minutes to begin the *process* of getting himself ready. The problem is the traffic inside his head, a snarl of brain commands. Bert Time, dissected: So much is going on up there—like the 405 Freeway—that the facilities that administer Bert's body to *get moving* are stuck in line behind the computing of what tools and accessories we'll need for the day. He's trying to anticipate not just the things we *will* need but things we *might* need. Do we have chain saw gas for the chain saws? Do we have bar oil? Do we have wedges? Do we need pry-bars? Do we have extra chains? Do we have . . . you get the idea. If I push Bert during this process, and I've ninja-trained myself not to, I'll disrupt the checklist and make him forget the one essential item we'll for sure end up needing. And so, I waited.

Twenty minutes later, I pulled into his driveway and honked the horn outside his house, a charming three-story turn-of-the-century Queen Anne. On this Saturday morning, Bert's pace was slowed even more. It was five below. So cold you could feel it in your nostrils. I tried to jostle him with a few more honks, and at last he emerged. We met eyes and saluted each other.

I rolled down the window. "What's up, tiger?"

"Morning," he said, with a trace of disorientation, his brain nearing circuit overload. He headed for the garage, the tabernacle, which sits detached from the house on the back of his driveway. He started rummaging for the checklist items.

I stayed in the truck. "Ready to go freeze our asses off?" I said.

He gave me a bleary-eyed harrumph, and I laughed.

"Suck it up, buttercup," I said, watching the mouth vapor float in the air.

Our plan this morning was to go into the woods with our chainsaws and clear fallen branches off our sap lines, one of the first, if not *the* first thing all sugarmakers do in preparation for an upcoming season. The shears, windstorms, and gust fronts that typically thrash the Northeast during summer and fall (with more and more frequency the last twenty years) inevitably knock branches across our lines and sometimes topple entire trees onto them.

I rubbed my hands over the heat duct on the dash. "Well at least we get to play with chainsaws today," I said. One of our favorite things to do. "That should put some pep to your pistol."

Twenty minutes later we rolled up on the sugarhouse and started unpacking the truck. Bright sunshine was cutting through the maples and baby blue sky. It was what I like to call an "Aldro Hibbard" day. Who the hell is Aldro Hibbard, you ask? Hibbard was a midcentury landscape painter famous for painting the winterscapes of Vermont. A master of light composition. No one has captured the exact angles, hues, and textures of the light on a midwinter Vermont day better than Hibbard. His oils were pitch perfect. The attitude of January sunlight up here throws lots of shadows, making the color of snow not true white, but dark blue, wolf grey, and sometimes even green. That's what made Hibbard's canvases so brilliant, *his snow*. Hibbard's snow was anything *but* white. He'd also add shadowed, almost purple ridgelines, tomato-red barns, pebbly brooks. Then he'd throw in blotchy green-brown dabs and strokes of maple and pine lined along a slope. If I ever make enough money in this business, I'm buying a Hibbard of my own to hang over the fireplace.

The temperature at the farm had risen to a balmy two above by the time we got there. Oddly, even in single digits in the middle of winter, if the sun is out and there are no clouds or wind—that's the key, no wind—you can sometimes work in just a hoodie. Of all the outdoor elements, I hate wind the worst. (Second worst is ice; third, rain; fourth, clouds; fifth and final worst, snow. Maybe I picked the wrong profession.) During the sugar season, not only will wind blow right into your bones, but it also makes a considerably dangerous job even more dangerous. The reason is because of our rapidly dying ash trees. Let me explain.

A once very populous tree species, the common North American ash are dying everywhere in the Northeast and Midwest. That's because of the emerald ash borer, a wood-eating beetle that is thought to have come over in the dunnage of cargo ships from Asia and escaped into the wild. The emerald ash borer ranks in the top ten of invasive species in America (with the spotted lanternfly gaining fast, a pest that loves to eat maples, we've been told).

Nearly every sugarmaker I know has a bunch of precarious dead ash standing in their woods that were murdered by the ash borer. And when the wind blows, down they come. The dead ash in our sugarbush we call "widow-makers."

Going into the woods on a windy day can be like Russian roulette. You might wonder why we don't just cut them all down if they're so dead and dangerous. I've talked to a lot of other sugarmakers about this, ones far more experienced than me with chainsaws. "Don't touch 'em," they always say. "Let them fall on their own." A standing dead ash is a viciously wicked tree that will contort and twist in every unpredictable way if you try and fell it yourself. If the whole tree doesn't crush you, dead branches, huge ones, shake out of the crown and come down on your skull. Another potential chart-topper on the dead-ash hit parade is it'll "barber chair" you in the chin. When a tree barber chairs, it means when you saw into it, the rotted tree rapidly splits until it hinges somewhere near your head, and then, without warning, it will kick out like the footrest of an old barber chair, snap your neck, and kill you, or worse, paralyze you.

Our woods are loaded with dead ash. The wind has been knocking many of them over, but there's still a bunch waiting to clobber some poor bastard on a blustery day. There's one dead ash still standing near the top of our hill that's so rotted you can literally see straight through it. It's terrifying. Even in the tiniest breeze, it creaks. We have a series of three or four sap lines that are routed beneath it. Every time I have to go near the tree, I literally *sprint* past.

We gassed up the saws and filled them with Itasca bar oil, which lubricates the chain and keeps it from overheating. We were using Bert's special blend of non-ethanol high-octane chainsaw gas that he mixes with a stabilizer fluid. The non-eth gas is only available at a gas station a couple towns over from where we live, and Bert makes a special trip a couple times a month with a dedicated gas can. Non-eth is crucial for running small-engine equipment.

Out of the heap of gear, Bert handed me one of our walkie-talkies and kept one for himself. The plastic casing was ice-cold to the touch. I switched it on, and it blipped to life.

Long-range walkie-talkies are useful in the woods, allowing us to check back and forth when we're on opposite sides of the mountain. We synced frequencies to Ch. 2 (because sometimes we overhear Truman and his crew in the sugarbush next door on Ch. 1).

We like to communicate with proper walkie-talkie jargon. I realize using the lingo is a little on-the-nose, but we do it because we think it's fun to make believe we're truckers. To begin a transmission, I go, "Come in Bert," and he'll say, "Roger." Our sentences, in radio-speak, are chirpy: "Copy" and if we want to know each other's location, "What's Your 20?" To end a conversation, we usually go, "Over." And "10-100" or "10-200" is the bathroom shorthand.

Bert twisted a knob. "Come in Pete. Are you there Pete? Testing. Over."

I looked back at him, expressionless. "Roger that. Standing right next to you. Out."

He squeezed a side button. "Copy. Test complete. Out," he squelched.

The folks at Stihl, the makers of my saw, have devised a riddling coding system on the choke switch that I can never quite figure out. There are four different symbols representing four different choke statuses etched into the plastic casing like hieroglyphics. I fiddled with the choke and its befuddling signs—pressing it fully on, then halfway on, then not at all on—each time while yanking on the starter rope, and my Stihl fired up on maybe the ninth or tenth pull.

Stihls have a reputation for being fussy, but I like that they're made in America. Chainsaw debates on Stihl vs. Husqvarna rage in the agricultural community like Chevy vs. Ford. Bert's chainsaw—or I should say *one* of his chainsaws; he's got four—is also a Stihl, a serious sucker called a "Farm Boss," which has a caricature of a bossy-looking farmer on its cowl.

I have no business messing around with chainsaws. Many sugarmakers and farmers in our area are taught to use chainsaws when they're around eleven or twelve, and by the time they reach adulthood, saws are as familiar in their hand as a toothbrush. The Dunns down the lane are like that. Truman taught his son Evan how to drop trees before Evan was a teenager. Bert has been using chainsaws since at least high school, when he worked on his grandfather's farm back in Yoe. Meanwhile, I didn't touch a chainsaw until my early forties. Chainsaws were totally foreign to me growing up in Mound. I didn't know *anyone* who owned a chainsaw. My dad certainly didn't have one. The notion of cutting down a tree would've never crossed his mind unless maybe one was standing in his way on the 16th hole dogleg at Hazeltine.

I've since become infatuated with chainsaws, with their ferociousness. But I worry about my thigh. And my foot. And my arteries. Yes, there are many chainsaw skill courses and great improvements in safety apparel—plus much-improved safety mechanisms on the saws themselves, particularly the chain brake—but there are still many gruesome accidents and deaths every year from cutting trees. I tend to be ultra-careful and circumspect with every move I make with a saw. I wear a helmet with a wire-mesh chip guard that flaps down over my face. I also wear chaps over my legs that are lined with a spaghetti nylon material that will tangle up the chain before it maws through your flesh. And I pray a lot.

Before we headed up the hill, I wanted to test my saw on some stray logs lying around the sugarhouse. I had just gotten the chain sharpened back in town at Salem Hardware—they only charge $3 to sharpen a chain there; a total bargain—and I wanted to break it in. But nothing was happening. I could barely make a notch in the log no matter how much pressure I applied.

"My saw's not cutting for shit," I hollered to Bert. He was still unpacking the truck.

Bert wondered out loud if I had let the tip hit the ground. "If you even kiss dirt with it, that's all it takes. It will dull the chain instantly," he said.

I was pretty sure I hadn't.

"I just put the chain back on yesterday," I said. "Just now is the first time I've used it."

Bert came over, grabbed the saw, and owlishly looked it over.

He laughed. "You got the chain on backward, buddy," he said.

He pointed to the pattern of links.

"The teeth need to be facing out and the rakers going in the other direction."

I disassembled the casing, flipped the chain around, and tried it again. This time the Stihl sawed effortlessly.

"Geez, an inside-out chain, who knew?" I said. "You handy with zippers too?"

Bert shrugged. "Sure. Chains. Zippers. You name it."

"Good to know," I said and revved the saw. "Because after I lop off my arms with this stupid thing—"

"Yeah?"

"When I need to take a leak, you can be my fly guy."

11

ENTER THE MAPLEX

Armed with our Stihls, Bert and I filed into the sugarbush.

The forest sizes up to twenty-five acres altogether, which in the overall farming world is tiny, but it's still a lot of ground to cover, and all that ground is vertical. At the bottom of the mountain, where the sugarhouse lies, there's an open field of goldenrod, which is split by a colonnade of our thickest and sugariest maples. The hedgerow. Above the fields, the sugarbush swells simultaneously with the rise of the mountain, all the way up in blanket formation.

The woods have an equal constituency of sugar maples and red maples. A sugar maple trunk has a particular look to its bark that makes it stand out from other trees—a faded shade of gray and distinct wrinkle pattern that resembles the skin of an elephant. This guise will almost always help us identify it. But sometimes not. In that case—maybe the tree has a funny growth pattern or something—we must look on the ground for leaf litter to confirm the signature five points of its blade to make sure it's a maple. Otherwise, we could end up accidentally tapping a hickory or poplar. Embarrassing. Red maples have a more jagged edge to their leaf, and often there'll be a light green moss growing on their bark that helps us distinguish them.

Sugar maples emit a tad more sugar in their sap than the reds. Some sugarmakers don't even bother tapping red maples, but we always do because we're chasing every drop of sweetened sap we can get, especially this season. *Five Pounders.*

A lot can happen in a sugarbush during the intervening eight months between seasons, all bearing their effects on the sap lines. Dead branches can fall across them. Whole trees too, ash in particular. Our job today was to clear away the debris so the lines would snap back tight. Tight lines are crucial to getting maximum vacuum and the most sap.

Trudging up Blossom Hill at the beginning of a new season always winds the hell out of me. Bert was huffing and puffing even worse.

He paused on the hill, pressed his palms to the flat of his back, and grimaced.

"The orthopedist is getting a call first thing Monday morning," he said.

I hunched over and rested an elbow on my knee.

"Man, I probably should've stretched first," I said.

Three kinds of sap lines innervate our woods. First are the *droplines*. These are short lengths of tubing—ours are thirty-six inches—that noodle down from the spout stuck in the taphole.

The droplines connect into much longer runs of tubing, sometimes hundreds of feet, called *lateral lines*, which are either three-sixteenths or five-sixteenths of an inch in diameter. The laterals zigzag from tree to tree. You can think of them as the avenues and the boulevards of the pipeline.

The laterals connect into *mainlines*, which are like the interstate highways of the system. Most of the mainline in our woods is either one inch or three-quarters of an inch in diameter. Mainline pipe transverses our hill in five separate runs, all of which connect to a 1,200-foot double trunkline—one pipe for the sap, another for air—that runs all the way down the side of the mountain back to a high-powered industrial pump behind the sugarhouse.

The mainline pipe, made of rigid blue plastic, is threaded through the woods by ratchet-tensioned wire. We lash the mainline to this wire with a series of heavy-duty twist ties.

At the bottom of the hill, the trunkline is hard-plumbed into something called a *releaser*, which is a blue canister about the size of a mop bucket that holds the vacuum in the pipeline while it dumps the incoming sucked sap into the tank. You need this middleman in the system to keep the vacuum level consistent. The releaser is hooked up to a five-horsepower pump the size of a dishwasher that sucks at twenty-six or twenty-seven inches of mercury vacuum.

All the pipeline sections are joined with barbed plastic fittings that are inserted inside the tubing. Each one forms a *Y* or a *T* or is straight. To lock them in place, we use a specialized tubing tool—basically a modified pair of vise grips—that scrunches the connections together.

And that's our pipeline system. It must always be airtight. There cannot be a single leak because even the tiniest hole will send our vacuum to zero, which means loss of sap.

Deeper in the woods, Bert and I decided to split up.

He waved. "Well, nice knowing ya," he said and began to march north.

I turned in the other direction. "Now might be a good time to mention I put you in my will."

"Am I gonna inherit anything good?" he asked, as he trudged farther away through the snow. "I've had my eye on your snow blower."

I cupped my hands around my mouth to answer. "Only if you agree to adopt my cat."

We were on patrol for anything that would prevent the free flow of sap through the pipe, especially fallen ash branches squeezing lines out of commission, or any telltale signs of leaks, even though they'd be harder to spot with no sap flowing through them just yet.

Aside from a dramatic branch or fallen tree, the most common leak-causers are squirrel chews. Nearly all sugarmakers, including this one, hate squirrels. Squirrels are barely not rats. Unbelievably destructive, especially in the woods. They're always biting into our plastic tubing. No one really knows why, although some theorize they're appetized by the salt residue left behind from our hands. You'd think it's the tasty sap they're after, but squirrels bite our lines year-round, and most of that time there's no sap in the tubing at all.

Other wildlife bite into our tubing, too, including bear, deer, racoons, porcupines, and fisher cats. Every sugarmaker has a horror story and a particular varmint that seems to pick on them the worst. One guy might have porcupine problems up the wazoo, while another has it bad with the bears (which can do far more damage to a pipeline—bears absolutely shred tubing).

Almost every day of sugaring season, we spend countless hours chasing leaks by hunting for little tooth holes. There are tricks to finding them. Sometimes we hear an audible hiss like a punctured tire. If we hear a leak, we're lucky. Usually, we find them with our eyes. Leaks present themselves with little clues. If there's a leak somewhere on our lateral line, for example, there'll be a *whoosh, whoosh, whoosh* pattern to the sap flowing through, caused by the air. If there's a hole in our mainline, an icicle will form underneath it, tipping us off. If there's a leak on a dropline, we can usually eyeball the chew marks from the little bastards.

Not long into my foray into the woods, I spotted some gnaw marks up and down a dropline, like someone had scored it with a carrot peeler. "Oy vey," I said.

To fix the chew I needed to splice out the damaged part with a pair of very sharp snips and reconnect it with a replacement fitting using the vise-gripping tubing tool. I was wearing a big orange apron that had a bunch of pockets for holding tools, pipeline fittings, and tape. I pulled out the tubing tool and clamped down on both sides of the chew then snipped out the chewed-up section in between. I positioned a fitting in the opening and closed the clamps together. The pipe slid nice and neat over the barbs. Repair complete.

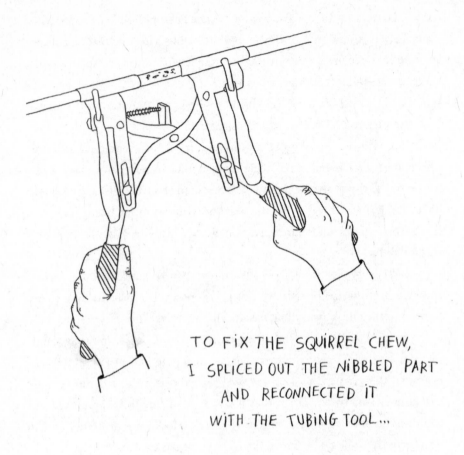

TO FIX THE SQUIRREL CHEW,
I SPLICED OUT THE NIBBLED PART
AND RECONNECTED IT
WITH THE TUBING TOOL...

"Like it never even happened," I muttered.

I snatched the walkie-talkie from a clip on my vest and squeezed the button.

"Come in, Bert." I wanted to ask him how the lines looked on his end.

Bert:

I tried again. "You got your ears on, son? Over."

Nothing. He was probably engaged with the saw. I kept moving.

Working in the woods with the tubing stretched everywhere means we do a lot of ducking under or stepping over. I turn into a contortionist out there.

In a clearing in the middle of the orchard, I came upon a flock of robins marching in formation across the snow. I counted sixteen of them. Suddenly a lead robin flew off, and the rest followed. Except for one stray robin who remained behind and wandered around by himself for a minute or two, seemingly wondering where the hell everybody went. Then the entire flock circled back around and swooped toward him, and he flapped himself off the ground to join them in the air.

Farther up the hill, I came upon a bunch of branches lying across my sap lines like a game of jackstraws. Most of the branches I could wrest off with my hands. A few would require a swipe or two with the chainsaw. I yanked on the cord about seven or eight times before it screeched to life. Sawing through wood is immensely satisfying. The chainsaw growls at louder decibels the harder it's working, and wood shavings kick out like a rooster tail from a Jet Ski. Fresh cut wood also has a great aroma, with a musk not unlike newly cut grass.

For most of the smaller branches, I barely had to apply any pressure to the saw. The fellas at Salem Hardware did an aces job sharpening my chain, which made the cutting easy. I let the weight of the saw carry it through the cut. I've learned that you want the saw to do the work, not your force. If you're putting too much muscle into a cut, that's when accidents can occur.

These were mostly small branches. Nothing too hard-core. Then I came upon a doozy.

A long-dead ash—the entire tree, with a trunk the length of a telephone pole—had fallen on a mainline, pinning it to the ground and pinching it shut. *Holy crap.* It was imperative to get it off there or not a single drop of sap would be able to travel through the pipe.

It was intimidating. *Maybe you should call Bert over to confer,* I thought. I grabbed my radio then stopped short. My ego stepped in.

Aw, don't be a wuss. You can handle this.

My first order of business was to lop off the jutting airborne side of the ash's lean. I tried to fire up the chainsaw again, but this time it wouldn't start. I fiddled with the Rubik's Cube choke setting and yanked the cord a bunch of times, getting more and more frustrated. "Damn Stihl!" I shouted.

I toyed with the stupid choke lever again. After a few more pulls, and a few more curses, the saw and I reached a bitter compromise—and with a breath of exhaust it let out its familiar combustion snarl.

I planted my feet on the uphill side and extended cross-body over the mainline to cut the span of tree hovering on the other side. When I sawed through the trunk, the remaining length of tree, which was still resting on the line, eased toward my torso with a groan. A warning sign.

Instead of making my next cut at the midsection of the leftover trunk, which would've been the smart thing to do, I instead cut a shorter length, maybe ten inches, just a tad adjacent to where the tree was garroting the pipe. As a visual, imagine a No. 2 pencil lying on a taut rubber band, with the eraser cap being the touchpoint. If you were to cut that piece off, the cap would slingshot in your face. Well, that's what happened with the log, except instead of a harmless eraser cap, it was a twenty-pound chunk of wood. And instead of a stretched-out rubber band, the log was sprung by a 500-foot span of high-tension wire.

The chunk rocketed into the air, grazing past my chin before hitting an apex above my head. It revolved in slow motion like it was preparing for a half gainer off an Olympic springboard, and then the chunk oriented itself for a return to earth, whereupon it landed butt-end on the vamp of my boot. More on that in a second.

During this explosion of force, keep in mind I held in my hand the fully throttled Stihl. In its velocity upward, the released pipe just missed the nose of the saw. Had it made contact, it would've bounced the ripping chain into my chest and gorged my heart or severed my windpipe.

Back to the boot. The good news here is I have "foot claustrophobia," meaning I prefer wiggle room in my footwear for my toes and enough space for heavy socks. Therefore, the boots I was wearing today were a size thirteen, even though I have a size twelve foot. So when the butt of the log landed, it only squished the very tip of my boot sparing my tootsies.

Cold sweating, the line still twanging like a mouth harp, I radioed Bert.

"Yo, you out there? Come in, Bert. Over," I squawked through the intermittent static.

"Stand by," he said, then, "Go ahead. Lots of cleaning up over here. Over."

"What's your 20?" I asked.

He was on the far side of our woods, where about ten different sap lines come into one spot on a manifold. "Spaghetti Junction. Over. Branches down everywhere. Haven't even got to any leaks yet. But seeing lots of squirrel scat around. How you making out? Over."

I told him what happened.

"Whoa, buddy. Maybe some scat in your long johns? Over," he said.

My voice was quivery. "Dude, it was like that log was shot out of a god-damn cannon."

"Insane tension on that pipe. Seriously bud, you okay?" Bert said.

"I wasn't killed, so I guess that's the good news. Bad news is you don't get my cat."

"I'm a dog person anyway," he said. "Maybe next time call for a second opinion. Over."

For the rest of the morning, I tried not to think about the slingshotted log. But at one point I noticed my hands shaking as I fixed more chew damage from the frigging squirrels.

12

FIREHOUSE BREAKFAST

T he next morning there was six inches of fresh snow—a run-of-the-mill accumulation that mostly just prettied everything up, rather than interfering too much with our lives. An Aldro Hibbard day, upbeat and clear. The town DPW crews had the roads passable by predawn. Up in the woods, it would be a different story. Six more inches to step through.

We were starting the morning the best way possible, at a firehouse breakfast hosted by the Salem Volunteer Fire Department. Many fire companies around here host breakfasts to raise money to defray the expense of their apparatus and gear. Firefighters can really cook. Throughout the year, they put on breakfasts, chicken BBQs, and pie sales. On Saturday nights in the summertime, they organize auctions where townsfolk empty their barns and attics then donate their old junk to the firehall. Other fire departments host carnivals. Over in Shushan, where Shakey lives, the fire department puts on a midway-style carnival under a big three-post, open-sided tent the first week in August. The amusements there are not to be missed. One of my favorites is the dime toss. The firemen box off an area surrounding a bench covered with donated teacups, saucers, salad plates, cocktail glasses, and coffee mugs, most of them vintage or even antique. We exchange our bills for dimes then toss or flip the coins into or onto a piece of dinnerware, and we keep whichever piece the coin lands in or on. The Shushan carnival also features milk-bottle knock-down games, dart-throw balloon-popping games, and other contests of skill and chance. Another favorite is the cake wheel. Attached to a countertop, an upright wheel divided into numbered wedges spins from one to twenty-six. Corresponding numbered slots are painted on the countertop, where we wager a quarter. If the wheel lands on our number, we pick a dessert. The prize rack contains frosted chocolate layer cakes, carrot cakes, brownies, berry-filled pies, Bundt cakes, and zip-locked bags of cookies—chocolate chip, oatmeal, butterscotch, and peanut butter mushed down with crisscrossed fork marks—all made by the ladies' auxiliary.

I'd been looking forward to the Salem breakfast for a solid two weeks. They'd been advertising it on a letterboard sign propped in front of the firehouse, which I pass by every day.

I got there first in the Tundra, and Bert pulled in about ten minutes later in Red Beauty. Bert Time. On this morning, another of our buddies was joining us, Tommy Benton. Tommy has participated in many of our sugarhouse shenanigans over the years. He knows his way around a farm. He grew up tossing straw bales on a dairy downstate. Now though, Tommy inhabits the white-shoe corporate world and lives a very ordered life, so the time he spends with us on Blossom Road allows him to channel his inner redneck. He's had some success in life and has earned some decent bank. While Bert and I arrived at the firehall in our trucks, Tommy rolled up in a red Jaguar coupe. When he climbed out, he was fitted in Filson outdoor wear like a catalog model. We dapped up, then I swung an arm across his shoulders and smiled. "Next time park that thing in the back so no one associates us with it." Flashy sportscars like Tommy's sometimes get the stinkeye around here, even though most guys in town probably spent more on their pickups than Tommy did on his Jag. We turned and admired the car, refracting the sunlight, surrounded by the grubby trucks in the parking lot; it looked like a ruby slipper in a boot locker. He took off his Ray Bans and laughed. "Yeah, I get it, maybe a tad conspicuous?" Tommy doesn't drive the car because he's a show-off. He drives it because it's a helluva car, and he's a *car guy*. He has a Wikpedic knowledge of all things car—makes, motors, models. He and I sometimes go to auto shows together to ogle the high-horse American muscle and watch them drag race. We also binge the Mecum auctions on cable and text back and forth our guesses of the winning bids.

The three of us arrived early enough to beat the rush, a little past 7:30. The firehouse banquet hall was organized with a grid of rectangular tables draped with white cloth. We hung our coats on the beige metal folding chairs, grabbed some thin, bendy paper plates, and queued up to the buffet. Ten bucks got us an all-you-can-eat buffet with a selection of scrambled eggs, home fries, pancakes (regular or blueberry), and a choice of meat: bacon or sausage or both.

The Salem firehouse breakfasts usually bring out most of the town, and we bumped into a couple other sugarmakers there. Jim Chambers, from Chambers Valley Farm, was volunteering behind one of the stainless-steel chafing pans filled with blueberry pancakes, kept warm by a can of diethylene fuel underneath. I asked him how things were going at the farm.

"There's a crew up in the woods tappin' today," he said, dropping pancakes onto my plate with a pair of salad tongs, "won't be long 'fore sap starts runnin' I bet."

I've become a connoisseur of firehouse breakfasts, and Salem's is top notch. There's one I like a little better though—the one over in West Pawlet. There, they arrange the seating in the garage between the shiny yellow firetrucks, which adds to the ambiance. West Pawlet's firehouse breakfasts are self-serve, which means . . . more bacon. We can thatch as much bacon on a plate as it can hold. The West Pawlet firemen also put maple syrup and butter right on the tables, so we can literally pour syrup and smear butter onto every bite of pancake. Here in Salem, they put all their syrup in a crockpot up front. Don't get me wrong, we can douse the pancakes as much as we want, but by the time we sit down, they sometimes dry up. We don't mind too much though. We want to support Salem's great fire department, so we never miss one of their fundraising events. If we ever have a fire at the sugarhouse (or I should say, *when* we have a fire at the sugarhouse), it's these men and women who will race up there to put it out.

"So do we have a workplan for today?" Bert asked, straining to keep his grease-moistened plate from drooping over as he eased it down onto the table.

I unfolded a napkin in my lap. "I figure we'd spout the lines," I said.

At a nearby table, this chucklehead who we've played poker with a few times, Eric Gerber, was sitting with his attractive bob-coiffed blond wife. They're a couple with a baffling disparity in appeal. Gerber is one of those dudes who takes his wife for granted and always acts henpecked. She was engaged in an animated conversation with what appeared to be, due to all the blond heads, her entire side of the family, while Gerber stared at his phone. I was hoping he wouldn't see us. But sure enough, he looked up, spotted us, and came over.

"Yo, bruhs. I could use a time-out from the in-laws," he said and straddled a seat next to Tommy, crossing his forearms over the backrest. He wore a goatee and had sunglasses perched on his ball cap. He smelled like clean laundry. "You cowboys still syruping?" he asked.

I told him we were. "I was just saying the first order of business today is we gotta go into the woods and spout the lines," I said.

"What the hell is that?" Gerber said.

I explained that we had to put new spouts on all the droplines for the season—spouting the lines.

Tommy made a confused look. "You replace the spouts every year? You don't reuse them?"

I unpeeled a tinfoil butter tab and squished it onto my pancakes. "Nah, they're plastic. They get filled up with bacteria at the end of a maple season after it gets warm and the leftover sap starts to ferment," I said.

"Can't you just wash them?" Tommy asked.

"Plastic is porous," Bert answered between bites. "You can scrub and scrub but at some point, anything plastic is impossible to get clean again."

Gerber laughed and tilted his head in the direction of his wife. "So I guess that means we shouldn't bother putting the, uh, you know, *marital aids* in the dishwasher anymore?"

Then he shifted in his chair closer to us. "Dudes, so I popped a gummy little bit ago."

Bert made a lemon face. "It's quarter to eight in the morning," he said.

Gerber held a finger up to his lips. "Uh-huh," he said, grinning. "I made the fireman give me an extra helping of eggs 'cause the omega-three is supposta help get ya wasted faster."

I raised my eyebrows. "Hadn't heard that one before," I said.

"I got 'em from Cheech and Chong! They make edibles now," he said. "So funny. Delta 9 high potent shit."

"Hmm. Good thing there's paramedics in the building I guess," Tommy said.

"It'd be nice if they served mimosas at these things, so a guy's gotta improvise," Gerber said.

After a little more chitchat, he got up to leave. We weren't too disappointed to see him go.

"This conversation has been ten times more interesting than what I gotta go back to, but it's queenie's birthday. Hope you understand."

"We do, we do," I said, catching Bert's and Tommy's eyes.

"I'm making smash burgers later."

"Nice, Gerber, tell the wife happy birthday," I said.

Gerber rolled his eyes. "Actually, it's not 'til Thursday but she gets the whole week."

Bert, Tommy, and I resumed. Like a lot of middle-aged males, the three of us become armchair historians when we get together and usually spend a lot of time ranking things, like best NFL ground gainers from the seventies (Sweetness, then, hate to say it, O. J., Earl Campbell, Dorsett, Chuck Foreman), best guitar players (my top five: Keef, Duane Allman, Page, Eddie, Terry Kath of Chicago), and, probably more than anything else, we talk about the World Wars. As we devoured our breakfast, our conversation went something like this: "—so the war in the Pacific was mostly won with napalm, not the atom bombs," I said, referencing a couple of books I'd read recently.

Tommy said he read the same books. "That's true, man," he said. "We'd been firebombing the crap out of Japan for six months. They were on the ropes. Hiroshima and Nagasaki were just exclamation points on a war that was already mostly won and close to over."

Bert slid his chair out and went back up for seconds then came back with three strips of bacon, a couple more sausage patties, and a *knoll* of home fries.

When he sat back down, Bert raised a finger. "The Japanese were never gonna surrender. MacArthur was planning an island invasion with a million troops for November of '45."

We prattled a bit more about World War II, and then Tommy dropped a bomb of his own.

He looked around the table. "So, I'm thinking of trading in the Jag for a truck," he said.

I stopped chewing. "Holy crap," I said. "I thought that'd be your forever car."

Tommy explained the Jag was too impractical for our winters.

"I can't even breach three inches of snow," he said. "It's totally useless around here. And I'm getting too old to climb down into it. The getting out part's even worse."

Bert and I nodded.

"But here's the thing," he said, "Jaguar announced the motor in my F-Type is gonna be the last gas engine they ever build."

"Oh yeah? What's it got in it?" I asked.

He straightened in his chair. "Supercharged five-liter V8. Five hundred fifty horsepower and 505 pounds of torque," he said. "Now they're gonna go all electric."

As Tommy spoke, I squirted a figure-eight of ketchup onto my potatoes. "Sounds like it's one-of-a-kind. You'll regret getting rid of it. Just find an old half-ton pickup for the winters and keep the Jag."

Bert shook some hot sauce onto his potatoes. "Yeah, keep it man," he said. "My dad got rid of his favorite car and regretted it."

Tommy perked. "Oh yeah? What'd he have?"

Bert pronged at the cubes of home fry. "A '64 and a half Ford Mustang," he said.

Tommy whistled with his tongue. "Damn, the '64 and a half? First Mustang off the line."

Bert nodded and chewed. "Yeah. It was a dark, dark metallic green," he said. "He sold it to a kid down the street for 200 bucks and a couple weeks later the dipshit wrapped it around a tree. Dad always kicked himself for selling it, and man, I wish we still had it. The car had a rusted-out hole in the floor behind the driver's seat. Dad covered it up with a piece of plywood and us kids would lift it up and watch the road fly by underneath."

I made a feet-running gesture with my fingers. "Flintstone car, that's totally boss," I said.

Bert looked back down at his plate. "It was the coolest car we ever owned," he said.

I also had a heartbreaking car story for Tommy.

"My dad got rid of his favorite car too," I said. "A '70 'Cuda."

Tommy reared back in his chair. "Whoa. Are you serious?" he said.

"Yup. Sassy Grass green with a 440 six pack, pistol grip shifter, and a Shaker hood," I said.

"Daaaang," he said. "Option loaded."

I speared a cushion of pancake. "When my sister was born, my parents needed a bigger house, but the stupid bank wouldn't give 'em a mortgage unless Dad sold the 'Cuda. They said his payments on it were too high."

Tommy shook his head. "How much were they?" he asked.

"Ninety-nine bucks a month."

The guys laughed.

"So, he did what he had to do for his family. He went back to the Plymouth dealer and traded in the 'Cuda for"—I curled my lip—"a four-speed piece of shit called a *Cricket.*"

Bert tilted his head. "What the hell is a Cricket?"

I explained. "It was a subcompact that Chrysler imported from England and rebadged. The boys at the dealership must've laughed Dad off the damn lot. That Cricket was a total rattletrap, my dad said. Thing frigging broke down every five minutes. But he got the mortgage, and they got the house. Meanwhile, that 'Cuda is probably worth a hundred grand today."

Tommy let out a long whew. "At least that much. Quite a story, holy shit."

I shook my head. "Still kills him to this day."

Tommy had a story, too. "Yeah, my dad's best car was a '63 Stingray," he said. "It was the roadster, not the split window that's the 'Vette Holy Grail. But still a sixties-era Corvette. He sold it when I went off to college. He always regretted it, I'm pretty sure."

We all sat there, wistful, thinking about our dads and their lost cars.

"Keep the Jag," Bert said, after a beat.

"Yeah, my vote also, buy a truck but keep the Jag," I said, crumpling my napkin and tossing it onto the plate.

Tommy slowly moved his head up and down as the realization became clear to him, too.

A line was starting to form at the door, and folks were eye-gesturing us to make room at the table. I stood up and put my coat on.

"Let's hup to it," I said.

13

CALL OF THE WILD

After breakfast, Tommy told us his low-slung Jag was no match for Blossom Road, so he motor-growled the V8 out of the firehouse lot and went home. He said he had a honey-do list waiting for him anyway. Bert and I sped to the sugarhouse—we had a honey-do list of our own. As soon as we got there, I hoofed it up the mountain while Bert stayed below to level up the new tank using some house jacks. We decided to give the tank a name, the *Edmund Fitzgerald*, after the iron-ore freighter that sank in Lake Superior and was immortalized in the Gordon Lightfoot song. "Yeah, that fits," Bert had said, when I first suggested it after Archie McClellan pulled us out of the gulch that day. Now the name stuck.

My job on this February morning was to attach new spouts to all the squiggly droplines—aka spouting the lines. The spouts are the fittings we stick into a maple tree after we drill a hole into it. Like we explained to Tommy and Gerber, spouts must be replaced every year.

Spouts, sometimes called *spiles*, used to be manufactured from cast iron, tin, or aluminum. Indigenous groups (especially Vermont's Abenaki people and the Iroquois nations) carved them out of sumac branches. There are a bewildering number of spout variations that have been sold over the 150-year history of the industrialized maple industry. I know several sugarmakers who obsessively collect and catalog old spouts and trade them with each other. Modern spouts—which are shaped like an uppercase *L* rotated one-quarter clockwise—are mostly made of polycarbonate plastic or nylon and cost about twenty-five to forty-five cents apiece. The spouts Bert and I use were invented by researchers at the University of Vermont. Each spout has a tiny rubber ball fitted inside it, like a pour spout on a liquor bottle, prevents sap from backflowing into the taphole during a freeze, which, when it happens, fosters bacteria growth and alerts the tree to compartmentalize off the hole, ending a season prematurely.

Halfway up Blossom Hill, I got to work inserting new spouts into the dangling droplines. This is my least favorite chore, a monotony made ten times worse today by the frigid cold. In my mitts, I held a two-handed tubing tool. I clamped down on the end of the tube and then, with my numb fingers, finessed the spout into position and squeezed the tool together, sliding the barbed end of the fitting into the open end of the tube. Easy-peasy. But tedious.

This is gonna be a long frigging day, I thought to myself after inserting a few more, with 800+ left to do.

Bert hit me up on the walkie-talkie. "Having fun yet? Over."

I fumbled for my radio and brought it close to my mouth. "Yeah, super fun wriggling little pieces of plastic with frozen fingers!" I barked.

Bert replied through the static. "Just checking on ya, crabbypants."

I mashed the talk button. "Know what else would be fun? I thought it'd be a real blast to lose the drawstring of my hoodie in the collar and then fish it back out again."

"Ugh—" he said.

"A thousand times in a row—"

"Double ugh—"

"—in the freezing cold," I said. "Get the idea?"

The radio hummed for a second, then, "Suck it up, buttercup," Bert said flatly.

I made air quotes. "For even more 'fun' I'm gonna assemble a bookcase later."

Some sugarmakers, after attaching a spout to the drop, immediately drill their tapholes and hammer the spouts into the tree. But for me, drilling tapholes the same day I replace the spouts makes the job even worse. I prefer to make one dedicated pass through the woods replacing spouts and then, a day or two later, after I recover, make another pass through the woods to awl the holes for the season and knock in the spouts with a tapping mallet.

The manufacturer of our spouts started offering them in a rainbow of colors a few years ago, and the ones we were using today were lucent red, which I thought would look cool connected to our light-blue tubing. Last year we used yellow ones.

Sunrays were kaleidoscoping off the crystals in the snow like a stained glass window. The week's aggregated accumulation of rain and ice and snow had mixed into a precipitation layer cake beneath my boots. Every step was like crushing a cardboard box.

Up and down this divide, we've set up dedicated runs of dry tubing to use as a handrail. Going up, I pulled myself along hand over hand like an alpine mountaineer. Today, ice had cohered to the tubing, which made the climb even harder. By the time I got to a break in the incline, I was gasping for air and had to stop to catch my breath.

"That's it. I'm swearing off Little Debbies," I said out loud.

Then my breath was taken away again.

Doubled over and looking down, I noticed that the fresh snow I'd been trudging through was gone, and I was now standing in a trampled tapestry of paw prints. I glanced around and saw clumps of tan hair littered about, and bright scarlet ellipses drizzled in all directions.

Then, into view came a figure, crumpled in the snow—it was the remains of a deer, ravaged and torn apart. Steam wisped off it and white and pink sinew stretched from the exposed rib cage. Its head was cockeyed and the eyes on its freckled face were open wide, resigned, just recently emptied of life.

Coyotes.

I'd known for years there were coyotes in these woods. I've heard them yip quite often. One rainy day last spring, I was out picking ramps (a type of onion that grows like a weed at the top of my hill), and a coyote passed below through the mist like in a movie, shadowy. Coyotes spook the shit out of me. Gauging by the number of paw prints, there must have been a half dozen who ganged up on this poor doe. I stared at the carnage a while, trying to puzzle together the forensics of the slaughter. The doe was not large; it might've been a fawn. Hard to tell, it was so *plundered*. Considering the way its shins and hooves were lying askew in the snow, the poor deer probably had already gone prone when the coyotes attacked.

I told Bert about it when I got back to the sugarhouse for a lunch break. He shook his head. "A crime scene, huh?" he said.

"Dude, they tore apart that doe like spareribs from Dave & Buster's."

Bert had been busy. He had the *Edmund Fitzgerald* hoisted up on three corners with house jacks, and a bubble level was lying on the rails. Later we would shim it up by Jenga-cribbing lengths of four-by-six hemlock posts and shoving other carpentry scrap underneath.

We talked about the deer. Bert knows how the wilderness works around here.

"My guess is the doe was weakened by the snow and the coyotes got an advantage," Bert said. "Or the doe could've had COVID-19"—it's been reported that many deer have been infected with the coronavirus around here. "Coyotes aren't like wolves, where they hang out in packs," he explained. "Coyotes usually roam around on their own, solitary, but when one of them has prey in its sights they'll collaborate for the kill. The coyotes will yelp out to each other with *whoop whoops* and all the others will come running."

Back up on the hill later, I noticed there were indeed coyote paw prints forming trails in every direction through the woods. *They must've come running from all edges of the forest to get a piece of this deer*, I thought. The unnerving part was they were likely still all around me, spying my every move. Coyotes do not generally mess with humans, "but it's happened a time or two," Bert told me. My only weapon of defense was my tubing tool, which I supposed I could use to thwack one on the snout. But if two or three or twelve of them were to gang up on me, I'd maybe end up like the deer. I hoped their stomachs were full.

A gun might be a good thing to have at a time like this, I thought. Most folks around here own several guns, primarily to hunt deer, a huge pastime. Deer hunting is a sanctified activity in our part of the world. Come mid-October, hunters like to do reconnaissance on the bucks, and they'll course up and down Blossom Road in their trucks trying to spot them, windows down, binoculars out, sometimes at night using high-wattage spotlights plugged into their cigarette lighters. When rifle season begins, exactly one half hour before sunrise on the third Saturday in November, they file into the woods and start blasting away. The gun thunder lasts until the week before Christmas. Unless you put POSTED signs on your land, hunters will freely and legally walk on your property to shoot deer, although they usually ask permission first.

Bert is a big-time hunter and maybe the best shot in the county. The cloven have no chance when Bert is around. He's one of those guys who truly hunts for the meat. The sport of it has almost no interest for him. For Bert, hunting is more like a job and, in the spirit of his off-the-grid dream of living in an abandoned school bus, he sees hunting solely as a means of getting free food and relying on his own wits to do it. He shoots his deer limit without fail every season—usually two tags for himself and two tags for Faith.

Bert always invites me over to his garage after he shoots his deer, and like a good friend, I ogle and praise the doe or buck that he'll have suspended on a trapeze apparatus from the rafters to drain the blood out of it. He'll spend all day carving for every single section of meat, efficient as the coyotes. He fills his freezer with the cuts, and he and Faith eat all kinds of venison recipes throughout the year: venison chili, venison sloppy joes, venison stew, venison tacos, venison pastrami for Reubens, venison enchiladas, venison sausage, venison jerky, venison spaghetti sauce, venison osso buco. When Bert cleans a deer, he wears a long white butcher bib and fills a garbage bag with the entrails. Like everything else he does, he carves it meticulously and with highly sharpened knives, usually taking all day.

He sometimes offers me the back strap or loin roast, which is like deer filet mignon, unbelievably tender with the mouth feel of venison cream cheese. Bert's deer meat is never gamey because when he hunts, Bert is so stealthy, the deer will die before it realizes it's even been shot, which makes a difference in the taste of the venison since there is no rush of adrenaline.

Back at the top of the sugarbush, toggling more spouts into the droplines, I was haunted by the doe for the rest of the day. It wasn't like it was the first time I'd ever seen a dead deer. Just about every day there's one croaked on the side of the road from having been hit by cars around here. But those are usually intact carcasses (until the turkey vultures get at them). And I've seen plenty of dead deer in Bert's ad hoc butcher shop every fall. But watching Bert clean a deer in his garage is like watching a surgical procedural on TV, no worse than an episode of *Grey's Anatomy*.

No, there was something different about the dead doe. It was the *violence* of her demise, attacked and eaten alive. The look in her eyes was not a look of terror as much as one of surrender—her pupils hemorrhaged, nothing left of her except bone and fur and face.

Piranhas could not have done a better job.

I wondered if I'd have a problem killing a coyote, especially after seeing what they're capable of. I've been told coyotes are shy and misunderstood. Tell that to the deer.

I am not a gun person, and I've never owned nor shot one (other than BB guns when I was a kid). I've had notions of arming the sugarhouse with a gun, and the coyote incident made me consider it even more. I've asked Bert about this and, of course, being Bert, he's in favor.

"Get a .12-gauge," he advised.

I made a gesture of cocking a gun. "Are those the kind that make the cool *shuck shuck* sound in the movies?"

He smirked. "Yeah, that's the one. It's a universal gun that can serve many purposes. It's a shotgun, so it sprays shot pellets. Just aim in the general vicinity, and you're likely to hit your target. Also, it has stopping power. If something's coming at you, a .12-gauge will make it not."

He'd been persuasive but I was still on the fence.

At the end of the afternoon, when I came upon Coyote Junction on my way back down to the sugarhouse, *the doe carcass was completely gone.* Head gone, legs gone, hooves gone. Just a Rorschach-shaped maroon blotch, the blood drips and some tufts of white-and-tan deer fur blowing around on top of the snow like tumbleweeds.

Thinking about guns and killing animals, or animals being killed by other animals, forced me to reckon with what I would be capable of as a man. Case in point: A couple months ago Bert and I were driving down the state highway in my Tundra and we came upon a possum that had been hit by a car. It was literally smashed into the road, but somehow still alive and violently squirming. I swerved to avoid him.

"Ooof," I said. "Poor fucker."

After a minute, Bert said, "That's maybe not what I would've done."

I looked at him. "Not have done what?"

He gestured backward with his thumb. "In Yoe, we probably would've run that possum over back there."

"Someone already did run him over."

He looked straight ahead, solemnly. "In Yoe, there's kind of a code we follow. You never want to see an animal suffer . . ."

"And?"

"That possum was clearly suffering. We should've run him over to end his misery."

I thought for a moment about turning around, but I just couldn't. I don't have the stomach for killing animals. I feel remorse if I kill a spider. One time, my cat dragged a river rat into the house. The rat was motionless but still alive (he blinked) when I discovered it on our dining room floor. I clubbed it with a fireplace shovel and felt terrible for a week.

Bert has invited me to go deer hunting if I ever do buy a .12-gauge. I've thought about it and decided that there's no way I could ever shoot a deer. Deer just have too much soul, I told him.

I've seen it in their eyes.

14
HURRY UP AND WAIT

When the sap starts to flow inside the maples—which occurs after a nighttime freeze and when daylight temperatures climb back over 32°F (0° Celsius)—we call that a *run*. It looked like we might get our first run by Wednesday. Our phone apps were forecasting temperatures in the mid-forties plus sun—perfect sap weather—which sent me into a panic since our holes weren't drilled yet. Tapping hadn't been on our minds since it was still early winter. But it was on my mind now. We wouldn't capture a single drop of that sap unless I got those holes drilled—and fast.

Global warming and climate change have had a real impact on the maple industry, speeding up the beginning of seasons. For decades, most Vermont sugarmakers had a tradition of tapping trees on Town Meeting Day, always the first Tuesday in March. That's the day when all 251 towns in Vermont hold their annual meeting and townsfolk gather in school gymnasiums and grange halls to debate issues, vote on budget allocations, and elect new selectboard leaders.

Back in the day, pre–global warming, sugarmakers would attend a town meeting in the morning, argue and vote, eat the potluck lunch, and then go home and tap trees all afternoon. A reliable bet. These days, maple season in Vermont can be halfway over by Town Meeting Day.

Making syrup in February was once unheard of around here, and now some guys make it as early as December. That's how warm the winters have become, and I was feeling that now, with the new season about to start only a few days after Groundhog Day.

Never debate a sugarmaker about the weather. Farmers in general pay closer attention to the weather than the average Joe, but maple producers in particular are obsessive, especially in January, February, March, and into April. When we obsess, it's not just over general trends like cold fronts or warm fronts or snow and rain. We home in on very small variations in temperature and barometric pressure. Television "meteorologists" frustrate us because they throw temperature predictions around with too much buffer, declaring temperatures will be in the 40s, when what sugarmakers want to know is will it be 45, 41, 48? Which? Small differences in temperature can mean big differences in sap. More importantly, we need to know if it is going to dip below freezing at night. That's vital for us since it's that temperature flux, and the internal pressure inside the tree that it creates, that gets the sap flowing in the trunks—the fall below, then rise above, the freezing mark.

For syrup production, we also want the trees to have a nice hard freeze over the winter, with a deep frost in the ground and lots of snowpack on top of it to seal that freeze in. When it thaws, that's when the trees wake up and start sending sugars and starches up to their crowns to make leaves in the spring.

But hard freezes don't happen like they used to. Climatologists have told us the weather we get now in our area is the same weather they used to get in Pennsylvania, 150 miles south, only twenty years ago. Researchers say a hundred years from now the prevailing tree in New York and Vermont may no longer be the sugar maple, which mostly thrives in colder climates, but instead a flowering dogwood or maybe the sweetgum, trees populous in Missouri and Tennessee.

By Tuesday temperatures had climbed into the high thirties, getting closer to sap flow weather. But it was a partly cloudy day with occasional gusts of wind, so there was still plenty of chill to the air. We were in a kind of maple limbo. It was warming up somewhat enough to get the trees to start their motors, but not quite enough to really get them fully juicing yet.

That night I called Shakey, and he told me he'd been in the woods all day, also racing with nature's clock to catch the earliest sap run.

He groaned. "I tapped this morning till one o'clock," he said. "In the woods it's goddamned cold yet. The snow was only just starting to get sticky in the sun at like twelve o'clock and then it was one slippery bastard out there, so I put chains on my boots and that helped immensely."

I asked him if he'd seen any sap yet.

"I haven't had a goddamned drop come out of the tree yet. Don't have anything connected anyways. Don't even have my buckets out. Hopefully, I'll be tapped by Sunday. Tomorrow it's supposed to warm up like a son of a bitch, Peter, better look out."

Tapping the trees—when we drill a hole and insert our plastic spouts for the sap to drain—is the most critical time of a sugarmaker's season. Almost immediately after we drill a hole, a maple will start compartmentalizing it off from the rest of its vascular system. That means we typically only have about a six-to-eight-week window to pull as much sap out of the hole as possible before it dries up, which coincides with the start of spring. Sugarmakers go into anxiety spirals on when exactly to commence this ritual. There's no set calendar date. We just go with our gut. On Blossom Road, we always start at the first thaw of winter, which was upon us now.

The next day indeed got warm, in the fifties, but not the sunny weather the TV and my phone apps had been promising. Intermittent rain. A diffused, miserable day.

I turned onto Blossom Road and spotted my neighbor Truman Dunn working on some new mainlines he'd installed near his sugarhouse. He was wearing rubber boots, a Carhartt field jacket, and a navy watch cap turned over his ears. He had a helper with him I didn't recognize. I rolled down the window to say hello.

"How are things looking?" I said, leaning forward. "Should we get the pancakes ready?"

Truman waved to acknowledge me then continued twiddling with his line. He was inserting a barbed T-fitting that connected a pipe coming down from his woods to another pipe that emptied to his tanks. "I wish I was a week ahead of where I'm at now, Pete," he said, not looking up. "We still got a lot of work left to get done yet before the sap starts to run."

I leaned toward the window again. "I got more work, too. Are we gonna miss out on sap?"

He pulled a wrench from his back pocket and walloped the pipe. "Naw, still pretty cold yet."

"But it's gonna hit fifty today," I argued.

He hit at it again. "We'll see. We might get some drips and drabs, but the ground is still plenty frozen," he said. "But I wouldn't dillydally getting your trees tapped."

It was unusual for Truman to concede he was behind schedule. Unlike me and Bert, who pretty much abandon the sugarhouse from mid-April, when a season ends, until early January, when we rush to get ready for a new one ahead, Truman and his wife, Shelley, along with their only child, Evan, work on their operation year-round, except for a week around the Fourth of July when they take their boat up to Lake St. Catherine to water-ski. Truman does a little construction work around town and grows potatoes and pumpkins to sell at their roadside stand, but his primary source of making a living is maple. The Dunns are usually the most prepared and organized sugarmakers in town. They always catch the earliest sap.

"Well, if you're not worried about it then I won't either," I said, but it was kind of a lie.

Truman stopped working, turned to me, and smiled. "Heard you had some trouble in your driveway the other day," he said.

Word travels fast.

"Yeah, we had to call Archie McClellan," I said and then played it off. "But no big deal. Got a sweet new tank. A supertank. You gotta stop by and see it. It's as big as the sugarhouse."

He laughed. "Is that right?" he said, pocketing the wrench and clapping dirt off his gloves.

He wondered aloud if we were trying to challenge his reign as the top-dog sugarmaker on Blossom Road. "Should I be worried?" he said.

I scratched my beard. "We're gunning for five pounds," I said.

He turned to his hired man and pointed his thumb back at me. "Big timers," he said.

Truman likes to rib me a little bit. I think he's always viewed me and Bert as a couple of flatlander hobbyists. Gradually, over the years, I'd like to think we've won his respect.

He changed the subject. "So, if you're wondering what to do for lunch you should head up to Mach's store," he said, referring to a general store nearby in Pawlet. "They're using our potatoes for their French fries, and they fry them in bacon fat."

I knitted my eyebrows. "*Bacon fat*, dammmmn, that sounds enticing," I said.

He nodded. "Me and Shelley were up there the other day, and they give you a sauce for the fries—I can't remember what they called it, some funny name, you dip your fries in it, like mayo, but with some Italian name."

"Aioli sauce?"

He blew out his cheeks. "Yeah, that sounds about right."

"I'll be darned."

Truman's hired man, a bigger guy, stood by during our entire exchange wearing a big smile on his face, nodding along in affirmation to everything we said, all the while holding the T-fitting they were cajoling into position before I interrupted them.

When I got to the sugarhouse, I right away got to unfurling a tarp over the *Edmund Fitzgerald*. One thing the tank did not come equipped with was a lid. All sixteen feet of the tank was open to the sky, so Bert suggested it would be a good idea to cover the thing with a tarp to keep the snow and rain out of it. It was the best solution to get us through the season until we could build a pavilion over it next summer. I frigging hate tarps. They're a huge pain in the ass. I was trying to secure the tarp with a series of bungee cords, but I couldn't get the stupid thing lined up right. Every time I'd hook the cord through a grommet on one end it would pull up the tarp on another end. I was getting more and more frustrated. As I walked around a corner of the tank, I began cussing a gibberish of jumbled swear words like I had Tourette's syndrome. And right then, I looked up and my neighbor Milt Hinchey just happened to be standing there.

He looked at me blankly. "Having a bad day?" he said.

Milt is maybe the biggest sugarmaker in West Pawlet. He claims to have 16,000 taps, although no one has gone into his woods to verify (all of us with these tap counts, we are on the honor system). Milt sustains a nappy chinstrap beard and wears black horn-rimmed glasses. On this day, he had on a frayed plaid shirt and twill Dickies chinos tucked into his over-the-calf green rubber boots.

Milt is as much a mechanic and long-haul trucker as he is a sugarmaker. He doesn't own any of his own taps. He leases trees from property owners all over the Ruperts and the Pawlets, over to Hebron, and as far away as Salem, and then hauls the sap back to his big sugarhouse near one of the abandoned slate quarries in West Pawlet. He even has a few taps on some rented woods farther up on Blossom Road, which was why he was in my neighborhood this morning, I assumed. He always stops in to say hi.

Milt's operation is a common setup for sugarmakers—renting taps from property owners around town. Usually, the sugarmaker pays a rate of about one dollar per tree, but sometimes more. In areas like Northern Vermont, the rate is as high as $2.50 per tree. These kinds of arrangements tend to work out pretty well for both parties. For the sugarmaker, he has access to a sugarbush that he may not have the capital to buy outright. For the landowners, especially ones in our area, who tend to be savvy millionaires from the city, they not only get the rent but also get what's called an "ag exemption," a property tax break that gives the landholders a much lower tax rate for acreage actively in agricultural use.

Milt owns a convoy of barely road-legal flatbed dually trucks—Chevys and GMCs—outfitted with huge white polythene tanks for holding sap. He drives around and collects sap from probably a dozen different locations. I don't know how he keeps up with it all.

We leaned across from each other on opposite sides of my truck bed.

Milt slowly yawned. "I started my pumps at 4:00 A.M. this morning," he said.

"Think you're gonna get any sap today?" I asked.

He rubbed his nose. "Oh, we might get a teensy-weensy," he said.

"Yeah, I just talked to Truman, and he wasn't thinking we'd get much of anything today, but geez it sure is gonna be warm," I said. "I bet the trees wake up a little bit?"

Milt made a face that seemed to say, "Possibly."

I clomped my boot against the ground to knock the mud off it. "'Cept I don't have a single tree tapped so it'd be just fine with me if they decided to wait another week," I said.

Milt thought about this, seemingly plotting each word about to come out of his mouth.

"Years ago, if it was early February, we'd be taking naps in our easy chairs rather than running around like chickens like we do now," he said. "I remember once, someone who used to tap the trees next to my uncle's house thought it'd be a good idea to start hanging his buckets on Valentine's Day and we all told 'im he'd gone plum crazy."

I laughed politely. "How'd it work out for him?"

Milt chuckled. "Oh, he got skunked all right and he never did it ag'in, but that was long before the days of high vacuum and tubing systems like we got now. And we just ain't gettin' the cold winters like we did back then. So it's not so gol'dang crazy now to git out there early as ya can."

I nodded and checked my watch.

Milt said his phone had been ringing off the hook the past couple days. Vermont's senior senator had been trying to reach him. "Bernie called me three times askin' me to be part of a 'visual.' So, I says to 'im, I says, 'now's not a good time.' But Bernie kept callin' back wantin' me to be on the visual and so I says to 'im finally 'don't you know I'm a sugarmaker? We're pretty busy this time of year, or maybe you didn't know that much about sugarmakers?'"

I tried to think what the hell Milt meant by a "visual" but then figured it was a Zoom, virtual town hall kind of thing. I didn't pry to see if it was Bernie Sanders himself who called Milt. It's possible. Bernie is that kind of guy. If it was Bernie in the flesh calling three times, Milt was right, the senator should've known better than to pester a sugarmaker during maple season.

Just then we spotted a robin, the quintessential early bird, stepping in the yard.

Milt said he'd been seeing robins a lot earlier than normal. "Yeah, they've been bouncing around in the snow for the past two weeks at my place."

I pointed up the hill. "I've actually seen robins all winter, like they didn't even bother to fly south this year," I said.

Milt cupped his ear and detected another bird singing. "That there's a Baltimore oriole."

I asked him if it was a bellwether for our season, like the robin maybe was. Early.

"Naw," he said, "it's just a bird."

15

NEW SADDLES AND A NUT DRIVER

I'd only been at the sugarhouse ten minutes and already I was close to having a freaking coronary to rival the old grouch. Before I could get started tapping the trees, I had to finish a project we began in the fall, adding new saddles on the mainlines. Saddles are the transition fittings that connect the lateral lines to the main. We were switching to ones that attach with a common hose clamp, and to fasten them down I had to use a screw gun with a specialized bit, which was hiding from me. "Where's the goddamned nut driver?" I muttered to myself.

After a few minutes, I found the driver bit lying in the cup holder of my truck, where a lot of small junk collects for some reason—guitar picks, jars of Carmex, ball-inflation needles. I grabbed the bit, marched back into the sugarhouse, affixed it to my drill, and then climbed into the sugarbush. I was replacing our saddles because the damn squirrels chewed up the old ones, which were made of plastic, their favorite meal. Man, they are voracious little SOBs. They totally gnawed the crap out of them, turning them to nubs. The replacement saddles were made of metal, so the squirrels would either leave them alone or give themselves a root canal.

The job was dreary, almost as bad as spouting the lines. I first had to cut the tubing off the old fitting with my scissor snips. Then I had to pry apart the piece with pliers and bang it off with a hammer. I twiddled the new hose clamp into position and attached it by screwing the nut tight with the screw gun. Four different tools to pick up and put down while handling the small pieces of the fittings with cold-numbed fingers. Ugh. Then, after the fitting was secured, I had to reconnect the line of tubing with my tubing tool—a *fifth* device to pick up and put down.

I kicked the snow. "This sucks big donkey balls," I shouted, after about the ninth clamp.

Higher up the hill I hit a denser concentration of maples, and the project quickened. I tend to get into a rhythm with these repetitive jobs. Still, by eleven thirty, I was wiped out and starving. A Five Pounder would've ignored the discomfort and finished the project. Had I done so, I'd then have been able to tap the trees. That's certainly what Truman, what Milt, and what Shakey were probably out doing right now—tapping and maybe even catching a little sap later today. But the bacon-fat-dipped fries at Mach's were too tempting, and I decided instead to knock off for lunch.

"Screw it, time to eat," I said to myself.

I spun out some gravel leaving the driveway and hurried along a back route to Rupert. Just past the Rupert post office, I took a left onto Pawlet Mountain Road, a single-lane half-paved/half-dirt road that goes from Rupert to Pawlet, where Mach's Market is located.

I passed by some of Milt Hinchey's leased woods but didn't notice anyone working. Farther up, I passed Bob Wood, a sugarmaker just outside of Pawlet Village who was setting out his sap tanks adjacent to the road. I honked and waved, and he waved back. I was too hungry to stop and chat. He looked busy anyway. I passed by a half-dozen more sugarhouses, and no one appeared to have any taps in the trees yet—all their droplines were still dangling—so I started to feel a lot better that mine weren't in yet, either.

I came down a gradual hill into Pawlet, Vermont. Looming above the slate-roofed buildings of the village was Haystack Mountain, which has a witches-hat outcropping at its peak giving it a slight resemblance to the Matterhorn.

Mach's Market is located in the center of the hamlet and just recently reopened after being closed a long time. The new operators have done a great job reviving this Pawlet landmark. They've added lots of local artisan foods, an insane lunch menu, and aisles of Vermont craft liquors and wines, all of it packed inside a solid brick mid-1800s grist mill that literally straddles the Flower Brook gorge. In the back of the store, there's a glass floor where you can peer thirty feet down and watch the brook rushing over the ice and rocks.

I parked and went inside. Scribbled in cursive on a chalkboard above the deli case was a list of all the local farms from which Mach's sources their food, and I noticed Truman's farm was up there, too, "Sugarbush Spuds." I ordered a Cubano sandwich and, of course, the bacon-fat French fries made from Truman's potatoes—the whole reason I was here. I mentioned to the woman behind the counter that the potatoes came from my neighbor's farm, and she went practically berserk talking about how much she loved the fries also.

She smiled with a lot of teeth. "Ooh la la, those are our best sellers," she said.

I smiled back. "I got here as fast as I could to get some."

Her badge said her name was Linnea. "It's so funny you're getting those," she said, in a cheery voice. "I sometimes order a bunch just before the end of my shift and then I bring them home to my boyfriend and we eat them all night."

"He's a lucky man," I said, maybe a tad disappointed she had a boyfriend.

She nodded her head vigorously. "They're so good. I get them all the time."

"I can't think of any better way of making French fries than deep frying them in bacon fat," I said. "The instant I heard the words 'bacon fat–dipped fries' I had to try them."

She held up two thumbs and made a click, click sound out of the side of her mouth. "Definitely the best."

I love Vermont stores like Mach's. General stores dot the state and kill you with quaint. Usually, they'll have lots of freshly baked goods, a deli counter to order sandwiches, and carafes of coffee from Green Mountain

Coffee Roasters (once a Vermont company; inventors of the Keurig) neatly lined in a row on a counter and always self-serve. A few other favorite generals are the South Woodstock Country Store in South Woodstock, the Castleton Village Store in Castleton, and the Wayside Country Store in West Arlington, which sits adjacent to a red covered bridge in front of Norman Rockwell's old house. (The bridge has a knotted rope swing that the kids and I used to fling ourselves from into the Battenkill River on hot summer days.)

Back at Mach's, the chef bellowed "Order up!" and dinged a call bell, startling me from my trance as I hovered over the peekaboo floor above the gorge. My meal was presented in two clamshell boxes, one for the Cubano and another for the bacon fries, which were sticking out past the edge, they filled it up so much. I also ordered a wedge of Mach's supreme flourless chocolate cake, and Linnea loaded it into yet another box.

She grinned at me. "Now that's a lunch. Want some fry sauce?" she asked. "It's included."

Linnea didn't call it aioli sauce, so I wasn't sure it was the same sauce they gave Truman and Shelley. I asked if I could have two—"I don't think one's gonna be enough"—and she happily obliged. Mach's also has one of those old-fashioned coolers built into the wall, with wooden doors, racked with hard-to-find pop brands in contoured glass bottles—Fresca, Sunkist, Mexican Cokes or Mexican 7-Ups, which are made of pure cane sugar instead of corn syrup. I got a Sprite.

I took my teetering stack up to the checkout register at the front of the store—two boxes of lunch, another one for the cake, two clear plastic containers for the mysterious fry sauce, and the Sprite. I carried my feast back to the truck, dropped the tailgate, and ate it there, watching the Flower Brook gurgle by, this time observing the stream from the outside instead of through the floor. I noted that the brook wasn't frozen over like it usually is in early February.

Everyone was right about the fries—Truman, Linnea, Linnea's stupid boyfriend—they were maybe the best French fries I'd ever eaten, even better than the Country Girl's. These were hand cut. Long, but not stringy, and a rusty, russety red-brown—as opposed to the beige fries they give you at McDonald's. Visible flecks of sea salt stuck to the savory grease. I couldn't definitively say I tasted bacon in them, but certainly the *concept* of French fries being lovingly deep-fried in bacon fat swayed my opinion, and I ate two or three handfuls before I even touched the Cubano, which turned out to be a close runner-up to the fries in terms of amazingness.

16

I'D TAP THAT

It was midafternoon by the time I got back to the sugarhouse from Mach's. Just as I was pulling into the driveway, another sugarmaker from the neighborhood, Frank Ardmore, drove up Blossom Road in a big Dodge Ram. He stopped, rolled down the window, and rested his elbow on the sill.

"Please tell me you ain't got ants in the pants to start tappin' like everyone's been doin'," he said.

I shrugged my shoulders. "Well, yeah, as a matter of fact—"

"—Jesus. You guys are all cuckoo for Cocoa Puffs, I'm tellin' ya," he said, shaking his head. "It's too early."

In addition to being a veteran sugarmaker, Ardmore is also a maple supply dealer—a subgroup of the supercenter supply stores like Bascom's, guys who sell lines of equipment out of a barn or their garage to take care of the locals. He's handy to have around. I've raced to his place quite a few times after breaking a hydrometer, which I'm notorious for doing. Today, he was on his way to Truman's to deliver a pump he'd repaired for him.

Ardmore is in his late sixties and falls into the demographic of retired-from-something-else-and-now-a-full-time-sugarmaker group of dudes. He lives in Argyle about ten miles cross-lots from the sugarhouse and operates a supply shop out of an old sheep barn.

I asked him why he wasn't out tapping today like everyone else.

He held his hands out. "I don't do nothin' 'til the fifteenth," he said. "I ain't never tapped a tree before the fifteenth of February and I ain't gonna start now. Just a matter of goddamned principle." As he was saying this, a cell phone in his coat pocket rang. He looked at it and declined the call with a frown. "Don't wanna talk to that guy." The phone immediately rang again, a country western ringtone I didn't recognize. "Don't wanna talk to that guy either," he said, finger-tapping the button.

"Geez," I said, "aren't you popular."

He looked at me. "It does this all day long," he said dismissively.

I laughed. "Who the hell's calling you all day long?"

"Sugarmakers!" he said, annoyed. "It warms up like this and they all a sudden need something to get going with the season that they shoulda bought in the fall."

Addled by my lunch, the last thing I felt like doing was attaching more hose clamps. But I somehow summoned the energy to make my Sisyphean hike back up the hill to connect four or five more then decided to go home. I didn't tap a single tree that day. Unfivepounderian.

That night, after dinner and a shower, I had a major FOMO panic attack. I phoned some other sugarmakers to find out if anyone today got sap and to get a gauge on how much production I might've squandered by not having my trees drilled yet during this weird thaw.

First, I tried Kevin Keyes over at the Chambers Farm, a few miles down the road in Salem. He was caught off-guard, too.

"We didn't get jack shit," he said.

"That makes me feel a little better," I said. "It's just too early, Christ."

I told him I spent my whole day attaching the stupid hose clamps.

"I was out fixin' our frigging vacuum pumps," Kevin said. "Half of 'em wouldn't start."

I made a *jeesh* sound. "It'd be nice if the seasons acted *seasonal* for a change," I said.

Then I called the other Kevin in my maple life, Kevin Mattison, who used to tap a bunch of trees on the back of Rupert Mountain in Kent Hollow before retiring from the sugar game a couple years ago. Mattison keeps his fingers in sugaring by helping a lot of us producers around Rupert and Salem. Especially me and especially when things break. He's also an electrician, and he's done all my sugarhouse wiring. I had him scheduled to come over later in the week to wire up this crazy new piece of equipment—a three-phased, high-voltage sap extractor—which would totally pimp out my pump, adding even more oomph to the continuous suction that pulls the sap out of our trees. But now, with the season bearing down, I was frantic to get him here sooner. Kevin has a strong Vermont accent—anything with an *i* sound changes to *oy*.

"You goys get all revved up just because of a couple warm days," Mattison said, referencing the phones buzzing between sugarmakers after the first warm-up of the winter, when all of us debrief each other on any signs of tree juice.

"I already feel like I'm way behind," I said. "Tryin' to hit five pounds this year."

He made a pshaw sound. "It's just a paper foyre, this heatwave, quick and hot," Mattison said. "It'll settle down soon. After it's over, the trees will take a nap and you'll have plenty of time to get the taps drilled, your tanks set, and the pumps turned on. Then it'll warm up again, the sap will start runnin' proper, and this time you'll be on it like a pit bull on a mailman."

He was right. I vowed to myself to get the hose clamps done tomorrow and move on to the most crucial step in our preparation for the season—tapping the damn trees.

"Come hell or high water," I reported to Bert that night on the phone.

The next day I felt more energetic. I raced through the last of the hose-clamp project and switched gears to drilling trees. I collected some tapping tools from the workshop in our utility barn, which sits at the top of the field at the base of the forest. Then I strapped a tool belt around my waist, stuffed the pockets with spouts, and headed back out the door.

I inhaled deeply and looked up the hill. "Let's get to frigging work," I said to myself.

Up I went. I attacked the steepest section of the mountain first, hugging the hillsides, zapping the spouts into the trees. It was warm enough that sap was oozing out of the tree immediately after I drilled the hole, like I was puncturing a watermelon.

Later I fell into a steady rhythm tapping the maples in a flatter relief section of the woods, where there also happens to be a cluster of beech trees about eye high. Beech trees have flimsy little spears at the ends of their branches, and I walked right into one, just catching the corner of my eyeball. It didn't poke through the sclera, but it still didn't feel too great.

A couple hours into the tapping, the DeWalt's batteries—I carry two spares with me—had all gone dead. That, and the growing soreness in my eye, made for a good excuse to go home for the day and take a hot bath in mineral salts and CBD oil. In the tub, I put a hot washrag over my face. My tapping tally for the day was about 250, a little less than a quarter of the way done.

"I made some progress," that night I told Bert, who'd been stuck in his office down in Schenectady and couldn't come up to help, "but still a long ways to go."

I popped five Advil before I fell asleep about eight-thirty. I was so tired I didn't even turn off the light on my nightstand.

The following morning, I came up to the sugarhouse and Kevin Mattison was already there, working on the wiring for that new electric releaser. The releaser is a component of the pump system that maintains steady vacuum in the lines while simultaneously dumping sap into the tank. It's a big canister that lies on its belly inside a warm room the size of a broom closet.

He waved hello from atop a ladder. "Know something? Oye hate working with woyre," he said.

I laughed. "Maybe you should've been a plumber," I said.

Kevin's a big palooka. His forearms are the size of mailboxes. If you've ever watched an electrician in action, you'd know why. About 90 percent of the job is twisting things—twisting wire, twisting screws, twisting nuts, twisting caps, twisting connectors. And when you're not twisting wire, you're bending it, snipping it, or stuffing it into little compartments.

He stopped and looked at me. "I think I'm just gonna say 'fuck this' and go and be like all the other old coots oye know and spend all my time buying and selling old junk," he said.

"Don't you have enough old junk already?" I said, smirking.

He unspooled a length of wire. "It's all cash money that goes right into my pocket and oye can stick it right up the government's ahss," he said.

Mattison is already doing this, the trading of old stuff, and he has a particular penchant for old engines. Not the kind under the hood of a car. No, Kevin deals in huge freestanding engines powered by steam or diesel gas. This is a thing, old-engine collecting—machines from the late 1800s and early 1900s, which usually spun some sort of flywheel that powered tools, farming equipment, and appliances. He and his wife travel all over the country to attend old-engine shows. He claims he has forty engines in his collection stored at his farm over in Arlington.

"What the hell do you do with these engines, just watch them run?" I asked him once.

He laughed. "Nah, oye actually use them. Oye have one that runs a shucker for shucking corn, another that runs a grist, another oye use to sharpen knives. Oye don't know why oye like them so much. My woyfe is always asking me the same thing."

Despite complaining a lot, Kevin is surprisingly cheerful when he works. While he threaded some ridiculously bulky conduit cable through some holes he had drilled into my walls, he sang the opening verses of "Yellow Submarine." In key.

Kevin told me he was just fine getting out of sugaring. He'd been struggling with his health. A tick had bitten him, and he's been fighting the debilitations of Lyme disease ever since.

"Oy'me only good for about two or three good hours a day," he's told me. "Sometoymes I'm so toyred it's hard to take my boots off at night."

Fear of Lyme disease is a common refrain in maple. Since we're in the woods all the time, tick bites are one of the major hazards we face. Ticks have proliferated over the past decade largely due to climate change. The winters don't kill ticks like they used to. Too mild. Even in the cold weather months on Blossom Hill, I'll see an occasional tick crawling on the thigh of my jeans. It doesn't take much to get ticks active. If temperatures rise a little above freezing on a sunny day, the ticks are ready to parachute in. Up in Maine, the moose commit suicide by head butting themselves into trees because their coats are absolutely carpet bombed with ticks. Last summer, Shakey also got bitten by a tick. He didn't get Lyme disease, but he got one of the other tick-borne illnesses that can knock the crap out of you. Shaky told me he's still not himself and may never fully recover. The ticks and the afflictions they bring have given me a full-blown case of *tickanoia*. I usually drench myself in Deep Woods Off! and check myself head to toe with a hand mirror when I get home after a day in the sugarbush.

Other than opossums and a few other mammals, there are no true natural predators of the tick, so the Lyme threat will likely get worse as our winters become even milder. Unless someone figures out a vaccine for us maple people, we'll have to continue to adapt, stay out of the woods, or retire from sugaring like Kevin.

The day was warming up fast, and I still had one last nagging repair to make on the mainline about halfway up the sugarbush. Up I went. Sun had the snowpack in the woods softening to the consistency of a snow cone, making the hills and crags greasy and dangerous. Not far from Coyote Junction, a busted plastic connector on a section of mainline was gaping wide open. Not fixing it would make it impossible to get even an inch of vacuum, and we needed 26 or 27.

When we're about to go fix something, Bert and I have this dorky inside joke; we point a finger in the air and make a pronouncement in a British accent—"I'm going to effect a repair." Bert wasn't here this morning, so I announced it to Kevin, who arched an eyebrow at me funny while holding three screws in his mouth. "You'ff go do dat den," he said through his teeth.

I hiked up with the tools for my fix: the DeWalt, a pair of channel locks, and some MAPP gas. What the hell is MAPP gas, you ask? Chemically known as *methylacetylene-propadiene*, a MAPP gas torch burns at 5,000°F, right there in your little ol' hand. I love the stuff because when you need to get something really hot, MAPP gas does not mess around.

I crouched in the wet snow next to the line and felt the moisture soak through the knees of my pants. I fired up the MAPP torch and held it to the plastic pipe for about twenty seconds, which loosened the busted fitting. Plastic loses all its strength under intense temperatures. So much so that I could wriggle the piece free with just my gloved fingers. I stuck in a replacement fitting, screwed on a couple hose clamps, and was back in business.

That night, Shakey called with an update from Shushan Sity.

"I got about 70 percent of my taps in, I guess," he said.

I yawned, wiped from another long day of going up and down the hill. "I got about two-fifty in. I keep getting sidetracked," I said, collapsed in a chair like my bones had dissolved.

He scoffed. "It's still early yet so don't worry about missing out on any sap. I know everyone's been doing sprints through their woods, but we ain't got no business getting started right now. It's only the first week in February for Christ's sake. And lemme tell you something, I tasted the sap trickles I got today and it tasted like fuckin' Alka-Seltzer. No sugar in it."

When sap comes out of the tree, it's typically 98 percent water and 2 percent sugar. At that rate, it takes about forty gallons of sap to make one gallon of syrup. But early-season sap is usually much lower in sugar content—like 1 percent, which means an *eighty*-gallons-to-one sap-to-syrup ratio. This early, the maples are barely getting an inkling that it's time to send starches up the trunk, sort of like they're slow getting out of bed in the morning.

"Tomorrow it's supposed to drop into the single digits and stay there for the next few days," Shakey reminded me. "That'll shut the trees back down."

The lull would give us an opportunity to catch up on tapping, maybe even finish it all, and hopefully be ready for sap run number two. But only if we got our asses in gear.

Shakey signed off with a particularly revolting joke and hung up without waiting to see if I laughed.

SAMARA:
SEEDS OF A LIFE IN MAPLE

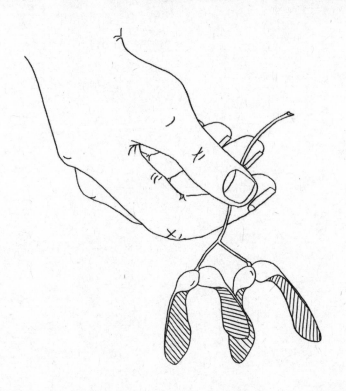

17

MY MAPLE HAZING

I grew up the son of a flavor man. My dad spent a forty-year career selling artificial food additives, calling on the big conglomerates around Minneapolis with a shoeshine and a smile. His claim to fame was developing the signature flavor in strawberry Yoplait, which made him "pretty well off," as they say in Minnesota. Dad's originally a New Yorker, born in Manhattan and raised in Jackson Heights, and he grew up playing stickball and watching the DC-3s take off at LaGuardia Airport. A city boy. He can never quite wrap his head around what the hell I'm doing making my own maple syrup up here in the sticks. "Why not just go to Zabar's?" he said to me once, with a palms-up shrug.

Mom also came from urban roots, growing up near 8 Mile in East Detroit. She later became a flower child of the seventies, and still kind of is. She appreciates the earthy aspect of maple. She loves the syrup we make but worries about me on the hill with the ice. "You're gonna fall and break your collarbone," she keeps saying. Always the collarbone for some reason. They both flew out from Mound a couple years ago to visit me at the sugarhouse—Dad wore buffed Johnston & Murphys; Mom in Teva sandals with socks—and they seemed genuinely impressed and asked a lot of questions about what all the pipes did on the evaporator and whatnot.

Dad put his arm over my shoulders. "Pretty neat contraption, I must say," he said.

But mostly I'm a mystery to them with all this maple stuff. I don't blame them.

I'm a mystery to myself.

I've always been drawn to the forest. As a kid in Minnesota, there was a pocket of woods behind our house—the suburban kind, flat and spread-out behind the split-level ramblers in our subdivision—and we kids would spend entire days screwing around back there.

We loved to build forts. We'd find scrapboard and scrounge up nails—there were always new houses under construction around us, so we'd raid them for building materials on weekends when no one was around—and we'd climb up in the branches of the cottonwoods, oaks, and Norway maples. We never called them treehouses or playhouses, we called them *forts*.

Later, in my latchkey teen years, the woods were where we organized BB gun wars. Sort of like paintball or laser tag, but with BB guns. Two teams, last kid standing wins. Most guys had Red Ryder or Daisy carbine-action guns, the sting from which would hurt, but maybe not any worse than a nut tap or a purple nurple. But some of the rich kids had pump-action guns that you could pump to ten, with each pump inflating more air pressure into the firing chamber. The rules of engagement with ten-pumpers were that you could only shoot a guy after two pumps. Yeah, right. What inevitably happened was the kid would forget he pumped the gun, and in the heat of battle he'd pump it *again*, adding two extra to the projectile velocity. Then he'd blast you and you'd coil on the ground in agony, screaming at him for cheating.

After the skirmishes, we'd sit on the far side of a creek on the immense trunk of a fallen willow that had been knocked over by a tornado years before. We'd chew Skoal Bandits or smoke Swisher Sweets and sometimes drink pull-tab cans of 3.2 beer if we could get our hands on some. We were fifteen, camouflaged from parents by the trees. Our guardians.

In my college years, in Vermont, I discovered the forests of New England. I became an avid hiker and attacked as many trails as I could. I owned a scuffed copy of the *Day Hiker's Guide to Vermont* and the *Long Trail Guide*, both published by the Green Mountain Club, of which I'm still a member. After each hike I'd check off the completion date in ballpoint pen.

My favorite is the Long Trail, a continuous 273-mile hike along the spine of Vermont from the Massachusetts to the Quebec border. Over the decades I've knocked off many ten-mile spurts of the LT and by now, altogether, I've completed roughly half of it. I hope to hike the Long Trail from end to end in one fell swoop sometime in the next couple of years.

I mostly hike for views—the payoff, and I especially enjoy hikes with distinguishing character features, like fire towers. In New England, and in the Adirondacks of New York, there are dozens of hikes that climax at old fire towers—erector set–looking structures where the government would post fire watchers to look for smoke. Fire towers bring you 200 feet in the air, above the peak of a mountain, offering an insane panoramic vantage. The final climb up a tower can be nerve-wracking because the stairs are usually very steep and narrow, and fire towers sway in the wind. At the top there is usually a little cabin—a fort!—where people sometimes carve obscene graffiti with pocketknives.

The transition into my maple career began not long after I graduated college and found myself drifting. I was at a stage in my young adult life when I was seeking something to help define me. A raison d'être. I had a lousy job. I drove a crappy car. I wasn't yet a father. At some point a lot of men pick a thing, and I felt I needed to also. You know, like a hobby. *Oh, you know Jim, you can never tear him away from his stamps.* My brother-in-law is obsessed with catching walleye. I know other dudes who've spent their lives searching for arrowheads in fields. These are the kinds of things that help characterize you, that they use to fill out the middle paragraphs of a man's obituary.

I tried to find my niche in many work endeavors. I sold a lot of junk. I sold car stereos at Best Buy. I sold TV sets at Sears. I sold pull-out beds, cellular phones, and car wash coupon books door-to-door. I sold *meat* door-to-door. I tried acting a couple times. I was cast as an extra in a hockey game scene in *The Mighty Ducks* and even got a walk-on part on an episode of *Cheers* (the one where Lilith breaks up with Frasier and he threatens to jump out a window. You can see me on the street below mouthing, "Don't jump!"). None of my star turns led to a movie career in Hollywood like I'd hoped. Instead, I settled into the world of journalism and public relations, got married, and started a family. A good life. But I always craved a more authentic, earthy experience. The only way I ever got my hands dirty was from ink or changing diapers.

Then I found maple.

Or I should say, serendipitously, maple found me. My first experience with real maple syrup was through a goofy dude named Dudley Jenkins, who was my colleague at a boring office job I once had in Rutland. I was fresh off the bus from Minnesota and didn't know squat about real maple syrup (until then, I'd been an Aunt Jemima man). Dudley was funny and congenial, one of the only people who brought color to our drab office suite. Dudley worshiped the Grateful Dead, and I moderately worshiped them, so we often swapped bootleg cassette tapes—although I only had a dozen or so (including my favorite Dead standards: Cornell 5/8/77; New Haven 5/5/77; Nassau Coliseum 3/30/90) and Dudley had like 130. In the spring, Dudley would sometimes come into the office with Mason jars of maple syrup and give it away to everyone. He was from central Indiana, with a rural twang, and would pronounce maple syrup as a one-word mashup, *maplesyrup*, the same way one might say *homemade* or *bubblegum*. He would proudly place a jar of it on someone's desk and say, "Here, try some of my homemade maplesyrup." I took notice of how everyone would go berserk for it. "I just love maple syrup!" they'd exclaim. On those days, he became the hero of the office, and something in me clicked. That stuff Dudley was bringing to the office, somehow derived from . . . ? I wanted to know more.

One Saturday in March, he invited me out to his hobby farm to "boil with him."

"Boil? Boil what?" I asked.

He laughed. "Sap, boy. Where do you think the syrup comes from?"

I had no idea what I was about to get into but went anyway.

Dudley owned a thirty-acre spread a few miles out of town and lived in a Greek Revival farmhouse with his wife and five kids. He had hung tapered galvanized sap buckets on the big maples spaced out across his property, and we went around collecting them in an old orchard tractor pulling a 3-bbl Grimm sap tank that was strapped to a hay wagon.

"What we do is tap the tree with this here spout, then the sap will drip out that hole and collect in the bucket, see? Idn't it great?" he said as we went from tree to tree, and I'd tip each bucket to reveal they were full of clear, shimmering sap. Dudley put me in charge of bucket dumping while he slalomed the tractor between the grid of maples.

Once we collected all the sap, we came back to a ramshackle chicken coop where Dudley had angled an evaporator into a corner. It remains kind of a blur, but before too long we were boiling the sap and sugary steam swallowed up the tiny room like we were taking a schvitz. My job was to toss logs into the firebox behind its glowing-red iron double doors. As the morning progressed, boiling sap with Dudley turned into more of a party. "The wife took the kids to her mother's," he said. This was an unusually warm early spring day. Woodstock was in the air. Dudley brought out a pair of guitars and some beers, and we sat on milk crates in the sun, strumming along while the sap boiled inside. Every fifteen minutes or so, we'd set down the guitars and step into the chicken coop, and I'd throw another log into the firebox.

From time to time, Dudley dipped a stainless-steel basting spoon into the sap and then held it vertically over the pan and let the clingy almost-syrup hang off the spoon like an apron.

"Comin' along nicely, won't be long now, dude," he said.

At some point during our jam, he stood up to go inside the house and gave me a conspiratorial glance. "I'm gonna be right back with a little sumptin' sumptin'," he said. When he returned, he unfurled his hand and produced a very fat joint. "Want to get hiiiigh?" he said, emoting the *iii*'s ironically with a gurgle. He stuck a twig in the firebox to flame it up. He took a whale of a puff and then passed it to me. I took a courtesy hit—I was mostly good with the beers—and he toked the rest of it. We played our guitars some more, and after a while, the fire and boiling sap became something of an afterthought to Dudley. But I was still completely captivated by the task at hand, syrup from sap—wow!—this is turning out to be some real interesting shit. It wasn't long before Dudley began to droop and fade. He excused himself and stumbled back to his house, presumably to nap off the high. "Watch the fire, man. When the thermometer hits the seven, take the syrup off." That's all the instruction he gave me.

It was as if he asked me to land a plane.

Sap turns into syrup at exactly 7°F above the boiling point of water (which can change from day to day depending on the barometer, but usually around 212°F). Thermometers on evaporators are marked with big 7s on the dials, the point of no return in maple alchemy. That's what Dudley meant. I sat on a milking stool at the side of the evaporator and stared intently at that dial, rapt, like I was waiting for a baby chick to hatch from an egg.

Over time, probably forty-five minutes, the thermometer needle inched closer and closer to the seven. At long last, it hit the mark. I twisted a knob on a spigot sticking out of the side of the evaporator, and it released a pilaster of orangey syrup, *glug, glug, glug*, into a pail that Dudley had set underneath. I wasn't quite sure when or if to close the damn valve or just leave it open and drain *all* the syrup out of the pan. I decided to keep the gate open until the syrup brimmed the pail. The sweet smell was intoxicating as Dudley's doobie.

Meanwhile, the dial retreated to about the three mark on the thermometer and then, rather quickly, climbed again back to seven. Holy shit. I scrambled around the chicken coop to find another pail and drained the pan again. This time, I only spigoted off about half as much since the needle dropped much faster on the second draw than the first.

Dudley eventually emerged from his house with some tuna fish sandwiches. "Let's see how you did," he said, eyeing the container of simmering syrup. He reached for a copper beer stein–looking thing—a hydrometer cup, he explained—and dunked it into the syrup. Then he dropped something called a *hydrometer* into the cup and pointed his finger at it to show how it measured the density of syrup by how deep or shallow it floated. A syrup hydrometer looks like a thermometer you stick under your tongue, but with a bulbous bottom. A red line on its proboscis indicates the proper thickness of the liquid, making it almost idiotproof. Most state agriculture laws deem standard maple-syrup density—where that red line is located—as 66.9° on the sucrose-measuring Brix scale, meaning it's more than two-thirds sugar. The "syrup" I let out of the spigot at Dudley's wasn't even close to that. The hydrometer barely stood upright in the cup. I'd drawn off way too much, thinning it. Dudley didn't care. "It still tastes good," he said, swishing his finger in the syrup and licking it off. "You did great!"

Dudley let me run the rig the remainder of the afternoon while he strummed his guitar and polished off the sandwiches. "Man, I got the munchies," he said. My next couple of draws improved each time, according to the hydrometer, and I started to get the hang of it. "Holy shit, does this make me a farmer now?" I said, and Dudley laughed. "Yeah, sure, man. We'll get you a straw hat."

I fell into a routine where I would draw off maybe a half a pail's worth of syrup and then check it with the hydrometer, occasionally pouring the syrup back into the evaporator to cook some more if the density wasn't correct.

It was one of the most memorable days of my life.

The following Monday, Dudley walked into my office gripping the copper hydrometer cup and clanked it down on my desk. "You earned this, man," he said. Dudley also gifted me a couple of sap buckets and some spiles and encouraged me to try my hand at producing maple at home.

"You make syrup once, you're gonna wanna make it the rest of your life," he said. "I hope to be a sugarmaker until the day I die. We call it 'the Bug.' It gets in your blood and never leaves. From what I saw on Saturday, I think you got it, too."

He was right. I was hooked.

18

THE O.G. OF
SUGARHOUSE BUILDERS

The sugarhouse that me, Bert, and the fellas from the dad band built on Blossom Road is my *second* sugarhouse. My *first* sugarhouse I built a few years after Dudley gave me his hydrometer cup and the buckets. I'd been tapping the huge maple trees around an abandoned cemetery behind my home and boiling sap in a washtub perched over some cinder blocks in my backyard, exposed to the snow and rain. I was having a hell of a good time, but decided I needed a roof over my head. So I went over to Salem Hardware, bought a hammer, a tape measure, and a Skilsaw, and got to work on a sugarhouse, my first construction project since the forts era.

My plan was to build it all by myself, in conscious appreciation of two men, a guy named Noel Perrin and another guy you might've heard of named Henry David Thoreau. Let me explain.

Thoreau built his famous cabin on Walden Pond solo. No help from anyone. Just Henry and his hammer and nails, a saw and some splintered clapboards, along with a notebook, where he wrote: "I went to the woods because I wished to live deliberately . . . and see if I could learn what it had to teach, and not, when I came to die, discover that I had not lived." Sounds like a sugarmaker. It's one my favorite quotes, one that always tugged at me.

Thoreau also aimed to hand-build his famous cabin for little or no money. Cheap, thrifty, or ascetic, take your pick, he mostly succeeded. In all, Thoreau spent just twenty-eight bucks.

When it came time to build my first sugarhouse, I called a guy who aspired to the same concept, a sugarmaker who wrote a book about building a sugarhouse in reverence to Thoreau's spiritual frugality—a farmer/writer named Noel Perrin. "Ned," as everyone called him, was a Dartmouth College professor who lived on a small farm in Thetford Center, Vermont. His short book, now long out of print, was called *Amateur Sugar Maker*, a copy of which I display on a shelf in my living room. (I'm sentimental about books.) I reread it every maple season.

Perrin was originally from the New York City suburb of Pelham Manor, an affluent village in Westchester County. He moved to Vermont to teach English literature and was a noted scholar on Robert Frost (another Vermonter and my favorite poet). Perrin's maple book featured *New Yorker*-style drawings by an illustrator named Robert MacLean, also from Vermont—Marlboro, near the Massachusetts border—which made the book even more Vermonty and cool. The running theme of the narrative was to see if Perrin could build his sugarhouse for as little money as possible, practicing the same Yankee thrift that Thoreau used to build his cabin.

Perrin came close. He scrounged around Thetford for reclaimed boards and nails and got his hands on some old sap buckets and tanks from some local farmers who had idle maple equipment rusting in their barns. Perrin chronicled his efforts of the 1969 sugaring season, during a notoriously depressed era for the maple industry, when syrup was only fetching three dollars per gallon and sugarmakers were going out of business left and right. Farmers then had no problem selling their unused maple equipment on the cheap to intrepids like Perrin, just to make room in their barns for something else.

Perrin did indulge himself by buying a new Grimm evaporator however, a splurge Thoreau never would have made. But then again, Thoreau never sugared. If he had, I suspect he might've at least been tempted to purchase some decent equipment to boil his sap with.

One autumn day, I pestered Perrin to meet, hoping I could appeal—from one suburban-raised farmer-slash-writer to another—for some help and advice in building a sugarhouse of my own. I looked him up in the phone book. "Sure, come on over," he said in a raspy voice. I think he was surprised someone had found a copy of *Amateur Sugar Maker* and was eager to put its prescriptions to use. "Not sure how much I can help you, but I always love to talk maple. I'll warn you though, the sugarhouse is in need of some repair."

Perrin's sugarhouse stood at the bottom of Thetford Hill along the Ompompanoosuc River, a short tributary of the Connecticut, next to the town's covered bridge, which spans it. We spent a rainy afternoon together touring his sap shack; the roof was leaking, and water was dripping everywhere. The flue pan and syrup pan were turned upside down on top of the evaporator, an old sugarmaker trick to keep field mice from nesting in them during the summer. Perrin was suffering from a neurodegenerative disease that killed him only a few months after our visit. He was hobbling around behind a cane, a sweater wrapped around his neck by the sleeves, spectacles sliding down the bridge of his nose. I could sense sugaring served a special purpose in his life, and the moment we got there, he tossed the sweater on a chair, squinted his eyes, and rolled up his sleeves. He began to tidy up the place, and with his cane, tried to bang some of the roofing tin into a better position overhead to shield us from the rain. "Scooch over, buster," he said to a sheet, just above a whisper. Without me knowing it at the time—but maybe he did—the tour ended up being Perrin's last goodbye to his sugarhouse and all it represented.

Perrin made syrup in that sugarhouse right up to the year he died—eight gallons, that previous spring. Truly impressive. In all, he enjoyed thirty-six seasons of syrup-making on the same evaporator in the same sugarhouse.

I asked him that day if he still considered himself an "amateur" sugarmaker after all those years of boiling sap. "If I'm no longer an amateur sugarmaker," he said, pushing his glasses up, "I feel like I'm at least a competent one now."

Perrin pulled off something most sugarmakers never do, with the exception of Bruce Bascom: he made a profit. He was as frugal as Thoreau in erecting his sugarhouse, and even though Perrin splurged on his evaporator, he used the same one all thirty-six seasons—a favorable amortization. Before I left, Perrin proudly showed me a check he'd just received from the Thetford Village Store—it was for $36—which was payment on a consignment batch of two-ounce syrup bottles the store had sold for him. I watched him slip the check straight into the pocket of his corduroy trousers.

After my visit, I raced home to get to work on *my* first sugarhouse. I built it adjacent to my garage, amid a tight cluster of 200-year-old village homes, which turned out to be an ill-suited location, since I almost burned down my house (and those of several neighbors) from the sparks shooting out of the evaporator. I designed it to the exact same proportions as Perrin's sugarhouse and Thoreau's cabin, eight feet by twelve feet. (I've since learned ol' Salinger had a hut about the same size up there in Cornish, and Arthur Miller hand-built an eight-by-twelve writing cabin in Connecticut and penned *Death of a Salesman* in it.)

The purple slates I shingled on the roof of my sugarhouse distinguished it from Perrin's roof, guaranteed to never leak. (I have a thing for slate.) While my roof was solid, I did a terrible job on the foundation, if you could call it that. In true Thoreau/Perrin spirit, I wanted to save money. Bothering to pour concrete would have been too expensive, I figured. More authentic to have a dirt floor anyway. I've since moved away from that home, and the new owners have converted my old sugarhouse into lawn mower and snowblower storage. Whenever I drive past, I notice it's tilting dramatically. Enough that I worry it will topple over.

One last confession about that first sugarhouse: I didn't build it entirely alone, hard as I tried. I recruited my father-in-law to help with the wiring, and an uncle came out from Michigan one weekend to lend a hand building the ventilator cupola, the trickiest part of any sugarhouse project. I also bribed a buddy with some pizza and Leinenkugel's to spend a day handing me slate tiles while I clung to a roof-jack and fastened them with copper nails. But I mostly built that sugarhouse by myself, at least enough that I think it would've impressed Perrin and Thoreau.

Even if its days are numbered.

PART II
THE FLOW BEGINS

LATE FEBRUARY 2022

19

TAPPING THE LIGHT FANTASTIC

On a Sunday morning in mid-February, I was given a great gift—sure footing. The melting snow of the past three days had hardened overnight as the temperatures dropped into the teens, transforming the pack into a sturdy hull.

Surface cover like this is rare, and I set my mind to tapping every one of our remaining trees before conditions reversed. I stretched the Amazon crampons over my hiking boots, and their teeth clung fast and easy to the crust as I went up the hill.

Up until now, we only had 250 (of our 856) trees tapped. During the warm-up last week, the 250 hooked-up trees seeped a little bit of sap into the pipeline. But neither the pump nor the tank was connected below, so the meager stream of sap just dribbled down the pipeline and spilled to the ground at the mouth near the sugarhouse. What a waste.

Very un-Five-Pounderish.

I was determined to get my ass in gear and get all the rest of them drilled, tapped, and connected, by hook or by crook. The forecast for the week ahead was promising another significant warm-up, one likely to linger. We might end up making a lot of syrup—but only if I got the trees tapped. "To-goddamned-day," I pledged to Bert in a text.

After my stoned, informal apprenticeship with Dudley and going out on my own, I got tutelage on proper tapping techniques from a legendary Vermont maple family up north in the town of Fairfield, which lies on a high ridge rising from Lake Champlain. Fairfield is a sugar town, the Silicon Valley of maple production, and where many of the biggest sugarmakers in the United States are concentrated. There are individual Fairfield sugarmakers—Gary Corey, J. R. Sloan, the Howrigan family—who produce more syrup on their one farm than the production totals of all the farmers in the Ruperts and Salem and Blossom Road combined, for example. One of the most prominent families up there are the Branons, who own a 2,600-acre sugarbush and tap somewhere around 80,000 trees. The Branons are very fussy about good tapping, an essential prerequisite for becoming a Five Pounder, which the Branons always are, season after season.

The Branon tapping method involves first circling the tree. "I want to see your bootprints in the snow around every trunk," Tom Branon, the steely-eyed family patriarch, told me during a tapping seminar he hosted at his farm not too long ago, where he shared his secrets. He was dressed the part of a Vermont sugarmaker, wearing a green plaid wool vest and matching plaid cap made by Johnson Woolen Mills in nearby Johnson, Vermont.

"You have to look for just the right tapping spot, far away from any old tapholes where the dead wood is," he said. Tapping a tree leaves a stain inside the trunk where the tree cauterizes the wound, turning it into nonconductive, or "dead," wood, he explained. "The telltale sign that you've hit dead wood is brown shavings will spin out of your drill instead of white."

Branon said he and his wife, Cecile, and sons, Evan and Kyle, had drilled hundreds of thousands of tapholes in their lifetimes. Maybe even a million. "Precision and consistency, that's what we strive for," he said. At the tree, Branon instructed me to make sure my drill was steady, gripping it with both hands and revving it all the way to full speed before it hit the bark. Then a fast in-and-out. "*Focus,*" he said. "That's the most important thing when you pull the trigger."

If you're sugaring the old-fashioned way, by hanging a sap bucket from the tree like ol' Ned Perrin used to do over in Thetford, or like Dudley behind his chicken coop, it doesn't matter what kind of hole you drill since the sap drips from gravity. But on a high-vacuum tubing system, like the one we have on Blossom Road, being airtight is essential, and that starts at the taphole. It matters how you drill it, Branon told me that day. "The better the hole, the better the seal," he said. The endgame for proper tapping is to avoid "wobbly" holes, which lead to vacuum leaks, costing time and money, he said.

Back on Blossom Hill I was so agile upon the sturdy crust with my crampons, it felt like I was levitating. I raced to each maple trunk gripping my DeWalt, then I'd pause, per the Branon method, and scan the bark to decipher where last year's taphole was. Then, when I found a clean spot, I maneuvered myself into place, pulled the trigger, and sank it into the tree.

There's a difference in the maples, between the sugars and the reds. Sugar maples are known as "hard" maples, and reds are commonly referred to as "soft" maples. The sugars have much more density and sometimes take two thrusts to reach proper tapping depth. With the reds, the bit just drives right in without much pressure at all. A friend from New York City once asked me if drilling holes hurts the tree. "Don't worry, it's painless," I told her. There are few trees hardier than a maple, and they're almost impossible to kill. In fact, the University of Vermont's Proctor Maple Research Center once ran an experiment where they purposely tried to tap a tree to death. They couldn't do it. They drilled something like fifty tapholes into a single maple. The tree was fine.

The only thing that really seems to kill maples are lightning strikes and road salt. One of or all the properties that make up the aggregate of most municipal road salt—sodium chloride, calcium magnesium acetate, and potassium acetate—have decimated roadside sugar maples over the past couple decades. Before that, much of New England and New York was tree-shaded with maples. In the mid to late 1800s, there was a government effort to encourage homeowners to plant maple trees in their front yards, so they'd have access to their own sugar. Those maples are now mostly gone, with only a few remaining pockets I know of where maples still umbrella the roadways—along a few backroads in central Vermont, and some twisty roads in the Berkshires, and luckily, on our Blossom Road. (The town crew doesn't use road salt on Blossom since it's a hardpan surface. They just use gravel or sand like Archie McClellan dumped on the driveway.)

In the woods the air was still, the sun was high, and I was working up a good sweat. The only indicator it was cold outside was the advancing numbness in my fingers. That small discomfort didn't bother me much because I was basking in the luxury of my traction.

I met another tree, shoved in the drill, and with it still spinning clockwise, reversed it back out of the hole, unspooling a helix of paper-white tree guts.

I seated a spout in the cavity and then knocked it a couple times with my tapping hammer, securing it tightly in the hole and linking it with the others in the pipeline.

It's possible we sugarmakers are putting these tools through a rigor the R&D department at the DeWalt company never envisioned, abruptly starting and stopping, pushing and retreating their drills hundreds of times per day in short, furious bursts.

Something weird was happening though. The DeWalt today was making a funny noise it had never made before, and at times it was outright resisting me, but I soldiered on. *"I'm getting every last one of these damn holes drilled today whether you like it or not,"* I said to the tool, *"so you best cooperate."*

I literally clung to the hillsides, *propelled* from tree to tree. Instead of curling my ankle to gain traction along the slope, I could traverse flat-footed and fast. I zipped to another trunk. A *whirrrrurrrert* of the drill and a *whap, whap, whap* of the mallet followed by the *crunch, crunch, crunch* of my boots buoyant atop the snow. On to the next one.

Late in the day, I heard static, then Bert chirping in on the walkie-talkie.

"Yo, you out there, good buddy? Come on back. Over," he said.

I pressed the talk button. "Copy, Rubber Duck. I'm blasting away at these trees. Be on my way back down soon. Drill batteries almost dead. Over," I said.

"Roger that."

The sky was cloudless and azure. The sugarbush so silent you could hear the rustle of the leaves clinging to the beech and the oaks, which they tend to do in winter. Every so often a jet airplane would interrupt the stillness, passing overhead leaving cottony contrails.

By daylight's end, I had tapped every last tree—the most maples I'd ever drilled in a single day, more than 600 of them.

A machine, I was.

I came off the mountain and reconnoitered with Bert, who was hobbling along the hedgerow using a pitchfork for stability on the ice crust. "I couldn't find my damn crampons," he said, inching toward me like he was using a tennis-ball walker.

"News flash, my friend, I think I got 'em all drilled," I said, a little cocky.

"Hallelujah," Bert said, and he draped an arm over the pitchfork handle.

I explained about the crust and the traction. "It was like walking on the moon."

"Good timing, because I predict there's gonna be a crapload of sap pouring out of those trees when it warms up this week, if the stupid forecasters are right," he said. "The full-on frigging maple season, brother. Get ready. The hurricane is about to make landfall."

As the words left Bert's mouth, I felt the same rush of anticipation and dread I get on a roller coaster when it crests over that first camelback rise.

20

EVERY GREAT FLOOD BEGINS
WITH A SINGLE FIRST DROP

Sap Day! We were tapped and ready for what was expected to be our first real-deal sap run of the 2022 season.

Personal regimens go out the window during maple season. From here on out, until maple season is over, you are on the schedule of the sap—and sap will flow any goddamn time it feels like it. Do you like to go for a jog every afternoon at five? Forget it. Like to sip a leisurely cup of Dunkin' and watch *SportsCenter* every morning? Not happening. Haircuts, therapy sessions, Tuesday night bowling league? All forfeited. I'm one of those people who has eyebrows that grow inordinately fast. I keep a pair of micro-scissors in my bathroom sink drawer just so I can whack away at those buggers as fast as they grow, probably twice a week. But during maple season? By the time it's over, I look like I have cheerleading pom poms latched to my forehead.

That morning of the sap I had an appointment to get a basal-cell carcinoma thingy carved out of my back—technically, skin cancer, although no one seemed to be taking it too seriously at the dermatologist's office. In fact, it was the office administrator, as opposed to an actual doctor, who had called a few weeks before to tell me I had the condition. I remember asking her (I think her name was Heather) "Is this cancer we're talking about here, Heather?"

"Um, yeah, it's cancer," she said, like she wasn't 100 percent sure but guessed so.

Heather told me I'd be in and out in twenty minutes, just a routine procedure to knife a football-shaped swatch out of my back. But here, on the appointed day, with the sap consuming my thoughts, I called Heather back to cancel, thinking I wouldn't be able to even spare twenty minutes.

"I'm expecting a lot of sap today so I can't make it to my appointment," I said to Heather who, I quickly realized, was not observing the same DEFCON level of responsibility to the sap as I was. "That's a new one," she said with a chuckle. "We still have to charge you the hundred-dollar cancellation fee."

"Way to be supportive, Heather," I said.

When I got to the sugarhouse, it was quiet except for a lone mosquito buzzing around. *That's weird. A mosquito on February 17?* I clapped it dead with my hands, and it left a black smoosh in my palm. *Not a good sign*, I thought and wiped it off on my jeans.

I smacked the toggle switch on the vacuum pump, and it started chugging. A brief note about pumps: In the maple business, there are many kinds of vacuum pumps that work many different ways. Mine is what's called a "rotary vane" pump, which is driven by belt-and-pulley on a two-horse electric motor. Inside the pump, there is a mechanism that floods the housing with a stream of oil to lubricate the spinning vane and keep it cool. On top of the pump there's a gauge that gives us a readout on the vacuum level in inches of mercury, or "hg," which is a unit of atmospheric pressure. It's marked off at 5, 10, 15, 20, 25, and 30, where it stops. I leaned against a wall and watched it climb. I wanted to see that sucker as close to 30 as possible (29.92hg is the highest possible vacuum at sea level). Today it stopped at 16. Dog shit. But expected, since Bert and I hadn't started repairing leaks in the tubing yet other than on that day of the log moonshot, so it was still a very holey pipeline up there in the woods.

The good news was that sap was still rushing in, the pump sucking it into that new releaser Kevin Mattison had wired up for me, which in turn dumped the sap down a drainpipe into the *Edmund Fitzgerald*. Bert and I had started to refer to it now as "the Fitzy." The sap splashed when it hit the bottom of the tank. Sap in the beginning of the season is usually clear, but today's was somewhat murky, which was as unusual as the mosquito and the robin in the snow the other day with Milt. "Cripes, the weather is funny this year," I said to myself.

The low level of vacuum likely indicated there were lots of fresh squirrel chews along the pipeline and probably also a lot of "Man Downs," our jargon for the dangling droplines that I evidently forgot to install in my haste to tap every tree in the sugarbush the other day. (A forest is not patterned; trees are scattered and sometimes it's easy to miss one or two, or twenty.) I clearly still had lots of work to do in the woods to get the lines leak-free and the vacuum up to twenty-six or twenty-seven inches, so back up the hill I went with my tubing tool, a pocket full of fittings, and my tapping hammer.

Sure enough, I found a bunch of Man Downs right around where the doe had been killed. With the vacuum on, it's easy to discover Man Downs because they hiss. You simply follow the hiss to the tree. I approached one, drilled a taphole for it, and plugged in a spile. Fixed. The trees today, with temperatures now in the fifties, reacted far differently than when I drilled them on Sunday when it was 20° and frozen. When I drilled the holes this time, sap drooled out in a way kind of like when you take a drink of water after being numbed at the dentist.

I spent two hours going up and down the hill attaching Man Downs and patching chews. I checked the vacuum gauge, and it had improved to 21, which was satisfying. I climbed up a ladder leaned against the Fitzy and watched sap pour into the tank. It was starting to fill. We usually wait for about 1,000 gallons of sap to accrue before we start boiling. The sap was coming in so fast that we were clearly on pace to get more than that after a few more hours. *Holy crap*, I thought. *I better ping Bert to get his butt up here soon.*

I took a break and headed over to Shushan to Yushak's Market, another great store we like to frequent. During maple season I usually have a big appetite for red meat, and I wanted to burn up a couple steaks on the Weber while Bert and I boiled the sap tonight.

Yushak's is in an Old West–looking building with a terra-cotta façade and sits just a maple leaf twirl down the street from Shakey's place. The store is a Shushan institution.

People mostly come to Yushak's for the meat selection. Denny Yushak, the owner, is a master butcher and can always be found behind the glass-paneled meat counter wearing a Mets cap and a long white apron covered with blood smears in various hues of dryness. The chuck always looks bright red and juicy, with well-infused striations of fat, perfect for meat loafs and hamburgers. Denny's specialty is sausage—patties for breakfasts, links for the grill. He even sells proprietary sausage-making spices, and, come autumn, Denny offers a class in sausage making so all the hunters can make venison sausage at home after they shoot their deer. (Bert's taken the class.) Denny also sells many prepared foods that he makes right in Yushak's kitchen—potato salads, pasta salads, potato and bacon salads, antipasto with chunks of cherry tomatoes and cheese.

Denny greeted me, and we exchanged some chit chat about pitchers and catchers reporting to spring training soon, and he seemed optimistic about the Mets' upcoming season, while I griped about the Twins. Then he tried to steer my gaze to a tray of hunky steaks on the middle shelf. "I got some nice Delmonicos today, Peter," he said.

Denny always asks about the maple season—a lot of sugarmakers come in and out of his store—and he's usually particularly in tune with the progress of Shakey's season since they're neighbors. Shakey also sells his syrup on consignment out of Yushak's.

He plopped a two-steak stack on a scale. "Sap running yet?" Denny asked.

I clasped my arms behind my body. "It's coming in good on Blossom Road as we speak," I said. "We're probably gonna boil tonight. It'll be our first boil of the season."

He wrapped my order in white butcher paper. "Okay, well good luck. How do you think this season's gonna be?" he asked, setting me up for a classic old sugarmaker retort:

"I'll tell you in April, Denny."

After Yushak's, I drove to Rupert to get my mail and passed by the McClellan farm. Steam was pouring out of the cupola of the sugarhouse, so I pulled in. Inside, the haze was so thick I couldn't see anyone. I hollered out and Archie McClellan appeared out of the cloud, and then his brother Walter followed behind. But there was no aroma of sugar in the air.

I looked at Walter. "You guys making syrup today?" I asked, confused.

"Naw, just boiling hot water, we're testing some new pans," he replied.

Walter said his tapping crew was way behind and they'd barely gotten started.

"We only got 500 drilled in or so," he said. "We're not hooked up yet."

The McClellans typically put in 16,000 taps for the year. *Five hundred drilled out of sixteen thousand . . . I guess we aren't so far behind everyone else,* I thought.

Walter grabbed a ladder, and he leaned it against the top pan, climbed up, and peered inside.

"Did Archie here tell you about our little, um, incident?" I asked him. They both smirked.

"Heard all about it," Walter said from above.

Archie waved his hand dismissively.

"The problem was those *tires*, you see. No *grip*," Archie said.

The first day of sap feels like an oil strike. All that work and preparation and now here it was, coming in big time. I got back to the sugarhouse and texted Bert at the office.

"It's pouring in the tank, buddy."

"Holy shit, enough to boil today?"

"Haul ass on up here, son. I got steaks from Yushak's. You bring the coleslaw!"

"I'll try."

The Fitzy was indeed filling up. But there were chunks of ice clogging the drain. I ran to the barn and found a broom handle to break it up with.

I went up the ladder, leaned over, and speared the ice until eventually little bergs chunked off in quarters, small enough that I could claw the blocks out with the prongs of a garden rake.

After about a half hour of this kerfuffle, and with the ice cleared, I noticed I'd riddled the bottom of the tank with small dents from the broom handle. "Did they make this damn tank out of aluminum foil?" I shouted and javelin-tossed the broom handle across the yard.

After I calmed down, the next order of business was to process the sap. To begin that, I would have to connect Edmund to an inlet pipe on the RO, the reverse osmosis machine, so it could start doing its job. I grabbed a long length of flexible hose. "Come with me, buddy," I said, dragging it through the mud. I connected one end to the tank's now-cleared drain and ran the other to a suction pipe sticking out of the wall from the room where we keep the RO. I opened the valve on the tank and watched a gulp of sap run through the hose.

I swung into the RO room and pushed a series of buttons to get it started. Remarkably, after sitting idle for the past nine months, the RO fired right up, and within a few minutes, the thing was sucking and squeezing sap, ultimately removing 85 percent of the water.

An up-and-running RO will keep sucking and squeezing sap until it completely empties the tank and then, on autopilot, it shuts itself off. So I had a couple of hours to kill before we would boil. I probably could've still made my dermatologist's appointment, but instead I took a disco nap in the truck, thinking I'd need to rest up for a big night of sap-boiling with Bert.

21

FIRST DAYS ALWAYS SUCK

I woke up—springing upright in my truck seat—just as the RO was finishing its job, sucking the last drops of sap out of the *Edmund Fitzgerald*,
and pumping the concentrate into another tank we call "Roundy." (It's
round.) Roundy was about to brim over with 300 gallons of what was once
2 percent sap and was now 12 percent concentrate. Got to it just in time.

I pinged Bert again.

"Let me guess, you're still at work?"

Bert:

Me, once more: *"Yo buddy, on your way? We got a pile of sap to boil."*

Twenty minutes later he texted: *"Sorry bud, stuck in meetings. Better start
without me."*

Shit. I don't mind boiling alone, but it goes more smoothly (and is a
lot more fun) if we do it together. Over the years, Bert and I have fallen
into a steady routine of how to handle boiling days, the who does what,
etc. Running a sap evaporator is a lot like being the commander of a ship.
When captains are at sea, they announce to everyone they are "at the conn,"
considered to be one of the most important principles of ship handling.
Being at the conn ensures there's no ambiguity as to who's controlling
the vessel. Same thing in the sugarhouse. The person positioned at the
side of the rig during a boil is the sugarmaker at the conn. For years, Bert

and I would take turns there, but after a while, the job fell mostly on me, primarily because boiling sap better fits my spazzy personality than Bert's contemplative one. I'll explain.

During a boil, there are a million things happening at once that demand immediate attention. I'm quick on my feet, literally, whereas Bert methodically processes everything happening around him and likes more time—Bert Time—to deliberate on a response. It's not that Bert's ever made bad syrup, he just makes slow syrup.

The bigger problem is Bert's lungs. Our evaporator cranks at about the same temperature as an iron forge. The forced air we blast into the firebox to get it that hot aerates fine particles of soot into the room, and this was wrecking Bert's delicate respiratory system. It's never really bothered me, but I smoked a pack of Camel Lights nearly every day of my twenties, so my lungs are accustomed to abuse. Long before wearing respirator masks was a thing, Bert would wear an N95 when he was boiling, which he found uncomfortable in a way all of us are now very familiar with. Over the years, he's just ceded all boiling responsibilities to me.

Bert has since assumed duties around the sugarhouse that fit far better with his meticulous nature. He is the tank cleaner and filtering man, and the one who is primarily responsible for the care and feeding of the RO. All are essential. When sap gathers in our tanks (in the past, the Centipede tanks, now the Fitzy), it leaves behind a residue that must be thoroughly cleaned so it doesn't contaminate the next quantity of sap that comes in. Bert spends a lot of time scrubbing and rinsing with hot water. He also washes the RO, which is even more demanding in its cleaning procedure. There are several step-by-step protocols for RO cleaning with various detergents and rinsing cycles that I would never have the patience for. Bert does.

Then there's the filtering. After syrup is drawn off the evaporator, Bert runs it through a filter press, which is a machine with a series of block plates that lie horizontally on a rack like a deflated accordion. Between each of the plates, he inserts a sheet of heavy-duty filter paper. The syrup is pressed through these papers with a pump. To aid in the filtering, he adds in a food-grade powder called *Diatomaceous earth*, the fossilized remains of mollusks from millions of years ago. He stirs a measuring cup or two into each batch of syrup with a whisk. Crazy as it sounds to be using this stuff, it's common in anything that requires a filtering procedure—beer making, wine making, swimming pool maintenance. It helps pass the syrup through the tiny holes in the plates of the press, removing various items of gunk—leaf chunks, dirt, the occasional moth—making it crystalline clear. Bert oversees all of that, almost like a safety officer.

Here's a little tip: never visit a sugarmaker on their first day of boiling. We'd love to have you stop by any other day during the season, but not on the first day of a big sap run because that's usually the day everything seems to go wrong, and we don't want any witnesses.

There was a part of me that thought maybe I should let the sap sit until Bert was available to boil it with me. But I was itchy to make some syrup and get the season officially underway. *To Hell with it*, I thought and went to fire up the evaporator without him.

The first order of business when you're about to boil a bunch of sap is start a fire. Seems so simple, but for years starting the damn boiling fire was one of my biggest challenges. It would sometimes take me two, three, even four tries. The successful attempt would always be the one when I took my time instead of rushing. Fire senses impatience. What I've learned is that besides taking it slow, it's important to also use lots of dry kindling—and then give it the frigging MAPP gas.

I balled up some newspaper inside the ceramic-lined firebox. Then I crisscrossed thin sticks of kindling over the newspaper, and on top of that a very narrow log of dead ash firewood. I arranged it like a teepee. Then I took the MAPP torch—a flamethrower—and blasted away at the tinder pile for a full minute. Once I had a good burn going, I closed the cast-iron chamber door. Inside the firebox, the blower blasted air across the flames. I leaned against a wall and kept my ears peeled, listening for the crackle of fire taking hold. "Come on, baby," I said.

I glanced at a thermometer we have wedged in the chimney that tells us how hot the fire is inside the arch. The needle began to revolve. It was catching.

"Let's goooo!" I shouted and clapped my hands.

The chimney—we call it a "stack"—is composed of lengths of stainless pipe that connect from the back of the evaporator and through a hole in the ceiling, sticking twenty feet above the roofline outside. When the fire is going full bore, the upcycling exhaust of heat and smoke and smoldering embers creates a buoyancy force so powerful, you could hover a bowling ball in it.

After the thermometer needle crossed 600°F, I flicked off the blower, threw open the firebox door, and quickly added a few more sticks to the blaze—now a bright yellow flare. I slammed the door shut and whacked the blower switch back on. The pin spun quickly this time, hitting 900°F. I repeated this process a few more times until the dial reached 1,200, as far as the needle would go.

With the arch now hot as a goddamned blast furnace, I scooted around the evaporator to scan all the pipes codified along the side of it. I always double-check the valves to make sure they're retained in the way I want liquid to go. I've learned that lesson the hard way, watching in horror as scalding hot syrup poured onto the sugarhouse floor because of an errant valve. It took me a long time to learn how to even *tell* if a valve was open or not; there's no light or signal. Then—duh!—I finally figured out the manufacturers designed the handle of the valve itself to use for this. When a handle is aligned parallel with the pipe, it's open, and when it's perpendicular, it's closed. I gave them all a good once-over. All looked good.

I'll give you a recap of the path of the sap: It starts in the tree, then is sucked by the vacuum through the taphole spout, down the dropline, across the lateral line until it merges onto the mainline superhighway and zips all the way to the releaser attached to the pump, where it will gather for a minute before the releaser dumps it into the Fitzy. Then the RO pump sucks it out of Fitzy, squeezes out much of the water, and sends the concentrate to Roundy. I use a utility pump to suck the concentrate out of Roundy and send it to a feeder tank sitting on a wooden platform ten feet over our heads inside the sugarhouse.

From there, the concentrate flows via gravity down a copper pipe into the first pan that sits on top of the evaporator, called a Steam-Away. Once inside the Steam-Away, sap travels through an array of more stainless-steel pipes—lying like a pipe organ—which are being heated by the steam rising from the pan beneath it. This is an efficiency invented by some wily Vermonters, designed to capture every bit of heat coming off the evaporator to keep the sap hot as hell wherever it might be in its travels through the machine toward becoming syrup.

In the Steam-Away the sap heats up to about 180°F. After passing through the pipe organ, the sap funnels into another long pan underneath. This pan is called the flue pan. The flue pan sits directly astride the superheated exposed fire, which makes the sap boil with a volcanic intensity. It features a sliding window so I can peek inside at my sap: today the heat detonation was sloshing the sap halfway up the side of the pan. Oh boy.

After being superheated in the flue pan, the sap then travels through *another* series of pipes and valves to reach its final destination: the front pan, also known as the syrup pan, or a finishing pan. This pan is short, and open to the air. During a boil we often loiter above it, sticking our noses into the steam blast of sugar bouquet, which is intense but pleasing.

The front pan has four channels, and the sap—in its magical metamorphosis into syrup—takes on its signature amber color in this pan. Here the liquid does a curious thing. No one knows exactly why, but sap, as it becomes thicker, moves forward in gradient, guiding itself through the four channels to its final stages of becoming syrup at a draw-off point above the spigot. The character of the boil also changes here, from the ferocious sloshing in the flue pan to a pleasing espresso froth in the front, where it spends time caramelizing. On the first boil of a season, like today, it can take a few hours of cooking in this pan before it becomes proper syrup.

I called Bert, still at work.

"Yo buddy, I fired it up. Sorry, I couldn't wait," I said.

He was cool about it. "I figured you would," he said. "No worries, man, I'm still stuck here anyway."

I cradled the phone in my neck and fiddled with a valve. "I think I can handle things. So far so good, I got a good boil going and—AW HELL!"

Like I said, things *always* seem to go wrong on the first day.

"—Dude, I'll call you back, we got a foam explosion!" I shouted.

Boiling sap creates foam. Foam in the evaporator is not good. It acts as a heat insulator and slows down a boil. Worse, if not controlled, foam can run wildly amok on you, sort of like dropping a Mentos into a two-liter bottle of Coke, creating an emergency for a sugarmaker.

That's exactly what happened. I tossed the phone aside.

Foam *erupted* out of the sliding window, over the rim of the pans, effusing everywhere.

I freaked. "Goddammit!"

I dashed to a nearby storage cabinet, desperate to find defoamer, one of the more aptly named substances in the maple business. Officially known as an anti-boil-over agent, defoamer is a food-grade waxy liquid made up of diglycerides that we're supposed to squirt into the pans every few minutes or so. But today, in my rush to get the season started, I forgot to do it.

Back in the day, sugarmakers would use butter to knock down head. Others would hang strips of bacon over the pans and let the meat drippings deflate the foam. Some guys would dangle an entire ham. More awareness of food allergies has put a screeching halt to these practices, although a few farmers still do it this way, with the butter I mean, not the ham.

The first boil of the season is the worst time not to have defoamer at the ready, like the situation at this moment. For some reason, which only the sap itself knows the answer to, the first boil of the season generates far more foam than any other time.

I got there too late.

A second tidal wave of foam oozed out. Actually, oozing is maybe not the right word—dynamited waterfall is more descriptive, the upsurge was so violent.

I unloaded an entire canister of defoamer into the lather—practically a whole season's worth of the stuff—but it was no use. Suds filled the room like a runaway bubble bath.

The sudden wetness in the sugarhouse tripped the GFCI electric breakers, and all the accessory equipment shut off—the blower, the lights, the digital thermometer.

I watched helplessly as my sap puddled on the floor in a swirling, steaming hot pool.

I hung my head.

"Fuck a goddamn duck."

When the disaster was over, I had a good cry and then called Kevin Mattison, who talked me through getting the breakers corrected and back in service. "You gotta jam a screwdroy'ver head into the little reset button on the outlet," he said.

Kevin's more pressing concern was not the junction box but my sap evaporator.

He made a long *ehhh* sound. "Did *all* of the sap foam out of the flue pan?" he asked.

I glanced though the peekaboo window. "I don't think so. Not *all* of it," I replied.

He let out a *phewf.* "You're lucky."

"Why's that?"

"With that amount of heat and all the sap gone from your evaporator, you woulda scorched the flue pan."

Besides a foam explosion, "scorching a pan" is another thing we sugar-makers never ever want to have happen. Especially on the same goddamn day as a foam explosion.

That last sentence, my friends, is a little storytelling technique called *foreshadowing . . .*

22

THE PHENOMENON OF THE SCORCH

In our sugarhouse there are two photographs hanging on a wall in ornate plastic frames. One is of Ned Perrin on our rainy day together in Thetford. The other is of a sugarmaker named Staffan Rascher, a brawny, cantankerous Swede who was my mentor in the ways of proper sap boiling. He died in a died tragically a few years ago. I might be the only one in maple who misses him.

Rascher owned the biggest sugarhouse in Shushan, down a bend from Yushak's and Shakey's Shushan Sity. He rubbed a lot of people the wrong way, especially Shakey. And Rascher disliked Shakey right back. Rascher was an unfoolish man, and it absolutely drove him nuts the way Shakey purposely misspelled the name of his sugarhouse. "Why *S*ity, it's *C*ity," Rascher would complain in my ear. To which Shakey would complain in my other ear, "Steve Rascher barged in here once and told me to my face that I didn't know the first thing about making good syrup and I said, 'You know what, get the hell out of here and don't come back.' And that was the last time I ever spoke to him. Good fucking riddance."

Rascher had a snarled shag of yellow eyebrow hair and a beet-purple face with a roadmap of burst blood vessels. He had only one functional eye, his right one, and it was ice blue. The unfunctioning one was jaundice-yellow and always welling. Or it could've been the other way around. I was never quite sure which eye was the one that worked.

He had a thriving tree service business and was probably the most skilled arborist in Washington County. I once watched him julienne a neighbor's seventy-five-foot hemlock like a carrot for a salad. Part of the nature of men in that profession is that they have no fear, and that was Rascher's demeanor, too. It's what gave him the balls to shoot off his mouth to other sugarmakers and not worry one iota about them kicking his ass. And that's what Rascher was most disliked for—he was a self-proclaimed expert in everything in maple and would go nose-to-nose with anyone to tell them so. He was a self-proclaimed expert on trees. He was a self-proclaimed expert on science. He was a self-proclaimed expert on syrup marketing. He was a self-proclaimed expert on equipment. He was a self-proclaimed expert on running an evaporator.

Except that last one was true. I saw it firsthand.

For some reason, Rascher took a liking to me early in my mapling career, not long after my visit to Dudley's. Likely because I was fresh meat to sugaring and a tabula rasa for him to instill his rabid opinions on impeccable syrup making. I spent a lot of time in Rascher's sugarhouse when he was boiling. He'd call me up in an urgent mayday whenever the sap was running. "Hey Peter! The trees are running like a graped ape today," he'd shout, using one of his strange euphemisms—and every time the sap was running was always the greatest amount of sap he'd ever goddamned seen. "It's unbelievable how much sap we're getting today—gonna break a record, that's for sure! All the tanks are overflowing! We're out collecting right now! You gotta get over here and see this and hurry! I'm firing up in five minutes!"

There was never a particular *need* for me to be in Rascher's sugarhouse—he never had me perform any kind of work other than to occasionally fetch him armloads of firewood—but he liked having me around, maybe because I was the only one left in town who didn't hate his guts.

Rascher ran a shipshape sugarhouse, spacious and appointed with the purple rosettes and etched trophy cups he amassed from his many victories in syrup-judging contests at the state fair. His sugarhouse was flanked by a mannered woodshed, impeccably stacked to the rafters with three-foot lengths of finely split and seasoned firewood.

I learned a lot from Rascher in those years about boiling sap and running an evaporator. Foremost was to stay attentive to every little thing, to be on high alert always.

One key lesson was to never allow beer in the sugarhouse, contrary to Shakey's policy of beer positivity. "Beer dulls reaction times," Rascher said, "and that's the last thing you want when you're boiling sap and making fire as hot as the underworld inside of your arch."

It was Rascher who first warned me about the phenomenon of the scorch.

Rascher's maniacal disposition served him well when he was boiling sap. During a boil, a sugarmaker must tend to a lot of things happening all at once: knocking down foam, firing the evaporator at consistent time intervals, watching the temperatures of the liquid, drawing it off at precisely the right time, and, very critical, ensuring sap levels in the pans are high enough.

Rascher would circle his evaporator like a hornet, constantly checking everything with his swiveling beady eye, like a submarine periscope. He'd throw slabs of firewood into the evaporator, dab defoamer into the boil with the tip of a coat hanger, and monitor draw-off temperatures on a digital readout mounted on a wall, madly working up a sweat that he sopped up with the felt of his Tyrolean hat and a yellowed bath towel wrapped around his neck.

He was most attentive to the sap depth in the pans, which he repetitively checked with a yardstick. "If you want to ruin your season in a hurry like all those other morons go ahead and scorch your pan," he said to me many times.

Scorching occurs when sap levels in the pan get precariously low. The intense heat cooks the sap rapidly past the syrup stage and dissolves all the liquid out of it, turning the sugars into charred, blackened ooze. Worse, if you don't catch a scorch, it can go beyond charred syrup into a much deeper hell realm and melt, warp, and otherwise permanently disfigure your front pan.

Back when pans were made of tin, a scorch would obliterate the lead solder at the seams and riddle your pan with leaks—that or a giant hole could burn through the thin tin surface from the inferno underneath. Not only would your day be over, but likely your entire season, too.

Today's pans are a lot tougher, made of stainless steel and TIG welded with tungsten electrodes, which is the same method they use to stitch up airplane fuselages. Now, when pans scorch, it may not be a death knell, but it can still leave serious and expensive damage, as well as high shame.

In the aftermath of the foam volcano, I refilled the pans with fresh, cold sap and basically started over. After an hour or so, I got back into a boiling groove. I was wearing some wool pants from Johnson Woolen Mills, a zip-up hoodie, and LaCrosse rubber boots, which have traction on the wet slippery floor, and protect my feet in case I spill scalding syrup onto them.

Let's see if we can make some syrup now, for chrissake, I thought.

Before long, I was catching up to where I was before the foam explosion, getting nearer and nearer to syrup density. The fire was burning nice and hot, the needle was buried at 1,200, and the boil was steady, no more crazy foam. I stuck a temperature probe into the pan, and it gave a readout of the sap to a tenth of a degree. The sap temperature began to steadily rise, 215, 216, 216.5, 217 . . . I sucked in a calming breath.

Remember, the draw-off temperature for sap becoming syrup is 7°F above the boiling point of water, just like it was in Dudley's chicken coop. A few minutes later, I looked at the probe's gauge again 219.5°F. Perfect. I opened the spigot and discharged a batch of brunette syrup into an old milking pail. Then some more, and some more, and more still.

Then something went very wrong.

Again.

After a draw-off, the temperature of the sap is supposed to drop. But instead, it shot up, and up and up, to 222°F and climbing: 222.5°F . . . 223°F . . .

"What the . . . ?"

The front pan changed smell, from sweet to acrid. And the boiling sap changed sound—from a baritone hum to a deep gurgle. The color of the steam in the front pan took on a green-blue tint. I stuck my face down close and got a blast of burning anneal.

It was scorching.

I smacked the side of the evaporator. "What the hell is wrong with you!"

For the second time today, I had to shut down. *Fast.*

I leaped for the air blower switch. Then I grabbed a nearby pail of water and threw it into the pan. A mushroom cloud of hissing fog vented into the room.

After a second or two, everything went dead. Just like before.

I hung my head.

"God hates me."

When the steam cleared, I saw the cause: a waffle-weave cotton dishrag buoying in the liquid like a jellyfish, left behind from when we were cleaning the pan last fall. The old rag had splayed in front of a channel gate, blocking the flow of fresh, new sap from backfilling the syrup I was drawing off, lowering the liquid level in the pan more and more until it hit the danger zone.

I knocked my head against a post, over and over. "Idiot, idiot, idiot."

What remained was a fizzling bath of ruined, charred, oozed syrup and gunk—and the goddamned rag, mired in the broth.

I reached for the phone and called Bert. He picked up right away.

"I got some news you're not gonna like," I said.

"I'm in a meeting," he said, whispering, "What's going on?"

"You know our syrup pan?"

"Uh huhhh?"

"Well . . . what comes to mind when you think of Chernobyl?"

"Nooooo."

"Mhmm. Scorched it."

I explained about the rag. I also told him about the foam eruption all over the floor earlier.

I could hear him slapping a hand to his forehead. "Ugh. How bad's the pan?" he asked.

I said it now resembled a campfire pit.

Bert stifled a laugh. "Aw c'mon, I'm sure it's not that bad," he said.

"Gonna need a whole *case* of Bounty quicker picker upper for this mess," I said.

If Bert was mad, he didn't show it much. In the history of our partnership, I can't recall him ever once getting pissed about any of my screwups. When he does get flustered, it's usually over something he himself did. And vice versa. If Bert had scorched the pan, my reaction likely would've been similar. I would've played it off. The question of what dope left behind the stupid dishrag in the pan in the first place wasn't even broached between the two of us (pretty sure it was me). Bert did remind me of one very salient point, however.

"We're off to a crackerjack start on that whole Five Pounder thing, aren't we?"

After we hung up, I tried to pull myself together and simply do what needed to be done next. I scraped out the black ooze with a spatula and then took a Scrub Daddy to it. "Look at this bilious schmaltz," I said to the grinning face on the sponge. After I cleared the gunk, a purplish splotch was revealed on the surface of the pan. The metal was warped, too. I lost it. I balled up the dishrag and hurled it out the door. "Remember the Maine!" I shouted, and it landed, splat, in the yard like when they throw dead octopuses on the ice at Detroit Red Wings games.

I walked outside, sat down on the tailgate of the Tundy and, for the second time today, dialed up Mattison. I fessed up to the scorch.

"Didn't I tell you once today not to do that?" he said, after he stopped laughing.

In sugarmaking, scorching a pan is not just about the damage it does to your expensive equipment and the money lost from destroying your sap. It's the humiliation. Scorching happens for one reason and one reason only: user error. It wasn't the dishrag's fault this happened, it was *my* fault, the sugarmaker, the one at the conn who steered the ship into an iceberg. And the mistake was so dumb—leaving a rag in the pan—I was sure I'd never hear the end of it around town.

Mattison picked up on my despair. "Peter, looky here," he said. "What oy'm about to say has been said many toymes in this business. Ready? Here it is—you ain't a real sugarmaker 'til you scorch a pan."

Word indeed got around town over the next few days.

"Heard you scorched some," Truman said when I saw him on the lane couple days later. Rather than rubbing my nose in it, Truman tried to salve my pride by repeating more or less what Kevin said: everybody scorches at least once in their sugaring careers. "Shake it off," he said.

Even Rascher scorched, Shakey pointed out with glee.

"That maniac even burnt down his whole goddamned sugarhouse once," he told me, which I hadn't known.

"So don't feel bad for one second," Shakey said.

"It *happens*. It's *fire*."

23

THE JUICE IS
WORTH THE SQUEEZE

Few things have disrupted the maple syrup industry more than the reverse osmosis machine. RO technology has been around more than seventy-five years, and it's best known for use on submarines, where ROs make freshwater out of saltwater. About forty years ago, the maple industry said, "Hey, those thingamabobs might work great for us." A nation of tinkerers.

The concept of reverse osmosis is simple—shove water through a giant sieve at extremely high pressure and segregate the molecules. In maple, the machine gives us a huge advantage by removing much of the water—upward of three-quarters of it or more—from the sap before we boil it into syrup.

The time-saving capability of the RO is maybe the single biggest reason why the maple industry has grown so exponentially over the past decade and a half. It's been as revolutionary to us as Eli Whitney's cotton gin.

In the past, big producers with thousands of taps would find themselves boiling raw sap thirty-six hours straight, or more. Now, with an RO, a guy can be in and out of a boiling session in a few hours (unless you foam or scorch).

ROs save a sugarmaker time, sleep, and fuel since we use only a fraction of the firewood or oil to run our evaporators. So much fuel is saved, in fact, that the federal government, during its Obama-era mania to subsidize energy conservation, created a grant through the USDA's Rural Energy for America Program that paid 75 percent of the price of an RO for sugaring. Everybody got one—well, almost everybody. Rascher didn't. "You'll never see one of those goddamned machines in this sugarhouse," he'd say to me.

On the downside, RO technology has taken some of the romance out of sugaring. Lengthy sugarhouse boiling sessions, with family and neighbors leisurely gathered around the evaporator for hours on end in the soothing ambience of the cooking sap—those days are gone. The routine now often goes like this: in the morning, turn on the vacuum; during the day, check the sugarbush and pipeline for leaks; late afternoon, start the RO, have dinner; in the evening, head to the sugarhouse, boil for a couple hours and go home. In bed before nine. All business.

The RO revolution has created a raging debate—maybe the biggest debate in all of maple: Do the machines affect the flavor of the syrup?

Rascher was convinced they did, and that's why he refused to buy one. "Everyone's syrup tastes like dog piss who uses one of those goddamned things," he would say.

For years I turned my nose up at RO'd syrup too, brainwashed by Rascher probably. I pretty much agreed with him that syrup from RO sugarhouses, while not exactly tasting like the urine of a dog, sometimes lacked the woody flavor of maple I always enjoyed. The pro-RO people say that's all nonsense, that the syrup tastes fine. The debate is unsettled.

Rascher had no problem boiling thirty-six hours straight—he loved it. But most sugarmakers aren't maniacs like he was. There comes a time when nearly every producer reaches a crossroads—*Should I get an RO or not?*—and usually decides the benefits outweigh the cons.

As for me, I've had plenty of fourteen-hour boiling sessions until two or three A.M. I always figured I was paying my dues as a sugarmaker, earning my cred. And I *like* boiling sap. Also, ROs intimidated the hell out of me—with their panels of dials and knobs and levers and buttons and lights and valves and gauges. Just like Rascher, I was firm on *never* buying an RO.

And then one day, I did.

I capitulated about three years ago, but on one condition: Bert would be in charge of it. "Meet your new girlfriend," I told him on the day I brought it home from Bascom's in the back of a rented box truck. "I don't wanna have anything to do with this stupid thing."

ROs require a tremendous amount of maintenance, which I have zero patience for. There's a bunch of complicated formulas on how to wash them, for example. Special chemical detergents must be used, and a couple three times per season. Bert also must give it an "acid wash" with a citric-acid formula to remove the mineral buildup in the membranes.

At first, I had a lot of buyer's remorse. "These things are more trouble than they're frigging worth," I said.

But Bert fell in love. "No, they're not. They're life-changers," he said.

He was right. Life indeed got better on Blossom Road once we got the RO, despite the pain-in-the-ass-ness of maintaining it. Because we weren't spending countless hours boiling, we were instead free to spend a lot more time in the woods chasing leaks and working on the pipeline, which improved our production dramatically. We made a lot more syrup.

Also, the boiling sessions, while being much shorter, were much more action-packed and fun—with the syrup draw-offs coming every five or ten minutes instead of every forty-five minutes like it was in the pre-RO days, when we'd wait and wait and wait for that dial to hit 7.

As for the flavor, I didn't notice a big difference. In fact, our syrup from that first season with the RO won a blue ribbon at the Washington County Fair and an honorable mention in the syrup judging contest at the Vermont Maplerama producer's conference that summer.

At the start of every new season, it's necessary to give the RO a thorough rinsing with fresh water to flush out a germicide we use in the off-season, so bacteria won't bloom in the summer heat. Since we don't have on-demand running water at the sugarhouse, we're forced to pull from the closest water source, the White Creek, a babbling brook that flows along Route 153 past all the hayfields and cornfields belonging to the Chambers Farm and a few other dairies.

Last year in February, when the new season was approaching, Bert broke the news that we had to perform this stupid RO-flushing chore before we could begin production.

"Listen, the rinse is gonna be a two-man job," Bert said.

I crossed my arms. "No way. We had a deal. Petey no touchy the RO machine," I said.

"Suck it up, buttercup," Bert said, "we can't start the season until we rinse it out."

One very cold, snowy February morning, we set up shop on the top of an I-beam bridge that crosses the White Creek. To suck up the water, we had a gas-powered transfer pump and a clear hundred-foot length of Tigerflex hose. I was to be the hose holder, Bert the pump minder.

He handed me the end of the hose. "March, soldier."

Bert sent me climbing down the bridge abutment and over to the 32.5°F creek. I waded in, dragging the Tigerflex behind. Water seeped over the tops of my rubber boots and down my calves, soaking into my socks. "Why did I get stuck with this end of the hose?" I asked.

"You're doing great, buddy. Just find a nice spot where there aren't any rocks," Bert said, feeding me the line from above.

I towed it along the creek bed until I found a little eddy where I could stick the pipe in the stream without it sucking a bunch of river gravel.

I turned and looked up to him on the bridge. "Good God, this water's cold. I don't think I've seen ice form in real time before," I said.

He leaned over a railing. "Are you just going to complain all day? Change your name to Karen," he said.

"Listen turkey, you're not the one in this water like a goddamned harp seal!" I shouted.

Up on the bridge, Bert had connected the other end of the hose to the pump, and he ran another length that would discharge the water into a 200-gallon tank on the back of Red Beauty.

There were many problems with Bert's plan.

For starters, we were asking the pump to pull water up the hose about fifteen feet in the air, from the bottom of the creek to the top of the bridge.

It went something like this: First, I'd yell up to Bert to start the pump. "Okay, start the pump!"

"Roger that!" Bert's voice echoed back.

Then I'd watch a sucked column of creek water climb up the hose, until, when it was just about all the way to the top, it would just stall and hang there, suspended, the column refusing to climb another inch, like a weary prospector's burro.

Keep in mind I could not *see* Bert or the pump from my vantage point.

Bert would throttle the pump, waiting for the water to reach him. "Nothing yet!" he shouted.

"I know! The damn water is just sitting there in the hose," I shouted back.

Problem number two was the pump inlet's rubber gasket, the O-ring, which is supposed to seal the intake valve. It was totally shot, which meant that once the slow burro of water finally arrived at Bert and the pump, it would douse him with a spray of the frigid creek water.

"Goddammit! It's like a busted fire hydrant up here!" Bert shouted.

Then all that water would roll off the bridge and cascade onto me.

"Yeah? Well the last fucker to get rained on this much was Noah!" I shouted back.

A *thesaurus-worth* of profanity combinations were unleashed under that bridge that morning. Birds fell out of trees and fish swam in retreat of the foulness.

"You're not my favorite person today," I said to Bert on the ride home, a shivering wreck.

This year, as February came back around, Bert had been quietly scheming a better plan to do the job we both knew we'd have to perform to start another season.

I had PTSD.

"Please don't make me go back to the river," I said to him, over and over.

"Not to worry buddy. I got it figured out. It will be better this time," Bert promised.

"I think we're gonna need to establish a safe word," I said.

On a mild day in February, we set out again for the White Creek. I went under protest. Bert pointed out several things in our favor this time around. For one, this day was much warmer, above freezing. Second, Bert wasn't kidding, he came prepared.

He'd spent weeks in his organized garage working on a doohickey that would allow us to pull from a different spot in the creek other than the bridge. So, no upright, lurching column of water (hopefully) and (also hopefully) I wouldn't have to hold the hose in the middle of the goddamned stream; we could simply lay it along one of the more modest banks of White Creek.

Bert found a low-lying cutout not far from the bridge and we pulled in.

He pulled the thingamajig out of the back of Red Beauty. "This bad boy is gonna do the trick," he said confidently.

On the bank, Bert assembled his "river sucker"—which was basically a long straw of PVC—and stuck it down into the creek, which was running nice and clear that day.

I wasn't convinced. "I need a Klonopin," I said.

Bert also bought a new O-ring for the pump, and he held the floppy circle of black rubber between his fingers and waved it in my face.

"We're gonna stay dry this time," he assured me.

A neighbor was out walking his dog and stopped to watch us. He kicked in his two cents on Bert's gadget, "Yeah, back when I was in the fertilizer business, we'd sometimes have to draw out of the river to fill our spray trucks," he said. "Just make sure you prime the shit out of the pump."

Bert filled the prime reservoir and pulled the rip cord.

Almost immediately we could see water sucked from the creek through the clear hose.

I pointed. "Oh, baby! Look at *that!*" I shouted.

It was working like a charm.

Bert put his hands in his pockets. "Exactly as I planned," he said, pleased with himself.

"Pretty slick," the neighbor said, his dog trying to tug him along.

It only took about ten minutes to suck 200 gallons of cold river water with Bert's whatchamacallit, and not a drop ended up on either of us. It was a moment of triumph for Bert. A self-satisfied smile emerged on his face, as he watched the tank fill the last bit of the way.

I watched it, too. "Don't rejoice too much, old pal," I said, "you know how it goes around here. Luck is about as fluid as that creek rushing behind you there."

24

KINKING THE LOYNE

It was dusk by the time we returned to the sugarhouse with the creek water, and I had an urge to relieve myself.

"I gotta take a 10-100," I told Bert and made off to the back of the yard.

"Okay, I'm gonna hook up the tank to the RO and start the rinse," Bert called after me.

I stepped into the field. As I issued into the snow, exposing myself to the tart air, I watched the emerging North Star glint in the sky. Another moment of Zen. Fleeting of course.

HA-WONK!—there was a concussive bang in the distance.

Then a howl.

"Nooooooooo!"

Bert. Something happened. I shook, zipped, and ran to the commotion. When I found him, he was stomping out of the RO room.

"Fuck. Fuck. Fuck. Fuck. Fuck. Fuck. FUCK!" he shouted.

"What the hell? Did you step on a nail or something?"

He put his palms on his forehead. "Worse. I kinked the line," he said.

"So?"

He pantomimed a grenade blast. "Kinked the frigging line—the RO, I blew it up."

RO pumps are so powerful that if you create any kind of blockage of its function for even a nanosecond—if you kink the hose feeding the raw sap into the machine or the hose discharging water—beware, the internal pressure is so high the RO will blow apart like a can of mushroom soup in a microwave.

I grabbed him by the arm. "So, wait, is the RO broken?"

Bert had been—"stupidly," his words—using the discharge water to hose down the Fitzy.

"I was spraying off the road salt that got on there during the ride home from Bascom's," he said, his eyes darting back and forth. "I was wrestling the hose around a corner and I kinked it for only a second, and that's all it took. The RO got really, really mad."

"And what happened?"

He jerked his thumb toward the RO room. "Take a look," he said.

I opened the door and turned it on. Water aerated from every valve. "Holy fuckannoli," I said under my breath. Now it was my turn to play it cool over someone's mistake—a mistake possibly far greater in consequence than my scorch. I slapped the red kill switch.

I came back out and Bert was shaking his fist in the air. "I can't believe I kinked that line," he shouted. "So stupid. Of all the stupid things not to do, the manual said this was the thing—the absolute *one* fucking thing—the manual said not to do the most. And I remember Mattison told me, *distinctly* fucking saying to me, 'Whatever you do—if you don't do nothing else—do *not* kink the line.' And what do I do? I fucking kink the line."

I put a hand on his shoulder. "Berty, calm down. Let's try it again. Maybe it'll self-correct," I said.

His eyes were wide and blackening. "Self-correct? Look at it!"

We went back over and started it up once more then stood back, watching. Again, water sprayed out of every valve like Buckingham Fountain.

"Sorry, man, our season's over. Our season's over!" he yelled at the sky, the North Star. "I really screwed the pooch on this one."

He was right. Without the RO, we'd be back to the dark ages.

In truth, though, I was more worried about Bert and the way he was reacting than I was about the goddamn machine. I'd never seen him so spun up.

"I screwed the pooch. I screwed the pooch," he kept saying over and over, and I tried to settle him down. "Listen bud, it's just goddamn maple syrup we're making here," I said, as he wrung his hands. "Not a cure for cancer. Let's chill for a sec. We'll figure something out."

But he and I both knew if the valves were blown beyond repair there was no way to get a brand-new RO installed and plumbed in time for the season, which was staring us in the face.

"Screwed the pooch," he said.

I didn't want to leave him alone with himself, but I had to go grab my phone from the truck. There was someone I needed to call.

⚭

"Someone get me a hand torch," said Kevin Mattison, who I'd hoped might save the day. Kevin was the only person we could turn to, just like when the evaporator exploded and blew all the circuits. He's a jack-of-all-trades in the repair of anything maple. If the blown RO could be fixed at all, Kevin would be the guy to do it. He wriggled his burly frame into the little closet where we kept the machine, the walls of which were wet and dripping. The floor a kiddie pool.

"Now oyme not sure why you boys never listen to me—maybe you got marshmallows stuffed in your ears—but oyme pretty sure oye said not to kink the loyne on our little friend here," Kevin said, tilting his head to the side. "Didn't oye say that, Bert? Remind me."

"You did, you did. 'Don't kink the line' is exactly what you said," Bert replied.

As Kevin worked his sorcery, Bert and I hovered in the doorway, at the ready to hand him a tool, like surgical attendants. He clenched a penlight in the side of his mouth. "Aw, I should have you up and running in no toyme.

I don't think it's too bahhd," he said in a tone like Bert had dropped his ice cream cone and Kevin promised to buy him a new one.

Kevin grabbed the MAPP gas torch and proceeded to loosen and disassemble every ball valve on the machine. Then he repositioned their O-rings. (Those damn O-rings are always the problem, just like on the pump at the bridge.) Meanwhile, Bert paced and chewed his nails like he was waiting on the results of a paternity test. Nighttime fell and Kevin continued working, which was a good thing. It was an indication that the machine might be fixable.

While he rapidly turned a wrench, Kevin notified us he was going to be gone for a couple of weeks because he and his wife were vacationing to an antique engine show in Florida.

"So try not to break anything until oye get back," he said.

Then he stepped away from the machine.

"We should be okay running hoye pressure now," he said and then nonchalantly started the RO up again, twisting a knob that cogged the pressure to the same psi as a steam locomotive.

Not one leak and no more spray.

Bert made an exaggerated bowing gesture with his arms outstretched. "You are the frigging man," he said to Kevin. "The frigging *man*."

"Runs foyne now," Kevin said, packing up his tools.

He put his fingers to his lips and made a chef's kiss.

"Voilà."

EARLY MARCH 2022

25

TAPPING WITH THE GOVERNOR

O n a Wednesday in early March, when it looked like the sap gods were going to make it gush like crazy, I had to race up to northern Vermont for the state's annual tree tapping ceremony with the governor, hosted by the Vermont Maple Sugar Makers' Association, of which I'm a member.

Sugarmakers are encouraged to provide a backdrop for this event, the ceremonial first tree tapped of the season. The media horde, as it exists in Vermont, scrambles for the best photo and video shots of the governor drilling a tree, which is then broadcast across the state and sometimes around the country to herald the opening of a new maple season.

I've been going to the governor's tree-tapping ceremonies for more than twenty years. They're always a fun event, and effective in helping rally the entire state around maybe its most famous byproduct besides Bernie Sanders, Ben & Jerry's, and Phish.

On this day, the event was being hosted by the University of Vermont's Proctor Maple Research Center in Underhill on the back slope of Mount Mansfield, Vermont's highest mountain.

Proctor is a bustling place. Four or five resident researchers spend their days running all kinds of experiments and studies on the nature of maple trees—trying to figure out why they do what they do and how we sugar-makers can become more efficient at siphoning them. UVM maintains

3,000 acres of sugarbush at the Proctor facility with two working sugar-houses equipped with three modern evaporators.

The Proctor Center was celebrating its seventy-fifth anniversary that year. The research program has done some really great work for the maple industry, so it certainly seemed worth celebrating their longevity by having the governor, a UVM alum, tap a ceremonial tree.

The Proctor Center is one of two such facilities dedicated to the research of maple in the United States. The other is operated by Cornell University in the Uihlein Maple Forest near Lake Placid, NY, which includes a sugar maple research field station. Cornell also has another separate facility near its campus in Ithaca. Where Proctor tends to focus more on the science of the tree, Cornell has been researching the potential of new products to be made from maple and finding ways to mass produce and market them—things like maple kombucha, maple sports drinks, maple beers and wine, maple marshmallows for your hot chocolate, and so on. Both organizations have been generous in sharing their research with the industry at large.

While we stood around waiting for the governor, I got to chatting with one of the young researchers, who said he was conducting an experiment to see how much pressure builds up inside a maple tree during a sugaring season. He said the maples build upward of 40 psi in their trunks, which astonished me. "That's enough to inflate a tire," he said.

The first familiar face I saw was Proctor's director, Dr. Timothy Perkins, who most sugarmakers call "Dr. Tim." Perkins is notable for maybe being the first guy in our industry to ring the bell on climate change and its effects on maple.

Fifteen years ago, Dr. Tim appeared on the front page of the *New York Times* warning about the possibility that the climate in Vermont could shift enough where the state might someday say goodbye to its iconic maples. "One hundred to 200 years from now," Dr. Perkins told the *Times*, "there may be very few maples here, mainly oak, hickory, and pine."

One day in the early 2000s, Dr. Tim and his team of researchers sat around a long conference table and brainstormed new ways to offset sap yield losses sugarmakers had been experiencing as the climate increasingly sizzled and maple seasons became shorter.

"We needed to come up with a hedge," Dr. Tim told me.

From that meeting on, UVM launched many of the methods and practices of high-yield maple production that serious sugarmakers now use to become Five Pounders. These techniques help maintain strong sap flows longer, so a sugarmaker can tap earlier in the winter and catch every available drop of sap before the trees shut down for the season. A lot of breakthrough stuff.

Dr. Tim and I chatted for a minute about the weird, warm start to the season.

"The sap started running at our place in early February," I mentioned to him.

"Yeah, that sounds about right," he said, understanding better than most folks that the warm winters are not so weird, but the new normal.

"I've already had mosquitoes in the sugarhouse like it was July," I said.

Vermont's governors recognize the importance of our industry and usu- ally have no problem making room in their schedules for this annual event. The first tree-tapping event I ever went to featured then-governor Howard Dean, who was an ornery and aggressive guy. Dean would grab a drill out of the hosting sugarmaker's hand and exclaim, "Let's get that hole drilled, we don't want to miss any sap!" and plunge into the job.

During these ceremonies, organizers sometimes make the events tor- tuous for the poor governors by requiring them to tap a tree with an old "bit-and-brace" U-shaped hand drill, which sugarmakers haven't used to tap a tree since the 1950s. The bits are always dull, forcing the otherwise desk-sitting governors to apply a massive amount of exertion to tap the damn tree—and they have to do it in front of a group of sugarmakers judging the crap out of them and the pack of Vermont media, who jostle each other to get as close as they can to capture the rather novel spectacle of watching a politician doing something other than talk.

Dean was followed by a long stretch of ceremonies with a governor by the name of Jim Douglas, who was more of a ham than Dean. Douglas had a special nuance to his tapping ceremonies, where he would stick his finger in the taphole and lick off some sap, and he'd furrow his face in delight and make "mmm *mmm*" sounds, as the cameras clicked away.

On this day, Governor Phil Scott arrived at the Proctor Center ceremony exactly on time in a vehicle entourage of one. He exited his Ford Excursion wearing an L.L.Bean hunting jacket, wool pants from Johnson Mills, and a ball cap with a logo for Darn Tough wool socks, which are Vermont made.

Governor Scott made a few welcoming remarks and was invited to the tree in question by one of the university's maple experts, who explained the basics of tree-tapping, reminiscent of the Branon method. "Look for a bare spot on the tree that hasn't been tapped before," he advised the governor. Mercifully, this year it was decided not to use the bit-and-brace drill. The fellow from UVM instead handed the governor a DeWalt. And instead of hanging a classic galvanized sap bucket on the tree like they'd always done for these ceremonies, they just had the governor connect a run of blue tubing exactly like the kind Bert and I use on our pipeline. Later, I was told by the UVM people that they wanted to portray the honest, modern version of maple in the twenty-first century, rather than the anti-quated version depicted in the *Saturday Evening Post* or something. Proctor was a research center after all, where many revolutionary technologies for the entire industry have been developed.

The governor popped the tap in the tree in about thirty seconds, and some sap salivated out right away. "Oh boy, look at that," he said. I thought the media people were going to kill each other trying to get a picture. A guy from the Fox News Channel—who I assume was from New York—was apparently sent to get a scoop on Governor Scott's rumored presidential ambitions, and he was throwing serious elbows to get to the front. The local media folk, not accustomed to this level of aggression to observe their modest governor, ganged up to shove the Fox guy back out of the way. The governor's trooper was forced to step in.

"Okay, everybody, just calm the hell down," he said.

On my way home from the tapping ceremony, I remembered I needed a new pair of gloves, so I swung over to the H.N. Williams store in Dorset. In the maple business, we go through gloves like surfers go through shorts. With the exception of boots, gloves are the most essential item of apparel sugarmakers use. If I'm in the woods working on the lines, I prefer tight-fitting elastic gloves so I can maintain dextral use of my fingers, since we're fiddling with those tiny fittings. For labor in and around the sugarhouse, thicker, more rugged gloves are necessary. When we're boiling sap, the gloves I've come to rely on, after much trial and error (and occasional searing pain), are oil hauler gloves. These are the gloves roughnecks wear on oil derricks and such. Freaking hard-core. Sap, when it's boiling, is somewhere between 200 and 220°F, skin-peeling temperatures. And scalding syrup spills all the time, especially when I'm checking the syrup density with Dudley's hydrometer cup. You need tough-ass gloves for that job. Hence, the oil haulers, which have a PVC coating and heat-protective insulation.

The H.N. Williams Store is one of the few remaining family-owned department stores left in Vermont, although there are a few others still around and thriving: Carl Durfee's Store in Fair Haven and the Pick & Shovel, way up in Newport, are two other favorites. There's also the Vermont Country Store in Rockingham, which is a little bit of a tourist trap, but the store is still loaded with a lot of cool stuff that is otherwise hard to find—carrot peelers, ice cube trays, patterned bed linens your grandma used to have, a selection of hard candies, butter dishes, clock radios, and stuff like that. They also have a great mail-order catalog that I receive every month.

H.N. Williams on Route 30 in Dorset Hollow was founded in the mid-1800s. The interior features the original well-worn wide-plank pine flooring that creaks when you walk on it. Their ample hardware department stocks a lot of things a Vermonter would likely need at some point, things like striking tools, post-hole diggers, mailboxes, bag seeders, bells, shovel handles, tank deicers, tip-ups for ice fishing, and a nice selection of pocketknives.

Today, H.N. Williams had a dedicated wall full of gloves hanging from stick-out hooks, and it was a little overwhelming, there were so many.

Most of the hooks were taken up by gloves a skier might wear. On the remaining hooks hung a selection of work gloves. I flipped over a few pair and checked the prices. The typical tanned cow leather ones ran about eighteen or twenty dollars. Then I spied a line of goat leather gloves manufactured by Vermont Glove of Randolph that were originally designed for pole linemen. I checked the tag, a hundred bucks. "*Dang,*" I said. The label suggested they'd last a lifetime, but I reckoned in the sugarhouse they'd last for, at best, one season. Almost every pair of my gloves either gets burned, torn, or chewed to smithereens by field mice who sometimes sneak into the sugarhouse in summer and love to munch on the sap-glazed material.

I felt guilty as hell for not supporting a Vermont glover, but I cheaped out and bought a twenty-dollar cowhide pair instead.

Then I put the hammer down and raced back to the sugarhouse.

26

THE MYSTERIOUS CASE OF THE MISSING MAPLE

At the governor's tapping event, none of us sugarmakers could believe what we were seeing on our phones—five straight days of perfect sugaring weather, pretty much all across New England.

"I think you might have a big week ahead," Dr. Tim said to me, as I was climbing into the Tundra to race home.

The whole ride back from Proctor, through Dorset and then back through the Ruperts, I saw sugarmakers hauling sloshing sap tanks in the backs of their trucks. Everywhere across the undulating countryside, there was steam pillowing out of sugarhouse cupolas. In West Rupert, I saw the McClellans boiling, then turning onto Blossom Road, I saw that Truman and Shelley were, too.

When I pulled into the sugarhouse, I jumped out of my truck and ran over to the Fitzy to see how much sap was in it. I was expecting a lot. I set the ladder against the side, climbed up to the edge, and peered over. "*What the . . . ?*" The tank was less than a third full, maybe 800 gallons, tops. Considering the weather and after seeing bloated tanks all over Vermont on my ride home, I thought we'd have twice as much sap as that. "You gotta be frigging kidding me," I muttered to myself.

I walked around the yard a few minutes checking to see if any of the feeder pipes had disconnected. Nope. I checked the pump to see if it was sucking properly. It was. I even looked to see if there was some big clog in the releaser, like maybe a mouse crawled inside and died—anything to explain why I didn't have way more sap in the tank like everyone in Vermont seemed to have on this day. "I can't believe this shit," I said, scratching my head.

I went back up the ladder, leaned over the pool of sap, and scowled at my reflection. *Something is seriously not right.*

Then a sinister thought crept into my head. I tried to push it away, but it kept creeping back.

I wondered if someone had stolen our goddamned sap.

Sap stealing happens in maple, as low-down as anything one sugarmaker can do to another, like cattle rustlers in old western movies. Arousing my suspicion, besides the very low tank level on what should have otherwise been our biggest sap day yet, were deep, fresh tire tracks in the driveway mud, gouged by something carrying a lot of weight. The tracks traveled perpendicular to the front of the sugarhouse, then curved around backward toward the rear of the building, like a vehicle had backed right up along-side the sugarhouse. Then I traced the tracks away from the sugarhouse, across the yard, and followed them right back onto Blossom Road.

I knew the tracks weren't made by me or Bert. And I also knew they wouldn't've been from any of my neighbors because they all drive "dually" trucks, which have two tires side-by-side on each end of their axles, while the tracks in the driveway were made by a vehicle with only one.

Nobody around here would do something like that anyway, I was certain of that. But over the years there've been whispers and gossips about certain people—invaders—from counties north of here, people I've never met but who are reputed sap stealers.

"Sons of bitches."

That evening, I came undone. I cussed around the house, unleashing the built-up stress and strain of the past couple of weeks and the run-up to the season. The scorch. The foam explosion. The busted RO, and now a disappointing, and possibly hijacked, tank.

At least I had Bert.

"What the hell are we busting our asses like this for?" I vented to him on the phone. "Stupid waste of time, this whole thing. Goddamned maple syrup. *You can buy the shit in a store!*"

My cat hid under the couch.

"The tank was barely filled," I said. "Everyone else had tons of sap. I don't get it."

Bert sighed a little. "Just wasn't our day," he said.

I got up from an easy chair and began pacing around the living room. I had taken my boots off at the edge of the chair, and I stubbed the crap out of my goddamned toe on a table. I clenched my teeth.

"So, I have a theory," I said. "I'm not sure I want to say it out loud, but . . ."

"What?" he said.

"Well, there were these tire tracks in the driveway—"

"So?"

"So, I think maybe someone ripped us off."

"Huh?"

"Pretty sure some motherfucker shanghaied our sap."

Bert burst out laughing. "C'mon. Are you serious? You really think someone stole our sap?"

I cradled the phone in the nook of my shoulder. "Dude, there's no other explanation."

Bert was very doubtful.

"There's lots of other explanations," he said. "First of all, Pete, it would take at least a half hour to offload that much sap into a truck tank. And the driveway is exposed all the way to the road, so there'd be a sizable risk of being spotted."

I massaged my foot. "Yeah, I guess," I said.

"Plus, you would have to have a very long transfer hose to get from the driveway"—where the tire tracks stopped—"to the back of the sugarhouse and over to Fitzy," he said. "That's 200 feet at least. Who the hell would cart around a hose that long? And why would anyone bother doing all that work anyway. For sucking what?"

"Our sap?"

Bert laughed again. "Yeah, but I mean how much sap does a truck tank hold? Maybe 300 gallons? Who would bother to take all that risk and make all that effort for just 300 gallons? In the middle of the day? There's just no way, man."

I hobbled to the kitchen and pulled a Sprite out of the fridge.

"It's just weird that there was hardly any sap in the tank," I said.

"Not that weird," Bert said.

I popped the can and it let out a hiss of carbonation. "How do you figure?"

"Our bush faces mostly west and north, and the sun doesn't hit us until at least midday. And even when it does it's still pretty cold. Our woods are just a touch colder than Truman's woods for example, even though he's only a mile down the lane," he said. "Truman's woods face mostly south and east, and his elevation is much lower than ours for the most part."

Bert was right. There have been many times when I've driven up Blossom Road, passing by Truman's sugarhouse, and it'd be raining, and by the time I got up to ours, it would be snowing. It's like two different climates only 5,000 feet apart.

"No one swiped our sap, buddy. Best to get that kind of thinking right out of your head, it'll drive you nuts. Our trees just aren't all the way thawed out yet," he said.

I walked back into the living room and set my soda on the coffee table.

Bert settled me down some more. "It might not be filled to the brim, but we still got 800 gallons of sap sitting in that tank. That ain't nothin' to blow your nose at."

Right again. The sap would also probably keep running for another day or two if the forecast held, maybe filling that tank all the way up after all. "Or pretty damn close," Bert said. "We could be on pace to have our biggest sap-boiling day so far coming up."

The cat poked her head out to see if I had cooled off yet.

"Get some rest, buddy, and try and chill," Bert said. "Try meditating or maybe call up Gerber and see if he's got an extra gummy to lend ya. Because dude, we're gonna make a shitload of syrup this weekend."

27

QUINLAN STORMS IN

On a Saturday in early March, a winter storm was supposed to hit us. They name them now, which seems a little contrived. By "they," I mean the producers at the Weather Channel, who were calling this storm "Quinlan," which sounds like it might've been the name of one of the interns there and they all thought it would be cute and funny to name the storm after him.

I woke up around 2:00 A.M. and couldn't fall back asleep, so I decided to go up to the sugarhouse and get the day started. Winterstorm Quinlan was supposed to arrive around midday, and I wanted to get our sap boiled before the snow pinned us in at the sugarhouse.

I hadn't checked the *Edmund Fitzgerald* since the afternoon I thought our sap was heisted, which was three days ago, and now I was panicking—also hoping—it might be overflowing. I dressed, slurped down a coffee, and jumped into my truck. I gunned the Tundy for Blossom Road, figuring there wouldn't be any cops patrolling the roads at this hour.

I was wrong.

I passed a state trooper while I was going probably a solid fifteen or twenty miles per hour over the speed limit. I crashed my foot on the brake, but it was too late. He whipped a U-turn and came up fast behind me. "Aw hell," I muttered. He hit the cherries, and I pulled over.

He side-sauntered along my truck to my window. Dude was a big 'un, maybe six-three or -four with an enormous round head, his Stetson perched on the crown of it. He didn't have as severe a bearing as most troopers, but he was still pretty imposing, getting his face—wide and flat as a sheet of plywood—closer to mine than I was comfortable with.

"So . . . you know what the speed limit is along here?" he asked.

I rested my hands on the steering wheel. "I'm pretty sure I do," I said.

He craned his Jupiter-head to check the inspection and vehicle registration stickers on my windshield. "Hmm, I don't know about that," he said.

"I'm assuming I wasn't going the speed limit?"

Big Head Todd coughed into the crotch of his elbow and side-eyed me. "No, you were not."

"Any chance I was going *less* than the speed limit?" I asked, probably a little too smartass-like.

There was a hint of a smirk. "No, you were not," he said. "I got you at 71."

I flicked my finger at the speedometer. "Noooo. Really? *That* fast?"

"Where you heading in such a hurry?" he asked.

I broke into a sob story about being on the way to boil a ton of sap and my tank, "probably right now!" overflowing and Winterstorm Quinlan about to bury us all and—

He squinted. "—Winterstorm who?"

"Winterstorm Quinlan's on the way. They're saying it'll be a two footer."

"So, wait, start over—you make maple syrup?" he said, looking maybe like he wanted to eat some atop a double stack of pancakes right then and there.

I raised my eyebrows. "Actually, I do . . ."

His lampshade face illuminated. "That's *cool*," he said.

Suddenly we were old pals, Big Head Todd and me.

"I was thinking about trying making syrup myself this year with my son," he said.

"Gee, that's *awesome*. How old's your son?" I asked, trying to keep momentum going on this newfound rapport.

"He's ten and he's been bugging me about it. They taught him something about maple syrup in school and he came home and said, 'Dad, can we tap some maple syrup trees?'"

I put my finger in the air. "That's the perfect age to get them started," I said and added that was the age my kids were excited about maple the most.

I dropped the names of a couple of troopers I knew back in town who I remembered made some backyard syrup, one of whom I even lent some sap buckets to once.

"*Those* guys make syrup?" he said. "Didn't know you knew those knuckleheads."

I chuckled along awkwardly. "Oh yeah, *those* two . . . ha-ha."

Big Head Todd let me off with just a warning and a tip of his hat. I decided not to press my luck by asking for a police escort the rest of the way to the sugarhouse.

A few minutes later I pulled up to the farm. When I shut off the headlights and stepped out, it was void black.

If you're one of those people in search of pure darkness—a place with literally no interruption from light pollution, Blossom Road at 3:00 A.M. is the place to come. The darkness messes with you when you're in the middle of nowhere like we are. Sometimes you'll mistake the blurred, spectral shape of a shrub or something in the distance and think it's someone coming to ax-murder you. Or a coyote. There's no electricity within a mile of our property except at the sugarhouse itself—so the production of light is completely at our control. More and more, we've been adding LED yardlights with massive quantities of lumens.

I used the flashlight on my phone to guide my way into the sugarhouse and flipped the breaker switches in the panel box. The compound lit up like one of those research outposts on an Antarctic glacier.

I walked around back, groggily placed the ladder against the tank, and looked in. The Fitzy wasn't overflowing, but it was as full as it'd been so far this season, probably a solid 2,200 or 2,300 gallons.

Hmmm, I thought, happy, but also a little disappointed at the same time.

Not *all-the-way full?*

The condition of the sap, looking phosphorescent in the flood of LED lights, had me a little worried, too. Usually at this early point in a season, the sap runs crystal clear, but this morning's sap was on the yellow-greenish side, which is typically the color of the sap toward the tail end of the season, when it's much warmer and bacteria starts to build up faster.

More ominous than the color of the sap was the moths swimming in it. There were two or three of them flailing, trapped by the surface meniscus. Moths in sap are notoriously interpreted by sugarmakers as a bellwether for the end of a season, and here we were at the beginning of one. I could reach in just far enough to cup them out with my hand. The sap was ice cold and slippery, and little cushions of white foam were floating in the corners of the tank.

When I reared back to toss the moths out, the notion of the *almost*-full-but-not-*all-the-way*-full tank triggered something that had been eating at me. I wasn't suspicious that someone plundered our sap again. Bert had talked me off the ledge on that one. No, this time it was something different.

This time I was worried I tapped the trees too shallow.

Let me explain.

There's a recommended hole penetration for tapping the trees: how deep into the trunk to drive the drill. Dr. Tim at the Proctor Center recommends two inches—he says that that's the best depth for maximum yields. But I couldn't recall even once drilling two inches during that great marathon day flying around on the weight-supporting snow in my crampons.

The problem had been the drill. It kept stopping out on me, making an *ack-ack-ack* sound when it ran out of force to bore deeper. At first, I thought it was the tapping bit. I was using an aggressively sharp one made in Quebec and thought it was biting into the wood too hard, jamming it up. So, I switched to a milder bit. That helped, but even then, when I drove the DeWalt to about an inch-and-a-quarter or so, the drill would run out of juice, bringing on that *ack-ack* sound again.

What I ended up doing that day was making two plunges, boring as deep as I could on the first thrust before backing the drill out, knocking off the shavings, and taking a second shot into it. But it still kept happening, that annoying halting sound. I should've consulted Bert about it at the time, called him on the walkie-talkie. He's the tool expert. But I was in such a race against the clock, and enjoying my great rhythm, that I pushed on, sometimes even skipping the second plunge, I recalled now, which left me far shy of Dr. Tim's recommended two-inch depth.

And so here, on my ladder peering back into the Fitzy, my tapping negligence was nagging at me. Even though the tank was filled with the most sap we'd ever collected in a three-day span, I thought . . .

. . . *there should be a lot more.*

I climbed off the ladder and got to work. The first step in my multistep pre-boiling routine was to change the RO's prefilters. Prefilters are exactly what their name implies, they filter out any detritus in the sap before it runs through the machine. The prefilter cylinders resemble a paper towel roll three-quarters unspooled. They're housed in a heavy stainless steel canister that hangs off the back of the RO like an appendix, and they function similarly.

To change them out, I had to unscrew the entire canister by hand. But I couldn't apply enough hand torque to untwist the damn thing. "Uff da," I said. Bert the Gorilla had overtightened it last time. One of Bert's favorite things to do is overtighten the crap out of things. I went inside the sugarhouse to dig around for the new gloves I bought at H.N. Williams the other day, which I thought would offer more grip. Sure enough, the leather palm gave me enough traction to loosen the chamber. I swapped out the filter then screwed it back to a reasonable tightness and was ready to start processing that *almost*-full-but-not-*all-the-way*-full tank of sap through the RO and boil it all into syrup before Quinlan arrived.

I was going to be cutting it close.

28
THIS IS WHAT IT ALL BOILS DOWN TO

The early edge of Quinlan began to dandruff up the yard. I stepped into the sugarhouse and turned on the radio, a mid-'90s-era Bose Wave that was a gift from my dad years ago. During sugaring is the only time I listen to local FM radio, and I always tune into 102.7 WEQX (The Black Keys, Cake, Florence + the Machine), an eclectic, independently owned alternative rock station out of Manchester. Comes in clear as a bell.

The storm was shaping up to be a real whopper, maybe a two-footer, which we hadn't seen around here in a couple of years. And, typical with Nor'easters, it was also going to be a fast dropper, with snowfall rates of two or three inches per hour. I tried to do the math on how much snow was going to accumulate before we boiled all the sap and would need to drive back home.

"This sap better boil in a hurry," I muttered to myself.

I texted Bert a wake-up call and alerted him I was getting an early start.

"Rise and shine sleepyhead"

The moat of mud around the sugarhouse was getting worse, and everywhere I stepped I sank ankle-deep. Bert and I have long called this phenomenon the "Western Front" because it reminds us of World War I troops bounded by the mud in the fortification trenches.

I traipsed back through the slop and over to the RO room. I pressed the launch-sequence of buttons to start up the machine, which worked flawlessly after Mattison's repair the other day, then I waded back through more mud to take a nap in my truck.

When I woke, I ran over to check the status of the RO, and it was just about done squeezing. I went to the evaporator and threw some balled-up newspaper into the arch, lit a fire with the MAPP-gas, and had a nice rolling boil in about ten minutes.

Daylight was just breaking, and I could feel the dampness in the air, a perceptible change of atmosphere whenever a big snowstorm is about to hit around here, especially a Nor'easter like Quinlan was supposed to be, sucking moisture off the Atlantic Ocean.

EQX kept updating their predictions of the snow amounts, now possibly two and a half feet, and warned that the storm was getting closer and closer. The station was goosing up the skiers. "Get pumped—it's gonna dump! Get your skis and boards ready!" the deejay shouted.

I texted Bert again: *"Get on up here, son. Keep your foot off them brakes."*

But there was no reply.

By this, the third boil of the season, the kinks were mostly worked out. The sap had been flowing nicely through the pipeline, and the leaks in the woods were mostly patched and spliced. The pump was pulling vacuum as it should, today at twenty-five inches. Not perfect, but a passable rate for now. The tanks were clean and the pipes in and out of them were connected properly. Inside, all the valves on the evaporator were either opened or closed in the positions we wanted them, and the sap boiled evenly and didn't foam over or scorch. All the accessory equipment behaved.

I've become a far better sap boiler thanks to a visit a few years ago from a sugarmaker named Bruce Gillilan, a salesman for Leader Evaporator, the Swanton, Vermont company that manufactured my rig. Gillilan comes from a multigenerational sugaring family in Fletcher, Vermont. Bruce just knocked on the door of my sugarhouse one March day and offered to boil with me. He had an athletic posture and a fringe of forehead bangs and was wearing a Green Bay Packers hoodie, his favorite team. Even though I'm a Vikings fan, I welcomed him in.

"I'm here to give you a few pointers I've learned along the way," he said and made himself at home.

Gillilan's principal lesson that afternoon was that I should make sure to operate the evaporator as evenly as possible. "An evaporator will perform as consistently as you do," he said and pulled something out of his pocket—an egg timer. "You might need some mechanical assistance."

The egg timer would snap me to attention and remind me to throw wood into the arch at precise intervals of time, which should be every five minutes, he explained. (Same concept as Skakey's red light.)

"An egg timer," Bruce said, rewinding it every time I threw more logs into the firebox, "make this little baby your best friend."

Making the syrup, the finishing part when it comes out of the spigot on the evaporator, is the money shot. This, we call *drawing off*. "I don't know about you," Gillilan said to me that day, "but every time I draw off a batch of syrup, I feel like I've accomplished something."

Here's how it works: When I'm at the conn, I'm positioned at the side of the evaporator, next to a run of pipes that leads to a valve with a faucet. From this angle, I can monitor a display on the far wall with a red digital readout of the syrup temperature.

At the appointed hotness—7°F above the boiling point of water, usually about 219 or 220°F—I throw open a valve, and rivulets of gorgeous amber liquid tumble into a small collection hopper. Then with my oil-hauler-gloved hand I reach for Dudley's hydrometer cup. I fill that with the freshly drawn syrup to make sure the density is correct. I do this by floating the hydrometer. If it sinks to the bottom of the cup, the density is too thin. So I'll wait a few more minutes for the syrup to cook some more. I'll play a little game a series of times—opening and closing the faucet, letting out just enough syrup to fill the cup, and then dunking the hydrometer again to see if it bobs on the red float line, telling me the density has reached 66.9° on the Brix scale. Once that red line plumbs with the surface of the syrup, Bingo! I drain out a batch of three or four gallons. I just open the faucet and leave it open.

Maple syrup.

Now I superglue my eyes to that red digital readout. As the syrup drains, the temperature will arc—it will go to 221°F, 222, 223, crest, and then cycle back down. Then I'll close the valve, and the temperature will cool even more—maybe down to 214 or 213°F—as a rush of cold raw sap gets invited into the evaporator to replace the finished syrup that just came out. Then the whole process starts over again.

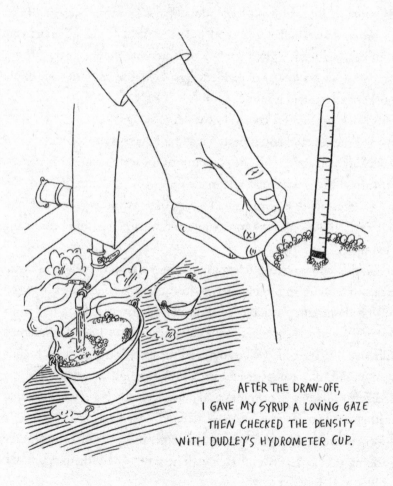

AFTER THE DRAW-OFF,
I GAVE MY SYRUP A LOVING GAZE
THEN CHECKED THE DENSITY
WITH DUDLEY'S HYDROMETER CUP.

I'll give the syrup a loving gaze then quickly resume my frantic duties to the evaporator, throwing more logs on the fire, resetting Gillilan's egg timer, squirting more defoamer into the pans, running out to the woodshed for more firewood, and wading through the Western Front to check on how much sap remains in the *Edmund Fitzgerald*.

I was in the middle of all this routine when Bert shuffled in around 8:30, just as the snow was really starting to accumulate in the yard.

"Up before the roosters, huh?" he said, yawning.

In one hand, he held a large coffee from Stewart's Shops, a ubiquitous convenience store chain around here, and in the other, a family-sized bag of BBQ potato chips. He and I keep lots of snacks in the sugarhouse to munch on while we boil. On a shelf near the rig, I hoard an enormous pouch of beef jerky, an eight-pack box of Entenmann's chocolate-frosted donuts, and a one-gallon jar of pickled eggs. He pulled a Sprite out of his coat pocket and handed it to me.

He took a slug from his cup. "How we doin' so far?"

I opened the can and laid it on thick about how early I woke up.

"Day's half over already," I said, pointing at my watch, smirking a little.

Bert turned his eyes upward and made the jerk off gesture. "Listen, I'm not a big waker-upper like you are. Think of me as you would think of a lizard. I gotta go lay on a rock for a while and warm up before I can really get moving."

Bert set down his coffee and began to filter the twenty gallons of syrup I'd already drawn off so far. He placed thin sheets of filter paper between each of the aluminum plates on the accordion filter press. Then he spun a screw clamp to mash the plates and the papers tightly together. He stomped on a foot pedal to start the gear pump, and the machine sucked my freshly made batch out of the hopper and pressed it through the plates and the paper, discharging clear syrup into a stainless steel forty-gallon drum that we'd ultimately take over to Bascom's.

As we worked, I told him about my run-in with Big Head Todd and the moths doing the backstroke in our sap. The moths were the bigger deal. He couldn't believe it.

"Moths are one of the signs of the Apocalypse," he said. Whenever a season begins, sugarmakers become hyperaware of harbingers of when it will end, moths in a tank being a big one. We concurred that we'd never seen moths this early in a season before. The biggest omen of all, far bigger than the moths, is when we start hearing "peepers," the frogs in the pond across the road, which make all kinds of racket when they start to mate. Almost in exact sync with the frogsong, the maples begin budding and a sugaring season will come to an abrupt end.

"Let's not have any anxiety attacks until we hear the ribbitts," Bert said.

After our morning chitchat, Bert and I fell into the rhythm of work. I was firing the rig consistently—the Gillilan way—and drawing off syrup almost every five minutes. It was coming out nice and smooth and rich. The barometric pressure was superbly low, around 209 millibars, which put the syrup draw-off temperature at about 217°F. Perfect.

After each draw, Bert pushed the maple syrup through the filter machine. We noticed it had lightened up at least two grades, from the very dark, burnt stuff I'd made the first couple days, to a nice medium amber this morning.

We both sipped some samples out of an old shot glass I won tossing dimes at the Shushan fireman's carnival and agreed it was the best tasting syrup we'd made in a long time.

I licked my lips. "Damn, this is some vintage shit," I said.

To determine syrup grade, we use an official Vermont state grading kit. It's a small wooden block with four slots, three of which have little square sample jars prefilled with colored water that designate the official tint for each grade. I dropped our syrup sample into the open slot and arranged the jars like an abacus to determine where it fit on the color scale.

Up until about ten years ago, the maple industry had a grading system based only on light transmittance. The old system dubbed the best syrup "Grade A," with three subcategories, Light, Medium, and Dark. Simple. Much darker syrup was categorized Grade B Extra Dark and Grade C. The top grades are what sugarmakers call "table grades," while the super dark stuff is called either commercial or processing grade—syrup you would never put on a pancake but might use to flavor pet kibble or mix into a BBQ sauce recipe. Industrial uses.

About ten years ago, the leaders of all the maple states and provinces got together and colluded to change the names of every grade of syrup. The new language of the grades was rewritten to help identify for consumers what the syrup *tastes* like, not just its color. The current table grades are Grade A: Golden Delicate Taste, Amber Rich Taste, Dark Robust Taste, and Very Dark Strong. Their hearts were in the right place, but I find the new system too wordy.

Today's sample—Grade A, Amber Rich—I set in line with some other sample jars I'd arranged on a windowpane, where we display all our syrup jars to show visitors the variation of color from boil to boil and also because they look so pretty backlit by the sun.

Bert stopped for a minute to munch on his chips.

I reached in his bag to poach a few. "I have to confess something."

"Uh oh," he said, swatting away my hand. "What now?"

"I think I drilled the holes too shallow."

He looked at me funny.

"What the hell are you talking about? You mean the tapholes?" he said, stuffing a cluster in his mouth.

I explained my problem with the drill on that big tapping day, how I couldn't sink it deep enough. "It kept stalling out and making an *ack-ack* noise," I said. "Like it was gagging."

The DeWalt was sitting there on a window ledge. "Okay, recreate the scene," he said.

I picked up the drill and showed him the perplexing collar on the barrel, which had settings from 1 to 15. I told him I'd adjusted this collar back and forth throughout my marathon tapping day and still couldn't get it to stop making that goddamn sound.

He set down the bag of chips, grabbed the drill out of my hands, and fired it while holding the collar tight.

It made the awful noise. "You mean it did that?" Bert asked.

"Yup. All day long, that whole day," I replied. "That's what it kept doing."

He laughed. "It's *supposed* to do that," he said. "That's the clutch."

Bert mansplained that the clutch on the drill is designed to purposely slip when it hits a certain threshold to prevent the overtightening of fasteners. The *1* setting is used when drilling a screw into drywall, for example. When the drill hits a torque limit, it makes that *ack-ack* sound to indicate to the user that the drive is disengaged, he said.

Bert pointed at the collar. "Lookie here," he said, "see the setting with a little emoji of a drill bit? That positions it to 'drill,' so the clutch won't slip like that."

It was the only setting I hadn't tried that day.

"I think I cost us getting to five pounds," I said. "That will be the difference. The stupid tool and the even bigger tool operating it. I didn't drill the holes deep enough."

Bert set the drill back on the ledge. "Dude, you're overthinking. There's no way we could've just collected more than 2,200 gallons of sap in three days if you drilled the holes too shallow."

I wasn't sure.

"I think I'm gonna go drill 'em again," I said.

He shook his head back and forth rapidly. "What?"

"I think I'm gonna go back up there and redrill all the trees," I said.

He looked at me like I'd lost my mind. "Dude, seriously? *All* of them?"

I shrugged. "It's the Five Pounder thing to do."

He pressed his palms into prayer hands. "Don't, man. C'mon. That's cray-cray. This storm is gonna leave two feet of snow in those woods and you wanna go back up there for sloppy seconds?"

He was right, it would probably take two days, maybe three, to retap all the trees wading through the fresh piles of Quinlan.

Did I really want to be a Five Pounder *that* badly?

Around noon we heard a honk in the driveway. Archie McClellan.

"What the hell you boys doing up here still?" he shouted from his Sierra, with the snowplow mounted to the bumper. "The roads in town are a goddamned mess."

I pointed to the cupola. "You see the steam don't cha?"

Archie smiled and spat on the ground. He understood. "Yeah, yeah. We just got done boiling ourselves. We filled eight barrels, all medium amber. Really good flavor, too."

I bounced up and down on my feet. "We're having our best day of the season so far, I don't wanna leave."

The snow was so wet and meaty the flakes stuck to my eyelashes. Each blink felt like a shade had been drawn.

Archie looked up at the heavy sky. "You might wanna rethink that. I'm gonna be plowing the next twenty-four hours straight, it looks like. I'll hit your driveway with a couple passes right now, see. I don't want to have to drag your butts out of here again later," he said with a wink.

After another hour we decided to take Archie's advice and start wrapping it up. Bert volunteered to go outside and scrub tanks. He filled a couple five-gallon pails with boiling hot condensation water and lugged them out the back door. Then, one after the other, he hefted the pails over his head and tossed the water into the Fitzy.

While Bert scrubbed the tanks with a long-handled brush, I paused alone inside, leaned against a wall, and took it all in—steam columns wriggling through the cupola, weighty snowflakes from Quinlan falling past the window, an aroma bath of caramelizing syrup. From EQX out of the Bose, a Jane's Addiction song with a guitar solo of spiraling pedal effects.

This is what it's all about. The toil, the problems, the broken crap, the physical toll on our bodies, the time, the risk, the huge investments of money, the weather, the ice, the failure, the humbling of the scorch—all worth it, in trade for just this kind of moment, just this kind of day. I drifted into a peaceful, dreamy, almost hallucinatory state for a minute or two. It was like falling asleep in church.

Then the egg timer snapped me out of it.

29

TO REDRILL OR NOT REDRILL?

The next day there was Hibbard-esque sunshine. The DPW plows had walled Quinlan's snow six feet high along Blossom Road, blocking the driveway to the sugarhouse. Coming up the lane I floored it and aimed for the drift. "Ramming speed!" I shouted and punched the Tundra through, obliterating the snow into the blue air like a dusty white particle bomb.

My goal for today was to climb into the sugarbush and do at least a trial run of redrilling the holes for the two inches. I couldn't help myself.

As I scaled the mountain, something interesting happened. Each bootprint in the snow immediately filled with dark blue snow fleas. What the hell are snow fleas, you ask? They're tiny wingless hexapods that have six legs like insects, but scientists say they are more closely related to crustaceans. In the snow, they looked like I had just spilled a pepper shaker. Millions of the little guys followed me up, jumping around like they were on a hot plate. Snow fleas are equipped with powerful tails that can spring them inches into the air. They used to freak the shit out of me, and whenever I encountered them, I'd shower like crazy when I got home to make sure none crawled into my crevices. I've since learned that was unwarranted. Snow fleas aren't parasitic, and they don't bite. Knowing that now, I love seeing them. They're cute as crap.

Bert was probably right; it would be crazy to redrill each of the 856 trees. It would steal all the energy I'd otherwise need to grind out the rest of the season. I was already taxed, running on fumes. But I figured I might as well try at least a couple to satisfy my guilt.

Midway up the hill, I approached one of my best sap-bearing trees. "Remember me?" I pried out the old spout with a prybar, redrilled the hole with the DeWalt, and knocked the spout back in with the mallet. I couldn't really tell if the hole had been too shallow or not. Some new shavings came out, but nothing dramatic, not enough to indicate that the hole was only drilled halfway the first time.

I drilled a few more trees and lost more and more enthusiasm. At every tap I had to switch out the tool in my hand three times—the prybar, the drill, and the mallet.

As I hiked farther up the hill through the deep drifted snow, each step was like climbing over a fence. I paused to catch my breath for a minute, braced my arm against a trunk, and took a good look at the forest through the trees, both literally and figuratively—did I *really* want to redrill all those holes? All on a *supposition* that I drilled them too shallow.

"This is bullshit," I said to myself.

I abandoned the idea.

The mad enormity of the task was outweighed by a more pressing matter anyway—the vacuum. It had been holding steady at 25hg, but it needed to be higher. More vacuum, more sap. Five Pounders check for leaks *every day*, and they're never happy with only twenty-five inches.

I trekked up to a haven above Coyote Junction where the squirrels love to hang out and chew the crap out of our lines. Anytime I'd been in this spot—a tight grove of some of our biggest trees—it looked like a giant jungle gym for the little peckerheads. I'd watch them scatter and sashay around, doing whatever it is squirrels do when they're not munching on our tubing.

What I've learned about squirrels is they generally stay in the same place. How I know this is because one of the squirrels in Squirrel Haven is a rare black one. Black squirrels are identical to Eastern gray squirrels, except for an abnormal pigment gene. Rodent biologists theorize the morph gives them a selective advantage, their black fur providing extra warmth for winter. Almost every time I've walked in this area of the woods over the past couple years, I've seen that same black squirrel prancing around with his gray pals. That's how I've determined they're territorial, not roamers. Call me the Squirrel Whisperer.

Fixing obvious munched-up leaks at Squirrel Haven took a couple tedious hours, but it was worth it. Back at the sugarhouse, the gauge on the pump increased to a far more respectable 26.5hg, which would give us more sap to fill that damn tank.

That afternoon, Kevin Mattison called from his engine show in Florida for an update on the season. After some preliminary chitchat, I told him about my day patching the chews.

"You're gaining," he said.

He told me Five Pounders are usually in the 27.5 to 28.5 vacuum range.

"Keep doing what you're doing and chase those leaks," he said. "In this business, the money is made in the woods. The more sap you get out of those trees, the more money goes into your change purse."

After hanging up with Kevin, I noticed my cell had a little red "1" over the phone widget. A message from Shakey—earth-shattering news: "Hey Peter I'm sure you're gonna hear about it around town but I decided this is the last year for Shushan Sity Sap Shack. Closing up shop. Everything in the sugarhouse is for sale. So, if you know anybody who needs any tanks or other equipment, I got a lot of shit collected from a lot of years. Already got someone coming to look at the evaporator. I'm at a point in my life that I rather not have to worry about anything, where if I want to just travel I can just up and do it and not be tied down by sugaring. I think I told you this one already but what does a one-legged turkey say? *Wobble, wobble.* Call me back, Peter."

I was dumbfounded. Shakey was maybe in his late sixties or maybe early seventies but carried himself like a college kid (and certainly partied like one). He always had tons of enthusiasm for sugaring, although I had noticed his energy starting to wane since his tick bite. Still, the last person I thought would be hanging up his drill was Shakey.

A couple days later we had a big night boiling. Bert came up after work, and we were making good syrup. The sap was boiling nicely, and we were filling another barrel with some Amber Rich. I was in the middle of a draw-off when my mom called—

"Are you in the sugarhouse?" she asked.

I dropped the phone in the breast pocket of my Chamois shirt to talk to her on speakerphone and keep working.

"Yes Mom. I'm making syrup right now, actually—"

"Ooh how does it taste?"

Good question. I hadn't tried any yet today.

I dunked a tin cup into the draw-off hopper, which was halfway full of fresh, hot syrup. I blew on the syrup to cool it down and took a slurp. Holy crap, this was good stuff, even better than the other day. I handed the cup to Bert and he agreed. "Wow," he signaled with his eyebrows.

Unlike processed foods, maple syrup is very subjective in its flavor. If you eat a bowl of Lucky Charms or some Mrs. Butterworth's or Strawberry Yoplait, it'll taste the exact same way every single time you eat it. But maple syrup flavor can vary from region to region, day to day, and year to year. Usually, on Blossom Road, the flavor quality tends to bell curve over the course of our season, and by the midpoint it hits a sweet spot—pun intended—where it adopts a buttery, vanilla-tinged, caramel flavor mixed with hints of smoked dirt and peat and chased with a blast of sweetness, which can even taste a little bit creamy. We call it "the Butter" when it gets like this. When we hit the Butter, we stop putting our syrup in drums for Bascom's and instead fill Mason jars for our own personal use and to give away to our friends and family, like my mother.

"Just tried some, Mom. Best so far this season," I said.

"Oh yay! There better be some postmarked for Minnesota."

I promised to ship her some when I got a break in the sap. With a Sharpie I scribbled BUTTER on the screw lid of one of the jars, which I would later put in the freezer at home and take out again in August to enter in the syrup judging contest at the Washington County Fair. I've won quite a few blue ribbons over the years with the Butter.

"So, how's it been going out there?" Mom asked.

I told her we had made about 150 gallons so far with a long way to go.

Bert scooped some chalky diatomaceous earth from a pail with a Pyrex measuring cup and emptied it into the draw-off hopper. Then he stirred the D.E. with a giant whisk before hitting a foot pedal on the filter press, which pulled the fresh syrup through a hose into the machine.

"Are you and Bert being careful on your mountain? I worry about you with those chainsaws and the ice," Mom said.

I told her about the slingshotted log incident.

"Oh, my goodness, I actually don't want you to tell me about these things."

I rolled my eyes. "I'm *fine* Mom. It just missed my toes."

"You are being too macho!"

This is my mom's favorite thing to get on my case about—being macho. Mom's a feminist, and a pacifist (I didn't tell her I was considering a .12-gauge . . .), and a vegetarian, a Unitarian, an environmentalist, an animal lover (. . . or that I might have to use it to fend off a coyote), and she comes from an era of modulated masculinity. Her icons of maleness are from the seventies, guys like Alan Alda, Rosey Grier, and George McGovern.

"This is a competition, Mom," I said. "Like a football game or a war."

"A *war*? Who are you in a war with?"

"It's us against the sap, Mom. Man versus tree."

"That *definitely* sounds too macho," Mom said.

I explained the Five-Pounder thing.

"I'm trying to hit a production goal that all the Vermonters hit, or the real ones anyway, the sugarmakers who are worth their salt," I said to her. "What the Vermonters do—it's kind of the gold standard around here. There's a mentality. Everyone holds me suspect anyway because I'm a flatlander from a state with a bunch of lakes and funny accents."

Mom made an audible scoff.

"Who gives a *hoot* about what anyone else might think, other than the people who are *eating* your syrup?" she said.

The egg timer dinged. Time to stoke the dragon.

I jerked on the latch to the firebox, opened the door, and as fast as I could, pitched four pieces of ash firewood into the blaze, then swung the door closed.

"Well maple—it's a social network," I said. "And I want people to respect me, Mom. But it's not just that. It's a little quixotic, this maple thing of ours. We're in a quarrel with nature."

Mom raised her voice a little. "I think someone wrote a book about that once, except in this case it was about a man and a giant whale—a man who was being way too macho. And guess who won *that* quarrel?"

She had a point. Her first question wasn't about how much syrup we'd made but about how good it tasted. I was becoming obsessed with the running tally of our production totals scribbled on the sugarhouse wall.

I was keeping score.

Maybe Mom was right. Maybe I was becoming too much like that certain peg-legged sea captain in my quest for the Five Pounder thing.

But I wasn't turning back, and I wasn't slowing down.

"By the way, it was the *whale*," Mom said, "in case you forgot."

MID-MARCH 2022

30

VERMONT ON A SUNNY DAY

On a stupendously bright morning in late March, the snow was melting fast. Temperatures rocketed into the upper fifties, and sap was fluming through the pipe. I fixed more squirrel leaks in the sugarbush—the snow now not as much of a challenge—which got the vacuum up to a solid 27hg.

On my way up Blossom Road, I passed by Truman's sugarhouse and saw steam coming out of his cupola—a familiar sight. The Dunns are skilled enough sugarmakers that almost every time I pass by their sugarhouse, they seem to be boiling.

The last time I had talked to Truman, that day when I took his French fry recommendation, he told me he was behind schedule. But judging by all the cupola steam I'd been seeing, I figured he must have caught up to and likely surpassed most everyone in the neighborhood by now.

I spun around and stopped in.

Truman and Shelley have a curved, puddled driveway through a grove of maples that comes off Blossom Road and dumps you in front of the sugar-house. There is a little bypass driveway that runs adjacent to the sugarhouse, on a rise, where Truman and their son, Evan, offload sap from their sap-hauling flatbed dually into enormous submarine milk tanks.

Truman and Evan had organized their split firewood, scattered ran-domly around the sugarhouse yard, into neatly corded rows, covered with blue tarps. The biggest stack is next to an open garage bay near the evaporator inside.

On boiling days, Truman opens the garage door and pulls girthy logs from the heap to pitch into the evaporator every five minutes or so.

The Dunn family has been making syrup in this area for several generations, and when you come up Blossom Road, most of the sap lines you see laced through the trees are Truman's.

The Dunns' sugarhouse is practically the size of a Pizza Hut, but it's still not enough room for them. Inside, they have a gigantic evaporator, six feet wide by sixteen feet long. It's got a two-tiered backpan setup like ours, and it towers over your head.

Along the side wall, the filter press and canner rest on a table made of plywood. In the back, there are two wing rooms: one for storage of filled syrup barrels and the other a workshop, where Truman can repair blown-out releasers and busted pumps and such. It has an impressive tool rack and little drawers for miscellaneous parts.

The Dunns are a reserved, modest family. Truman has always been encouraging, and he likes to keep sentry on our sugarhouse, like a neighborhood watch. He's been the best neighbor one could ask for, and he's helped us out of countless jams.

"How it's going, stranger?" Truman said when I walked in. He was holding a pail of hot syrup in each hand. "You look like a semitrailer backed over you."

I rubbed my eyes. "That bad, huh? I've been chasing leaks instead of sleeping," I said.

I watched Shelley draw off syrup from the side of the evaporator, filling an assembly of three-gallon draw-off pails that were set up on milk crates.

Shelley is a petite woman and does all the boiling for the operation. Instead of using a hydrometer cup, she floated a hydrometer directly in a pail, and if the syrup in one pail was too thin, she'd balance it out by pouring in thicker syrup from another pail. She was quick on her feet, the syrup coming off the rig fast and in huge batches, like a wide-open bathtub faucet.

It looked chaotic but Shelley never appeared panicked; she remained silently in control, knowing exactly what she was doing.

"Man, I don't know how you keep up with draw-offs this big," I said to her.

She dropped a hydrometer into another pail. "Oh, you get the hang of it after a while," she said in a quiet voice.

When the syrup in a pail was the proper density, Shelley would set it aside and Truman would step in, heft it up by the looping carrying handle, and dump it into a tub near the filter press.

While the two of them continued working, I stepped over to the evaporator and stood cross-armed, mesmerized by the sap boiling in the front pan, illuminated by a clamp light from above.

The front pan on their evaporator is long and wide. Today it was deluged with vibrating sap, brown and foamy like a head of root beer. The sap progressed all the way down one compartment, turned around, and came back up another, back and forth in gradient through six partitioned channels, finding its way to the spigot in front of Shelley.

Truman walked around to the front of the rig and opened the hinged, vault-like door exposing the inferno inside the firebox. "How's the sugar content up at your place?" Truman asked. He heaved in three or four logs of dead ash, each the breadth of a railroad tie.

"We've had mostly 2 percent so far," I said.

He slammed the door shut and flicked the firebox blower back on. "We had 2.1 the other day," he said. "How much syrup you make so far?"

"Oh, about 150 gallons or so, maybe," I said, fudging a little bit.

He stopped and grinned, "That's what we made last night."

Truman likes to rub it in, good naturedly, about the disparity between our operations. Before the season is over, the Dunns will likely make ten times more syrup than me and Bert.

"Got your vacuum up?" he asked.

I smiled. "Yeah, been prowling the woods this season like a coyote."

"Oh really? Where are you at?"

I squared my shoulders. "Twenty-seven as of the last time I checked," I said.

He creased his brow. "Is that right?" he said. Then he wondered about the status of our neighbors. "How's everybody else doing?"

I rubbed my nose. "I haven't seen the McClellans in a couple days," I said. "I'm gonna visit Kevin and Bob over at Chamber's Farm for the open house breakfast on Saturday. Looking forward to that. And, bombshell, I got a message from Shakey last night and he said he's quitting."

Truman looked at me. "What? Does he know it's only March?" he said.

"No, not quitting for the season, I mean for good. Retiring. He says his heart isn't in it anymore so he's hanging up his drill. He already has someone lined up to buy his evaporator."

"That's what he told you, huh?"

"Yeah. Was very surprised," I said.

He pulled some more logs off the pile. "Maybe you can take over his taps," he said.

I tilted my head. "Eh. That crossed my mind, but I don't know if I want to haul sap from all the way over in Shushan," I said. "That's ten miles."

He nodded. "Yeah, just make the most of what you got right here on Blossom Road."

Evan walked in, wearing a Yankees cap. Evan is only a year out of high school, where he was a three-sport athlete. He waited for a break in the conversation between me and Truman and then, almost offhandedly, mentioned that my Tundra was blocking his dually from getting to the offload dock beside the sugarhouse.

"I was wondering if you could move your truck out of the way," he said politely.

"Oh geez, sorry Evan," I said and made my way to the door. "You got a big tank of sap to unload?"

He grinned. "Yep, sure do," he said.

I told everyone I had sap to boil too, waved goodbye, and skedaddled up the lane.

"Keep that vacuum up," Truman said on my way out the door.

When I got to the sugarhouse, the Fitzy was two-thirds loaded again, probably a good 2,000 gallons of sap and this time, nice and clear and clean. Whatever was yellowing our sap the other day vacated itself from the lines. This was the best-looking sap all season. It would probably make a nice light amber after I boiled it. I connected the tank and RO and started it up.

"Time for lunch," I said to myself, even though it was only 10:30.

On sunny, warm March days like today, homes empty as everyone heads outside. Driving, I saw children wildly pedaling their bikes across the ice-melt ponds, kicking their legs into a flying V to avoid the up-spray as they glided through. Teenagers were digging their basketballs out of hibernation and shooting hoops. And old men fussy about their driveways were pecking at the winterlong ice buildup with their chippers, trying to find the asphalt again.

A lot of people hate March, and I used to be one of those people—not quite spring when you're fed up with winter. But for a sugarmaker, March is Christmas. Traditionally, March is the biggest maple month across the Maple Belt, which stretches from Minnesota to Maine.

A warm March day can invigorate all the senses at once. There's an angle to the sun this time of year that makes the braided streams of melting snow glisten like Christmas tree tinsel. The sun will feel as warm on your body as it does at the beach. Folks shed their layers of Gore-Tex and flannel and run around outside in T-shirts. Up in the mountains, the softened snow is perfect for spring skiing if you're so inclined. Tourists leave the resorts, and the locals get the slopes back to themselves.

March also helps you hydrate again. After being bone-dry all winter, the evaporating snowpack puts humidity back into the air, which feels good on the skin.

With March also arrives the mud. On Blossom Road, and on all the lanes and long driveways in rural New England, what used to be a road will turn into something resembling beef stew. Vermonters call this "mud season."

Mud season delivers the best days for sugaring—twenties at night, forties and fifties during the day, with sun or haze. We love it like this. That freeze-thaw cycle is what gets the sap flowing in the trunks. But if the weather gets too warm, it might mislead the trees into thinking it's spring. We don't want that. We just want them to think it's *almost* spring.

As we drove through town past the fire department, the firemen were washing their trucks in the driveway with their attack hoses. Everywhere I looked, laundry was draped over clotheslines, people airing out the heavy, dusty quilts that had been covering their beds all winter.

In the villages at this time of year, it seems like we're all driving drunk, swerving to avoid the spring potholes, which the highway crews ornament with bright-orange road cones.

I landed at Sherman's Store in West Rupert for a sandwich, which I ate on the tailgate of my truck, absorbing sun and much-needed vitamin D. I waved at the other sugarmakers who were driving back and forth with loads of sap. You know it's sugaring season again when all the pickup trucks in town switch from snowplow blades in the front to sap tanks in the back.

Sherman's makes serviceable sandwiches and sells bags of chips for only a dollar. They treat everyone like family. It's an economical place to stop for lunch, and close to the sugarhouse. I got pastrami on rye along with a brownie wrapped in Saran wrap from a stack in a basket sitting next to the cash register.

As I was enjoying my tailgate picnic, an old woman, maybe in her early eighties, got out of a car next to me and trained her face to the sun's glare.

"Finally, a nice day," she said.

There was relief in her countenance, like she'd just stepped off a plane in Hawaii and someone draped a lei around her neck. "I just want to put on a halter top and go out in the yard," she said.

We both enjoyed the sunbath for a moment.

"Our friends keep inviting us to move to Florida—"

I interrupted her. "Bet you wouldn't trade places with Florida on a day like today," I said.

"Yeah, but I don't know how many more Vermont winters I can take," she said.

Winters here can take a toll on people. They're getting shorter, but they're still hard. Unless you're in the maple business or love to ski, waiting out January and February for March or April can be isolating as hell. Many surrender, decamp, and race down I-95 to Florida. Usually, it'll be a close call with the ice, or, worse, a flat-out faceplant on the sidewalk; or maybe it'll be a heart attack shoveling the driveway that gets them to the decision to get the hell out.

A look of resolve came across the old woman's face. "Think I'll go for a long walk later," she said, and she turned and went into Sherman's.

As I was finishing my sandwich, a red Ford F-250 pulled in next to mine. A clean-cut guy about my age wearing green coveralls and muck boots stepped out.

He glanced at the blue tubing coiled in the back of my truck, which must've tipped him off I was a sugarmaker. "Sap running much today?" he asked.

I smiled. "Running great," I said. "I'll be boiling later."

He introduced himself as the local bovine vet, who takes care of the big dairy herds around Rupert and Salem.

"Man, I love sugaring," he said. "I used to tap trees when I was a kid in the backyard. But when I got to high school all I wanted to do was play basketball and that took over the winter months. And the sugaring, well, I just stopped doing it, I guess."

He shook his head a little, like he was frustrated with himself that he gave it up.

"Today seems like it would be a great bucket day, doesn't it?" he said, and he was right. Warm, sunny days like this are the type of days sap flows best on sheer gravity. Ideal dripping weather for the ol' sap bucket guys, like I used to be and what Ned Perrin and Dudley Jenkins were.

I took a bite of my sandwich. "Yeah, the sap's running hard today—a great day to put buckets out for sure," I said.

"Man, I need to get back into sugaring," the man said. "I love buckets. I love collecting sap. I love putting up firewood. My boys are nine and fifteen. I think it'd be fun for them, too."

"Perfect ages for kids and maple," I said, just like I had told Big Head Todd.

He turned and looked toward the mountains in the distance. "Yeah, I think they'd love it. I know I did when I was their age. We got about thirty or forty trees on our property we can tap."

"Why not do it?" I asked.

The guy turned back to me. "Would I have any trouble finding a little evaporator to boil on?"

I pointed behind me toward New Hampshire. "You could drive over to Bascom's this afternoon and pick one out. There's still some season in front of us yet," I said.

He made a *hmmm* sound. "I'm really gonna hav'ta give that some thought," he said. Then he turned his face sunward and squinted. "Nothing like being outside on a day like today."

He stepped over and shook my hand.

"I need a cup a coffee and then I got cows to see to."

After lunch, I drove to Shushan and visited Shakey. Despite his retirement announcement, he was boiling today as furiously as ever, firing the evaporator every five minutes when the red lightbulb came on.

Shakey's sugarhouse has about the same level of rusticity as mine—lots of rough-cut pine, except his boards have burn scars from a few flash fires over the years. Scribbled across the wall are the crude production records of each of his seasons. This is something most sugarmakers do, including me and Bert. With a Sharpie, we mark on the wall the date of each boil and the gallons produced that day. Shakey also displays lots of Irish knickknacks inside Shushan Sity—empty whiskey bottles mostly, and pinups of half-naked women.

Shakey sighed. "I've been making syrup for thirty-two years, a nice stretch," he said.

I was expecting him to be in a lot worse mood than he was, but he was cracking cringy jokes like usual. "Why don't witches have babies?" he asked. "Their husbands have hollow weenies."

I told him about my situation with the shallow tapholes, and he agreed with Bert, it would be stupid to go and redrill them all, especially when we were already more than halfway through the season.

"That sounds like absolutely no fun at all, and this shit is supposed to be *fun*, damn it. Don't do it," he said.

A white-bearded hobby sugarmaker from a town near Saratoga Springs was in there with him, sizing up the evaporator, which he planned to buy from Shakey at the end of the season. Word was out about Shakey's retirement, and sugarmakers were swarming in.

I asked Shakey if he was feeling emotional about his decision.

He began chewing on his thumbnail. "My wife could see it coming," he said. "It didn't seem like I was having fun anymore and she said exactly what I just told you, 'If it's not fun then why do it?'"

He reached for a can of Coors sitting on a makeshift bar next to a window. "I tore up one of my knees this winter and I gotta have it completely replaced. It's gotten to the point in the woods where I'm just petrified I'm gonna fall and tear up the other knee."

He tilted his head way back, drained the beer, then swished the can into an orange trash barrel. "I love being in here, in the sap house," he said, "but the woods? Forget it. I just can't go into the woods no more, so I said you know what? *Fuck it*, I'm outta here."

Just like the old lady at Sherman's earlier, the winters had done him in.

The white-bearded guy had agreed on Shakey's asking price for the evaporator, "but I gotta get permission from my wife," he said and looked down at the floor.

The sum was $5,000, which was a great deal for both. Great for beard-guy, because if he were to buy an evaporator brand-new at Bascom's, it would cost him four times as much. And a great deal for Shakey because, as he told me after the fella left, it was the same price Shakey paid for the evaporator when he bought it twenty years ago.

"The Irish aren't so dumb," he said with a sly grin.

Then he twisted off another Coors from a plastic six-pack ring and held it out to me.

"Need a cold one?"

I waved him off. He shrugged and popped it open for himself.

"Gotta run, I got sap to boil too," I said, turning to vamoose.

My ears waited for another parting zinger, but none came.

Shakey was already busy throwing more firewood into the evaporator.

The red light was flashing on and off.

LATE MARCH 2022

31

THE NEIGHBORHOOD WATCH

I knocked my knuckles on one of the sugarhouse girts. "We're having a good season," I said to Bert in almost a whisper, so no one in the universe except Bert could hear.

"Maybe we're doing something right for once," he said.

I made the *shush* gesture to my lips. "Don't jinx it," I said.

Mother Nature was certainly doing her part. We were getting ideal weather conditions for making the sap gush from the woods—day after day of freezes at night and forties and fifties in the daytime. The trees were going bonkers.

"Holy crap is it coming in hard," I reported to Bert one morning on the phone, as sap sprayed into the releaser. "It's a goddamned firehose."

Not only that, but another critical element was going in our favor—the sugar content in the sap was high, around 2 percent or so, just like I'd mentioned to Truman the other day.

In so many ways the trees are unknowable. Not even the experts at the Proctor Center or Cornell can tell you with certainty why maple trees have more sugar in their sap some years than others. Regardless, this season was much better than last year, when the sugar in the sap was as low as 1.2 percent, meaning it took nearly twice as much sap to make the same amount of syrup.

On a Saturday in late March, it was probably going to hit seventy in the sun, and we were getting a stampede of sap into the *Edmund Fitzgerald*.

In the sugarhouse, it took all day to boil it.

It was a big day for Bert. He was Paul Freaking Bunyan. He spent most of the morning splitting firewood. We had boiled so many times, we were running out. There are two log bays in our woodshed, and we were already getting to the end of one of them—three cords, burned.

It was warm enough that Bert shed his flannel and wore only a white tank top as he hefted a maul over his head and brought it down onto a log with a *wa-schunk*, his pale arms as long as canoe oars.

On a clipboard in the sugarhouse, I had been keeping a running logbook on each day of the season, and the entries were bearing out how kick-ass a year we were having:

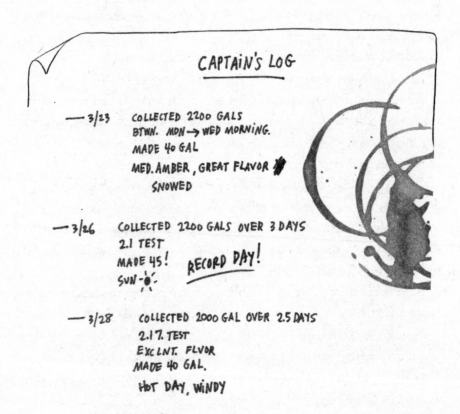

CAPTAIN'S LOG

— 3/23   COLLECTED 2200 GALS
          BTWN. MON → WED MORNING.
          MADE 40 GAL
          MED. AMBER, GREAT FLAVOR
          SNOWED

— 3/26   COLLECTED 2200 GALS OVER 3 DAYS
          2.1 TEST
          MADE 45!   RECORD DAY!
          SUN -

— 3/28   COLLECTED 2000 GAL OVER 2.5 DAYS
          2.1% TEST
          EXCLNT. FLVOR
          MADE 40 GAL.
          HOT DAY, WINDY

I've never, not once, not been able to strike up a conversation with another sugarmaker. For males involved in maple, being able to do this is a nice perk. Most dudes never know what the hell to say to one another, which is why, at a party for example, men who've just met will nearly always end up talking about the same three things: sports, real estate, and commutes. Common ground. But it's different with sugarmakers. Dialog prompts come easily. "How many taps do you have?" or "How was your season?" We usually have instant rapport since we're bonded by mutual adversity. Over the years, I've met a lot of sugarmakers. I've generally liked them all. Except one. Cubby.

Art Cubbins, who makes syrup over in Sandgate, just past Rupert, has almost the same number of taps as me, so we're a similar cohort. Except Cubbins started sugaring *after* I started sugaring, but he acts like he has maple figured out better than anyone and certainly thinks he's better at it. Trust me, making maple syrup is an infinite universe; there's no one in this industry who has it all figured out. And no one ever will. But try telling that to Cubbins. He carries himself like he's the most perfected specimen of sugarmaker who's ever lived.

I was boiling on a cloudy Tuesday, a run-of-the-mill kind of day. A medium amount of sap in the tank, maybe 1,500 gallons. Sugar content in the sap was about 1.9 percent, decent. The sap was boiling evenly, and I was making on the darker side of medium amber.

It was a relaxing morning. I love morning boils because the vibe is mellow. Less pressure (unless a snowstorm is coming). You can take your sweet-ass time boiling the sap, instead of nighttime boils, when you're in a race to finish so you can get home and go to frigging bed.

The thing about sugarmakers and sugarmaking is this: when you're boiling sap and steam is rising out of your cupola, that becomes a tacit invitation for anyone to stop in and see what the hell's going on inside. If there's steam, someone will be stopping by. Count on it.

Sure enough, through the front window I saw Cubbins pull into the driveway in a champagne-colored Chevy 1500. It had a rusted-out bumper and so much grime smirched over the green license plate you could barely read the vanity lettering, MPL KING. Cubbins opened the door and swung his legs out then carefully eased himself down from the cab while a chocolate beagle leaped behind him and started running around the yard, sniffing the ground.

I turned away from the window. "Just wonderful," I said to myself.

When Cubbins let himself into the sugarhouse, neither one of us greeted the other. He just down-nodded at me, and I up-nodded back but didn't say anything.

Cubbins is a ruddy-faced, beefy guy with a white handlebar mustache. Everyone calls him "Cubby." He was walking with a limp for some reason that I didn't ask about.

He drag-footed over to the front pan and stuck his snout down close to it. I just kept working. He had on flat-front polyester work slacks held up with rainbow colored *Mork from Ork* suspenders.

He pulled his face away from the steam. "Have your ears been ringin'?" he asked.

I felt my haunches go up. "No. Why?"

"Well, me and the fellas was talkin' at coffee the other morning, askin' 'bout how everybody's been doin' with their seasons and whatnot, and we got to talkin' about you and one guy said he heard you was shootin' to make a lot more syrup this year."

"That's the plan," I said. "Five pounds."

Cubbins made a slight frown. "Uh huh. That's quite a plucky goal for the new kid on the block, don't cha think?"

I climbed up a stepladder and squirted defoamer into a float box.

"Been making syrup longer than you have, Cubby," I said.

"Now don't get defensive, just sayin' that's a hard thing to pull off, is all," he said.

He limped over to the draw-off hopper and stuck a meaty finger into the syrup I'd just made, swirled it around a little, and then poked it into his mouth. No reaction. Then he double dipped for a second taste and this time crinkled his upper lip.

I could feel my face redden. "Have *you* ever got to five pounds?" I asked him.

"Of course. Last year we did close ta six," he said.

I knew this was a steaming pile of horseshit. No one had a good year in '21, except maybe Truman and Shelley down the lane, and if they hit five pounds it would've been just barely.

I stepped off the ladder. "I'd offer you a seat, but I don't want you to stay," I said half-jokingly, even though I meant it.

He shot me a hurt look.

"Aw just messin' with ya, Cubby," I said, walking past him. "Make yourself comfortable."

Cubbins grabbed a wooden stool, sat down, and folded his arms across his man-titted chest. I trotted in firewood sticks from the woodshed and stacked them next to the evaporator.

He tried to center himself on the seat. "Filled a barrel of Fancy last night," he said.

"Fancy" is an old-school syrup grading category in Vermont that was phased out about ten years ago when the powers-that-be changed all the grading names. But some stubborn Vermont sugarmakers still refer to the absolute lightest syrup they make as Fancy. There's a little bit of history behind this. Back in the day—pre–global warming—the winters used to be a lot colder and same for the springs. The result was sugarmakers in Vermont tended to make much lighter syrup, because typically the colder the weather, the lighter the syrup. Since there was so much light syrup being made, the powers-that-be invented the Fancy grade to trick consumers into thinking it was better syrup, according to lore. The thing is, it's not, in my opinion. It has *less* maple flavor. But the "Fancy" term has hung on. And a lot of sugarmakers still like to stick their thumbs in their britches and brag about making Fancy. Cubby is famous for this.

He lifted his chin. "It was lighter than fish piss," he said.

I edged past him to climb back up the stepladder again and squirted more defoamer into the pan.

"Fish piss is light colored?"

"Why sure it is," he said. "Fish piss is so light you can't even tell they're pissing. It's same color as the water."

"I don't know about that. Do fish even piss?"

He narrowed his eyes. "Of course fish piss. Everything pisses."

"Not fish."

"Sure they do," he said, raising his voice. (I actually knew fish peed. I just wanted to irritate him.)

He got off the stool and shuffled outside to snoop at my vacuum gauge, which is screwed into the releaser just beyond a sliding barn door in the back of the sugarhouse.

"You're at 26," he shouted, and then he came back inside to sit on the stool again. "That's baby shit compared to what we're doin'."

I didn't want to ask, but I did. "Why, what's yours been?"

He puffed out his chest. "Oh 'bout twenty-eight point five."

I narrowed my eyes suspiciously—more horseshit—but bit my lip. "Well, if you're insisting on staying you can run the filter press," I said.

Even though he's annoying, Cubbins is still a sugarmaker, and if one sugarmaker has an opportunity to help another sugarmaker, that's usually what the sugarmaker will do. Cubbins dug into a tote box for the filter papers and started arranging them up in the plates.

"I don't know how you get anything done in here. It's like working in a hallway," he said.

"I like it just fine. It's cozy."

He snickered. "Oh yeah, it's a *cute* sugarhouse and all. Just that most sugarhouses have a lot more room than this to move around."

He's always calling the sugarhouse cute, which I really hate.

Cubbins straightened and put his hands on his hips. "When I was pouring the floor for my sugarhouse, I asked everybody how big it should be, and then I doubled it," he said.

"Yeah well, I like that everything's close at hand."

"Can say that again," he said.

Just then Cubbins's beagle wandered in and started sniffing around.

I shooed the hound out the back door with my foot. "No dogs in the sugarhouse, Cubby, you know the rules," I said. "State regulation."

Cubbins waved a hand at me. "Oh, he's a good boy. He don't bother nobody."

It was bothering me immensely. "C'mon now, git," I said to the mutt as his hind cleared the threshold.

"Easy now," Cubbins said. "You don't need to be such a *meany* about it."

I scowled back at him. "If the state inspector saw a dog in here, I'd get fined."

Cubbins scoffed. "Aw you ain't gonna get no inspectors comin' around ta Blossom Road. They wouldn't wanna get mud on their loafers."

I looked out the window and saw the beagle begin to pace back and forth and then squat next to the woodshed.

I threw my hands up. "Now your dog is crapping in the goddamned yard, Cubby."

He craned his head to look out the window and laughed.

"Aw yeah, I guess he is."

"So now I gotta worry about stepping in it," I said.

"Aw, it'll dissolve when the snow melts," he said and went back to assembling the press.

Cubby hung around another forty-five minutes, which was forty-five minutes longer than I wanted him to.

As much as I hated to admit it, he was a little bit right when he was snarking about my vacuum level. Twenty-six was not going to cut it. I was not doing enough to get to five pounds. Skipping out for too many French fry runs. Taking too many naps.

Over the next few days, I strengthened my resolve and became a maniac with the leak checking, making sortie after sortie up Blossom Hill, chasing away squirrels, searching for the tiniest little nibble. I got the vacuum to 27 and even hit 27.5 a couple of times. I texted Bert a twenty-second video of the gauge holding near 27 and a torrent of sap emptying into the releaser.

"*Watching this is better than porn,*" I captioned.

"Not really but I get the idea," he replied.

The good news was the evaporator was performing well, seemingly not bothered by the scorch from the first day and the warped pan. Sap boiled just fine. A nice gingery froth.

Bert meanwhile proved himself an animal in keeping the tanks sparkling clean, making sure the RO was happy, and running the filter press, squeezing out handsome ambery syrup.

For a week and a half, we fell into a pattern of collecting sap for a couple of days, then boiling on the third. Defying Bert Time, he'd tear ass up to the sugarhouse after work, at his Schenectady job, excited to hang out and boil into the evening.

The sugarhouse usually ends up being where he and I find ourselves discussing a lot of life shit, things like: my DOA love life and the riddles of dating, or Bert's occasional office politics; COVID disruptions (all our kids caught it, but neither of us did); global politics and foreign policy (a niche interest of Bert's); restoring fiberglass motorboats (a niche interest of mine); World War II of course; and updates on the adventures of our far-flung adult children.

I checked on the neighbors almost daily, stopping by the McClellans' and the Dunns', who both said they were working at record-breaking paces. I paid visits to John and Michele Reid down the road at Sugar Mill Farm in Greenwich, and to Brian Adams over in Shushan, and Brian Ducharme at Wild Hill Maple in Jackson. All of them, killing it. Everyone I knew seemed to be having a great, even ecstatic sugar season. Maple was back! Everyone, that is, except Shakey, who surprised me with a call one night when I was in the middle of a boil. He was toast.

"Peter . . . I had to quit a few days ago," he told me. "My leg is just . . . every time I go down a hill, my leg hurts like hell. The knees are just completely shot. I didn't do good at all. I made only about seventy gallons altogether and that was it. Done. Just pulled the plug."

Shakey's news was sad to hear. He was missing out, and I knew it had to pain him. It was the end of an era. Meanwhile, for everyone everywhere across the U.S. Maple Belt, there was a riot of sun and sap. It was shaping up to be the biggest year ever in maple history, with Vermont and New York sugarmakers leading the way.

The five pounds was within reach, but only if the weather held up, as well as my body.

The accrual of fatigue was becoming an obstacle. I was buzzing too much on steam and sugar to fall asleep properly after I'd get home from boiling. Then when I'd finally conk out, I'd have the REM cycle of a rhesus monkey, waking up off and on all night. Then I'd get up early the next morning to race up to Blossom Road and check for leaks and fix lines. All my waking hours I felt exhausted. During boiling sessions, I'd sometimes doze off, slumped on a stool with my arms dangling and head tilted back against a wall, only to jerk awake to the egg timer.

"FYI, you're a snorer," Bert said.

One morning, I was at a convenience store grabbing an armload of 5-hour Energy shots, and who happened to be in line behind me but ol' Gerber, armchair pharmacist.

He pointed at the stout bottles in my hands. "What'ja bothering with those for, bro?"

I explained about my lack of sleep and the daytime fatigue catching up with me.

He gave me a once-over. "Yeah, your color's not looking so good," he said. "You sure the low energy is from the insomnia?"

I half-shrugged. "I'm in this vicious cycle—wide awake at night, a zombie in the day."

He made a tight-lipped smile. "Maybe you got Low T, man," he said.

I rolled my eyes. I'd listened to enough sports talk radio to know what he meant, low testosterone. The remedy pills and creams are advertised constantly to male-dominated media audiences and on my Facebook-feed thingy. Gerber is exactly the kind of guy you'd expect to be an advocate for the stuff. He gave me the contact for a place called "Supreme Male T Clinic" down in Florida. I looked it up online in desperation, but it just seemed too sketchy. He also suggested herbal therapy. "There's a gummy for that," he said, waggling his eyebrows.

Instead, I turned to Big Pharma. I began self-medicating with ZzzQuil. The stuff worked amazingly well—for a while. It'd knock me right out at night and keep me out for most of it, too. But then the next day I would feel druggy, which slowed me down in the woods.

There was no obvious solution to my problem. I was just going to have to suffer.

I know what Rascher would've said: "Sleep all you goddamned want when maple season's over."

I popped in on Milt Hinchey one morning over in West Pawlet. He and an older hired man were knee deep inside the RO room, where he stores two mega-ROs with multiple membranes. The men were covered in grease and sap.

He waved at the machines with a pipe wrench. "I don't know who made the O-rings on these goldarned ROs but whoever did oughta have his head examined," Milt said. "They're not the right size, not a one of 'em. They's all were leaking. We've's spent half a day takin' part the valves and replacing each O-ring. Each one takes 'bout an hour and we've's got eight more."

Always with the damn O-rings.

We were all eagle-eyed on the trees to see if the end was nigh. By this point in a season, we look closely at the tree buds to see if they start to expand. Once they do, that means the trees are close to done shooting sugar through their xylem vessels and our season will soon be over.

I bumped into Cubby at Sherman's Store, and of course his trees were behaving. "I was in the woods today and the buds—they are *tight*, tighter than a boar's ass," he said. "Ain't moved one bit."

Bert, too, had been a pillar of optimism, offsetting my cynical nature. One night when I was predicting that we were getting close to the end of our season, Bert kept effusing about how we had a solid two weeks left.

"Not hearing the peepers yet," he kept repeating. "And we're not seeing moths."

It was true, I hadn't seen any moths since that first sap run when I found those three or four flopping around in the sap tank.

"And we're still making good syrup," he said.

Still, I thought we were late in the third quarter.

"I don't know, man, my gut tells me it's almost over," I said.

On the way back to town that night in my truck, with the windows rolled down and cool air streaming in, I didn't hear any frogs on Blossom Road—but I did hear peepers chirruping from a roadside pond about three miles away, on Route 153 outside of Salem.

They were getting goddamned close.

We started out the next day with a pancake breakfast at Dry Brook Sugar House, operated by Kevin Keyes and his brother-in-law Bobby Chambers, who is also probably the biggest dairy farmer and landowner in this area. Their sugarhouse is tucked in a sustained hollow that starts in Salem, New York, and runs into Sandgate, Vermont, probably ten miles long.

It was Maple Open House Weekend. Bert brought Faith along for the pancakes.

"Hope I'm not being a third wheel," she said.

Sugarmaker associations in almost every maple state will organize at least one weekend in March as an open house, inviting civilians to come and see sugaring in action.

Open house weekends can be a mixed bag. Some sugarmakers love them because they sell a ton of syrup and maple confections to the tourists. Many producers unload their whole crop in a single weekend and entertain literally thousands of visitors if they're located near a metropolitan area. I've been to some open houses where people wait for hours in line just to *look* at an evaporator boiling. Then they wait in another long line to buy maple products—syrup, candy, coated nuts, maple cotton candy, lollypops, maple cream, granulated sugar, maple taffy on a stick. The whole event falls into the category of "agritourism." Folks make a day of it.

Rascher used to participate in the open houses, and he'd get a lot of visitors, but often they'd stir up his unbalanced ire. I once saw him evict an entire family because they tracked mud into his sugarhouse. "Get the hell out of here!" he screamed, terrifying the family and scattering everyone else there, too. "Would you walk into your own house with filthy shoes like that?" he bellowed as they sprinted for their cars. "What the hell's the matter with you?"

At Dry Brook, Kevin and Bob have a big enough extended family that they have no problem accommodating so many people. There are probably a dozen Keyeses of various generations seating people, flipping pancakes, taking breakfast orders, and working the sales counter selling syrup jugs and boxes of maple candy. All of them are usually smiling.

Today Kevin and Bob were buzzing around the evaporator, boiling sap and chatting and answering questions for the masses.

"It takes forty gallons of sap to make just one gallon of syrup," I overheard Bob explain to one young couple, who, judging by their patterned scarves, waxy Carhartt coats, and fashionable white sneakers, were maybe from Williamsburg or Bushwick.

Bob and Kevin's sugarhouse is a board and batten–style like ours, with a main boiling room and many wing additions, situated between the cow barns of Bob's dairy. They have long rows of picnic tables covered with patterned oilcloth set up in a back seating area. Visitors can watch the sap boil, eat some pancakes, and then wander around the farm with the little ones in a stroller and shove them right in front of an 800-pound Holstein munching on a mound of grain.

Breakfast at Dry Brook is just eight dollars, and they undercharge in my opinion. You get all-you-can-eat pancakes, all-you-can-eat sausage patties or links, and coffee, milk, or orange juice to wash it down.

I walked over to Bob, a slender man with a profuse mustache. He likes to grill me on what other sugarmakers are up to and how their seasons are going, just like Truman does.

"What are you hearing from everyone else?" he said, as he climbed up a stepladder next to the evaporator to throw defoamer into the top pan, ten feet in the air.

I told him we were having a good year on Blossom Road. "We've been getting a pile of sap, and everyone I've talked to has been saying the same."

As he climbed back down the ladder, Bob made mention of the lack of cold nights in the forecast, something I was noticing on my weather app, too.

"No freezes beyond Tuesday as far as I can see," he said. "What do you think?"

I blew out my cheeks. "Yeah, that's got me worried too," I said.

Kevin walked over and fist-bumped with me. He was wearing a camouflage ball cap and had an unlit cigar compressed in his teeth. "We had people frigging lining up outside at 7:00 A.M.," he said. "Can you believe that?"

I laughed. "That's cause you're giving away almost-free breakfasts," I said.

Bob grinned and tilted his head toward Kevin. "Yeah, I keep saying we should raise our prices but someone around here doesn't agree."

Kevin continued. "We don't flip a pancake until eight. And I told the early birds we don't open for another hour, but they didn't care. 'We'll wait,' they said, ha-ha. So, we just said 'aw, what the frig' and sat them at a table anyway."

Kevin is the chief mingler at these events. He likes to shoot the bull and has a lot of friends in town, who all make the pilgrimage for the flapjacks.

He looked around the room. "We're gonna be hella busy today I can feel it," he said.

By some miracle, Bert, Faith, and I found an open spot at a table, and I swung a leg over the bench and sat down across from the two of them. Almost immediately, a Keyes family member dropped platefuls of breakfast in front of us. Another one poured some coffee, and a third came around with a pitcher of orange juice.

After some chitchat, Faith wondered when Bert might return to a normal schedule.

She rubbed his shoulder. "Am I getting my husband back anytime soon?"

"That's up to the sap," I said, and Bert nodded, his mouth full of what was probably already his ninth link of sausage.

Faith moved a bowl of foil-wrapped butter pats out of Bert's reach. "I'm signing him up for Zumba classes as soon as you guys wrap up," she said.

I pointed my fork at Bert. "Your husband here predicts we still have a few weeks to go with the season, but I disagree," I said. "I heard some peepers outside of town the other night."

Faith raised an eyebrow. "And those are?"

"Frogs. They're the canary in the coal mine," I said. "The moment we hear the frogs start to peep in the pond behind the sugarhouse, that'll be the end."

I lifted a jug of syrup off the table and shellacked my pancakes.

"That's pretty interesting," Faith said.

"It's almost simultaneous. When the frogs start peeping the trees start budding," I said.

"And when the trees start budding, the sap changes from sweet to sour," Bert said.

I checked my phone. High sixties by Wednesday and beyond. "Looks like a heat wave by midweek," I said. "So, you might get Bert back sooner rather than later."

Bert smiled at me through his chews. "Why you gotta be such a Debbie Downer?"

I looked at Faith. "Thanks for agreeing to be a maple widow the past two months," I said.

"Beats being made to watch the History Channel every night," she said, elbowing Bert.

She turned to him. "I've decided it's gonna be your turn to take the trash to the curb for the rest of the year," she said.

We finished breakfast and Bert and Faith said they wanted to go for a ride through the hollow on a horse-drawn wagon, part of the open-house festivities they were offering outside.

On our way out, we hunched our shoulders to navigate through the throngs of people filling up the sugarhouse. "I'm getting claustrophobic," I said to Bert. I made eye contact with Kevin across the room, and we both stood on our tippy toes to see each other better over all the heads.

He cupped his hands around his mouth. "Leaving so soon?" he hollered.

"It's like a Taylor Swift concert in here!" I shouted back, and he shrugged.

I spotted Bob, waved goodbye, and mouthed to him good luck on the rest of the season.

When we got outside Bert and Faith stood in line for the hayride. The queue stretched all the way down to the road. Folks were stepping up a small ladder into the wagon and playing musical chairs to claim a seat on the bales. Young women in shiny puffer jackets were Instagram posing beside the two horses with lidded, deadpan eyes, chewing globs of straw.

"Meet you back at the sugarhouse after the wagon ride, buddy," Bert said.

I started walking to my truck. "Roger that. I'll get the RO rippin'," I said.

Then I burned rubber for Blossom Road, zooming past the incoming traffic of white SUVs and gunmetal Teslas.

32

ALPENGLOW AND MOONGLOW

On a Tuesday in late March, the invisible hand that induces sap flow in the trees had them running silly, and the Fitzy was brimmed, 3,106 gallons. "*Full boat!*" I texted Bert, with a picture of the lake of sap. "*Hell yeah!*" he replied.

I got busy preparing to boil, zipping back and forth between the RO room, the tank yard, and the woodshed. It was another almighty sun-dappled day. Morale was high.

At one point, I was carrying an armload of firewood across the yard, and I noticed a windowless white van unhurriedly slip sliding down the lane, the surface of which had been transformed to a bog by the heaving frost and warm temperatures. The van was fishtailing each time the driver tapped on the gas to clear a rut, every few feet or so.

Geez, rear-wheel drive, I thought. *Pretty much useless on Blossom Road in the spring.*

About a half hour later, I was knocking around on the side of the sugarhouse, bent over connecting a hose to Roundy, and I happened to look up and noticed it again, the van, this time sluggishly making his way back in the other direction, toward Truman and Shelley's place.

Who is this guy? DEA surveillance van thinking we're a meth lab?

After a bit, with the RO up and running and a few minutes to kill, I decided to run over to Sherman's Store for a Sprite and a sandwich. I jumped in the Tundy and slithered through the Hasenpfeffer until, about halfway down the lane, there he was again, the white van now pulled over far to the right—so far over I wondered if he was lodged in the quicksand.

I came up broadside to him and tooted the horn. Inside was a hunched, weather-lined old guy, wearing a heavy coat, ballcap, and wide sunglasses. He didn't look up. I could see he had something attached to his steering wheel that looked like some sort of makeshift painter's easel apparatus. He was holding a long-bristled brush, flailing at a canvas.

I rolled down my window. "Everything okay buddy?" I asked him.

He was swooshing away. "Oh yes, just in a bit of a hurry," he said.

I leaned over and got a better look inside his cab. I noticed the passenger seat had been removed, and the bare metal of the door and chassis was paint-spattered with pigments of every imaginable color, like a melted bag of Skittles.

"Are you stuck in the mud?" I asked him.

"No, just trying to get this nice blue sky before the clouds *shersh* in."

"*Shersh?*"

He laughed. "Old Ukrainian term," he said.

While continuing to stroke the brush back and forth, he told me he'd been a painter for forty-nine years. "I just drive around, looking for things to paint," he said.

He said his name was Harry Orlyk. I recognized it, a well-known local artist.

"Then I sit here in my van and work and don't bother anyone."

He reached down and then stuck his hand out the window holding a flyer.

"I have a show going on this month if you want to see some of my work," he said.

I got out of my truck, walked around, and took it from him.

The pamphlet teased some samples of his art, on exhibition at a gallery along the Hudson River. In one of the paintings, a familiar scene. It was of Truman's sugarhouse during a boil.

"I like seasonal stages," he said when I pointed it out. "Sugaring is great for that."

I asked him if he'd ever heard of Hibbard.

"Of course," he said, still whooshing at the linen panel attached to his steering wheel.

I said I thought Hibbard was a master at capturing winter scenes.

He looked at me for the first time. "Well, I'd like to think I'm not so bad at that myself."

I mentioned my observations about Hibbard's snow—the colors he chose, none of them white.

Orlyk nodded and resumed painting. "Yes, you wanna to save your white when it comes to snow," he said. "There's an old artists' secret—something called 'Alpenglow'—that's when the sunlight hits one bank of snow and reflects onto another. And Hibbard knew about that."

I watched him paint for beat or two more. He was in the zone.

"Well, I'll let you to it," I said, "just wanted to make sure you weren't stuck in the slop," and I promised to check out his exhibition when I had a break in the sap.

He waved at me with one hand without breaking stride with his brush in the other. "Sorry I'm not more talkative. Just trying to capture this before it goes away," he said and chuckled. "Hibbard was a slave to the light, and so am I."

⬥

I hadn't seen Milt Hinchey in a couple weeks, so I took a detour to West Pawlet to see if he was boiling. Sure enough, there were cumulonimbus clouds of steam drifting over his farm.

Milt's sugarhouse is at the end of a long, climbing driveway, and at the top there were three or four GMC pickups parked akimbo. Backed up to the front of the sugarhouse was Milt's big International S2500 dually with a 2,000-gallon sap tank strapped to the dumper.

I walked inside and there were several very old hatted men in various junctures of activity, all of them shuffling around Milt's mammoth evaporator, which was rippling with hot, sudsy sap.

Milt emerged from a fog of steam that was hovering shoulder-high throughout the room. Unlike our wood-fired setup on Blossom Road, Milt's evaporator was being fueled with flaming oil, sprayed into the arch by three atomizing pressure guns.

He nodded as he brushed past me, scooting from one side of the rig to the other.

"We're just starting up," he said matter-of-factly.

His sugarhouse was utilitarian in contrast to many of the aesthetical post-and-beam sugarhouses common in Vermont. Milt's was a basic 2x4 light frame building with pressboard siding. It felt a little bit more like I was in an auto repair shop than a sugarhouse.

Along the walls, Milt had steel racks populated with a mad arrangement of old parts and junk. On one shelf there were not one, but two Makita skill saws, a gas station windshield squeegee, a hoard of wrenches and pliers, coffee cans full of nails, a couple of fan belts, some random chain links, a crisscrossed pile of pipe lengths, and a swimming pool ladder.

Milt was issuing commands—actually, they were more like suggestions—to one man to run the filter press, another to monitor the incoming sap, and a third to mind the barrels filling with fresh syrup and to make sure they didn't overflow.

They all looked confused.

There was something reassuring about being in the sugarhouse with Milt. A veteran sugarmaker in firm control at the conn. He was unfazed that the octogenarians, while appearing eager to help, seemed to have no clear understanding of what the hell Milt wanted them to do.

One of the gentlemen I was somewhat acquainted with, who used to make syrup off 1,000 taps in North Rupert until about five years ago when his hip gave out. He was standing off to the side. "I just had a second hip replacement, and the doctor told me that this is my last chance—there won't be another one," he told me. "So I gotta stay out of the woods for good."

I asked him if he missed sugaring much.

"Oh boy I miss it something fierce," he said, gazing at the floor. "That's why I like to hang around here. Milt don't seem to mind."

After a while, I cornered Milt beside the evaporator and started grilling him about how his season was going.

He adjusted a screw on the sap intake float box as he talked. "I had one pump run out of gas and it's in the middle of the woods in two feet of snow and I can't get to it," he said in his muffled voice. "We've been too busy anyways."

Milt told me he hauled approximately 10,000 gallons of sap this morning, roughly a third of the amount of sap Bert and I would probably get the entire season on Blossom Road.

He leaned back and stroked his beard. "I remember March 12, 1981, we had a sap run big as the one we've been havin' yesterday 'n' today—lasted three days straight and we all's were drinkin' pot after pot of the coffee justa keep up," Milt said in monotone. "Course we were on sap buckets then and they were's all spilling over the brim by time we got to 'em, elsa we'd've had even more sap and we'd've probably been boilin' for four days straight."

Then I did something stupid. I got in his way.

We were pinned in a narrow corridor between the draw-off station and the wall, and without realizing it, I had been blocking the draw-off pipe while Milt told his anecdote. I also blocked Milt's sightline to the temperature gauge, and he was too polite to tell me to get the hell out of the way. In an instant, the sap temperature shot up to 223°F, probably 4°F above proper density. The sap bubbles in the pan changed texture, turning heavy and umber.

Scorching.

Milt's face abruptly turned serious. He quickly reached above his head and smacked a red-button emergency kill switch.

The evaporator shut off, and all the old men turned to us with puzzled faces.

"Ooopsy," Milt said.

Milt didn't scorch beyond the point of no return but came pretty damn close, thanks to me. In fact, the syrup didn't even thicken up that much. He'd stopped it just in time. If we'd been boiling on my wood-fired evaporator, there'd be no way to instantly kill the heat like Milt was able to do with his rig.

"Nice thing about oil evaporators," Milt said loud enough so everyone could hear, "slap a button and it quits." The old men looked at each other and nodded.

I felt terrible. I apologized to Milt profusely for distracting him, and he shrugged it off.

"Aw, nothin' to get too worked up about," he said.

Milt reflooded the front pan with fresh, cold sap, he hit another button, and the rig fired right back up again. About ten minutes later he returned to boiling at the velocity he was at before.

I got out of there with a succession of more apologies and hurried back to Blossom Road.

"I've overstayed my welcome," I said, tipping my hat. "Good luck the rest of the way."

Milt wouldn't let me leave so quickly, though. "Hold on," he said.

He grabbed a plastic bag full of Dixie cups and filled one with some hot syrup, then handed it to me. "Tell me what you think," he said, with an anticipatory look.

I took a sip, gave it a second to register with my taste buds, and then took another.

"Well, it doesn't taste burnt, if that's what you're worried about," I said.

That night, Bert and I filled another barrel and a half. Altogether, a five-hour boil or so. After we shut down the evaporator, Bert got busy cleaning tanks again, his specialty around here. He keeps them as clean as he does Red Beauty. He's fastidious with washing, which is a good thing since we're making a food product. Bert insisted on scouring the 150-gallon head tank, which is where we hold the concentrate to feed into the evaporator. It sits on a ledge inside the sugarhouse about ten feet over our heads, supported by 2x8 Hemlock trusses. To access it, Bert had to clamber high on a ladder with a pail of hot water and a scrub brush. Him being up there was like King Kong clinging to the Empire State Building. I stood below and held the ladder for him. Although if he fell, I'm not sure I'd be much use, I told him.

"I'll catch you on the first bounce," I said.

Meanwhile, I kept a tidy sugarhouse, another practice I learned from Rascher. He was a neat freak and liked everything in its proper place and would shriek at anyone who disturbed the orderliness of his workspace. I'm the same way. Not the hollering, but the obsessive-compulsive. I have all my tools—wrenches, hammers, pipe cutters, scoops, snips, ladles, brushes, hatchets—hanging on a row of nail hooks on the wall, ordered by size. Arranged alongside the evaporator I've neatly positioned lots of colorful old milk crates—collected from various dairies that have gone out of business around New England; I love them like I love Grimm tanks. They make handy resting places for pails, hydrometer cups, and the gloves that I'm always putting on and taking off, things like that. To keep the outside of the pans mirror-shined, I smear on Bar Keepers Friend with *Karate Kid* "wax on, wax off" hand circles and then wipe it off with a specialized cellulose spongecloth that the dairy farmers use to clean udders. The concrete floor of the sugarhouse is also immaculate. If I spill some syrup, or if we track in mud from the Western Front, I'll take a pail of the residual hot condensation water and slosh it across.

I was doing exactly that when suddenly there was a cry from Bert.

"Holy fuckannoli! Look at the vacuum," he shouted from outside.

I ran over, peered at the gauge, and did a double take. The vacuum had dropped to 13, less than half of what it should be. Bert tapped at the dial, thinking maybe it was stuck.

"Something major happened up there," he said, thumbing toward the woods.

I agreed. "Spout blew out of a tree, I bet," I said. "One of us better go check. I nominate you."

"Negatory," he said. "I'm staying right here. I hav'ta run a long rinse cycle on the RO."

I looked up toward the mountain. "I guess that leaves me then."

I'd never gone into the woods at night before. Too chicken. Grown-ass man afraid of the dark. Lots of the big Five Pounders in Fairfield perform nighttime leak checks wearing headlamps and then post about it on Facebook. Right now, hunting for that leak up on Blossom Hill was the last thing I wanted to do. But the situation demanded it. A Five Pounderian move.

I had a couple things in my favor. There was snowpack and it was mostly crusty, conditions like that big tapping day I enjoyed six weeks earlier. So, I'd have good footing up there. The other thing was the moon—it was a full one. (The full moon in March is often called the Sugar Moon.) It would maybe offer comfort like a night-light in a bedroom. I collected up some gear and felt my pulse quicken.

Before I left, I unscrewed the lid on the jar of pickled eggs sitting in a snack cubby. I rolled up a sleeve, immersed my arm deep in the brine, and snatched one of the slippery little suckers. Then I popped it, whole, in my mouth, and Bert gave me a look.

"Last supper," I said with an eye roll on my way out the door.

I marched to the top of the field above the sugarhouse then paused and squeezed the walkie-talkie. "If I'm not back in an hour, send a rescue party. Over."

Bert radioed back. "Watch out for coyotes, old buddy. Over," he said.

That, I did not need reminding of. It was top of mind. I'd armed myself with a hatchet, which I wedged through my belt loop, and a tapping hammer on a lanyard around my neck.

I took a deep breath and stepped into the forest.

Up I went.

The higher I got, the more on alert I became for coyotes.

At first, I was spooked, the moon was casting ghostly shadows onto the snow. I hummed a few bars of "Moonlight in Vermont" to settle myself down and held a tense grip on the hatchet handle. I didn't see any paw prints in the snow, so that helped ease my mind. Also reassuring, it was a tranquil night. No wind to blow a dead ash onto my skull.

I kept getting clotheslined by filament runs of tubing, which I could barely see despite the luminosity. I stuck my hands out in front of me as I went along. I should've worn safety glasses because I got poked by the damn beech trees a couple times and some saplings snapped back at my face.

About halfway up, I turned around and, in the distance, I could see the pattern of the ski runs at West Mountain, a resort way over in Queensbury, lit up for night skiing. It was a solid forty miles away, but from here it looked close enough to throw a football at it.

For a while, as I tromped, I could still hear Bert clattering around. But the noise dissipated the deeper into the woods I went.

As I neared the crest of the mountain, I cupped my ear trying to detect that blown tap. It turned out there were two of them, hissing at the very top of the line. They were both on the opposite side of the tree from the moonglow, so I had to feel around the trunk braille-like to find the hole they popped out of. I knocked the spouts back in with the mallet, nice and tight.

And then, silence.

I leaned against a tree.

All I could hear was my heartbeat rapidly vibrating in my eardrum and some tinnitus left over from the dad band days. I let myself enjoy the moment.

Zen.

I was at a vantage where I could look down on the scatter of houses in Rupert Valley, wash-lit like holograms by the moon, yellow wattage blushing through the tic-tac-toe-paned windows. Inside, West Ruperters were, who knows? Maybe folding laundry, watching puzzle shows, loading the dishwasher—living lives of domestic routine while I eavesdropped in the peace from half a mile above.

After a minute or two, I started walking back to the sugarhouse, my boots smashing the snow like a Styrofoam cup.

Then, klutz, I tripped over an exposed root branch. "AAUGH!" I contorted midair and landed on my back in a deep pile of snow, *whump*, like a flop onto a pole vault mat.

But instead of getting back up, for some reason I decided to lie there, and I stared up through the spiraling trees. Their craggy branches, backlit by the moon, looked like the meandering squiggles of alveoli and capillaries on a cardiovascular X-ray.

Must've been ten minutes, I just gazed at the maples.

It looked like they were breathing.

In and out. Expanding and contracting like enormous lungs.

Holy shit, these trees really are alive, I thought to myself.

This turned out to be just the communion with nature I needed. I'd been too focused lately on production, on the five pounds, on the exploitation of these *creatures*, the trees.

I swear I could feel their energy, I told Bert later.

After a while, my backside turned numb from the snow icing up underneath me.

I reached for my radio. "Found the blown spouts. Over," I squawked to Bert.

His reply pierced the air. "Copy that. Vacuum gauge back up to twenty-six and climbing. Good job. Glad you didn't end up as coyote kibble. Over."

I got up, brushed the snow off my fleece, and made my way back down the hill through the night.

THE FIRST WEEK
OF APRIL 2022

33

THE GRIND

One late winter day, a few years after the end of my unofficial apprenticeship with Rascher—and after I had started my own operation in
earnest—Rascher chewed out his only helper and right-hand man, a guy
named Monte. I had witnessed Rascher berate poor Monte countless times
over the years, and on this day, for some reason, the dude finally up and
quit. I had always wondered why Monte hadn't done it sooner. Rascher
was too old by that point to try to run his entire operation alone. And he
had perhaps alienated himself from so many folks in town that it would've
been impossible to find someone to take Monte's place at the last minute.
It wasn't going to be me, that's for sure. In Rascher's eyes, I was too much
of a newbie and a flatlander to be any help. It was March and the season
was right on top of him, and when the weather broke, Rascher didn't have
a single one of his maples tapped or any of his tanks set out—the sap fixing
to run like a grape ape, and he was going to lose it all.

Later that day, Rascher called me in great despair. I guess maybe I was
the only shoulder he could cry on.

"What the hell am I going to do now?" he said between sniffs.

The mighty Rascher, his sugaring career finished.

That's what a maple season can do to people.

Most sugarmakers call it the Grind, the last days of the season when every cell of your body is screaming, *Give it up already!* We'd boiled more than 20,000 gallons of sap into 300 gallons of maple syrup for the season, enough to fill a hot tub. The trees hung on through the no-freeze spell that Bob Chambers and I were worried about—the buds stayed tight—and after that we got a weeklong stretch of perfect sugaring weather again.

I entered a heart of darkness. Maple every day, climbing Blossom Hill, chasing leaks, fixing broke stuff, hefting barrels around, checking tanks, obsessing about the weather, hooking up the RO, unhooking the RO, chipping ice, slogging through the Western Front, splitting firewood, all while buzzing on syrup and Sprites, sweating away at the conn.

But things were changing. The sugar content in the sap was beginning to weaken, and the syrup was starting to darken and change flavor:

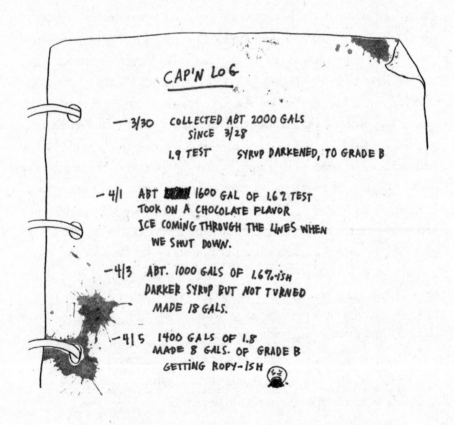

CAP'N LOG

— 3/30   COLLECTED ABT 2000 GALS
           SINCE 3/28
         1.9 TEST   SYRUP DARKENED, TO GRADE B

— 4/1   ABT 1600 GAL OF 1.6% TEST
        TOOK ON A CHOCOLATE FLAVOR
        ICE COMING THROUGH THE LINES WHEN
        WE SHUT DOWN.

— 4/3   ABT. 1000 GALS OF 1.6%-ISH
        DARKER SYRUP BUT NOT TURNED
        MADE 18 GALS.

— 4/5   1400 GALS OF 1.8
        MADE 8 GALS. OF GRADE B
        GETTING ROPY-ISH

One morning, I dashed up to Pratt's Farm Supply in Tinmouth, Vermont. Whitey Pratt, the father, and Ethan Pratt, the son, run the store, where they mostly sell dairy supplies, but also carry a good selection of sugarmaking supplies. They're big into sugaring themselves and have some 8,500 taps. They boil inside a cathedral-like timber-framed sugarhouse a few miles from the store. Ethan is assigned duty to the sugarwoods, keeping the lines tight and the vacuum high, and he also hauls all the sap, while Whitey stays in the sugarhouse and boils it.

Ethan, in his early thirties, is also a journeyman tubing installer. He's done much of the pipeline installation in our sugarbush, and he's the one who masterfully plumbed in our new releaser. He's a maniac in the woods, running lengths of one-inch mainline with a lit cigarette dangling out of his mouth. He usually brings another wooly dude with him to help on the install jobs, and together they can pull wire and hang pipe through the woods like nobody's business.

I was there at Pratt's to pick up some liquid acid detergent they had set aside for me. In this last stage of the sugaring season, something called *nitre* builds up as a hard mineral scale on the surface of the front pan. It's important to remove scale or you can scorch. I'd already scorched once this season and would never be able to live it down if I scorched *twice*.

The only effective way of removing scale is with phosphoric acid. Some say vinegar works, but only if you soak your pan with it for a month.

The Pratts are sharp-featured men, and on this day, both were looking haggard. Hair was falling over their ears, and they carried heavy beard weight on their chins.

Ethan wore a North Face puffer with ripped sleeves that he had patched with a weave of duct tape, and it was sheeting off and flapping around. Whitey was wearing a well-worn hoodie and syrup-crusted jeans, with spectacles pinched to the peak of his nose.

I loitered around the evaporator, trying not to get in their way like I had with Milt the other day. Whitey was drawing off syrup into a container the size of a laundry bin.

Ethan stepped inside, returning with a truckload full of sap, guzzled into a 1,000-gallon poly tank strapped onto a flatbed dually. "How much you bring in?" Whitey shouted across the room to his son.

"Oh, I filled it again," Ethan shouted back. "You just keep boilin', old feller."

Ethan turned to me. "I think that's my 300th trip this season."

He threw a lever to drain the sap into a tank inside the sugarhouse. "So that's 300,000 gallons of sap I've hauled," he said, astonishing himself as much as me.

"Three hundred thousand. Jesus," I said.

He wiped his brow with his sleeve. "The thing with maple is, this time of year you're pinned to it," he said. Then he fished around in his jacket for his pack of cigarettes and shook one out.

He asked me how my season was going. "You at five pounds yet?" he said.

I put my hands in my pockets. "Getting there. My vacuum's been at 27," I said.

His eyes went wide. "Shit, ya crazy bastard, nice job."

I rubbed the back of my neck. "I'm tired as hell though, holy cripes," I said.

He struck a match on the wall to light his cigarette, took a drag, and exhaled. "We've had sap every day for six days straight."

He peeked his head outside to check on the progress of the emptying sap. "The last two weeks of a season are the hardest syrup you're ever going to make," he said and took another drag. "But dude, you just gotta keep pounding it," and he blew the smoke through his nostrils.

The forecast was calling for a hard freeze to start that night, with temps dropping into the mid-teens for a couple days. Ethan noted that this would give us all a break from the sap and provide one last reset for the trees, who'd be tricked into thinking it was winter for just a little while longer.

Ethan leaned against the doorjamb. "Not gonna lie, I'll enjoy a few days off," he said.

The cold snap came and went, and we hit the part of the season when the trees lose their ability to buttress against the tilting of the earth and the angle of the sun, which apexes higher and higher in the sky as April becomes sovereign. When that happens, even a day in the thirties can feel like a day in the sixties or seventies to a tree, with the sunlight cooking its bark all day.

The season would be over any day now, I was certain.

I soaked the front pan overnight in the scarlet-colored acid that I brought home from Pratt's. The pans shined right up, and it revealed where I'd scorched back in February like a relief map, with two channels completely warped and rippled. Corrosive liquids can be dangerous if not handled properly. I was so groggy, I splashed acid down my boot and felt it burn through my sock and into my skin, like a beesting.

The part that sucks about using acid is removing it. For this, I wore goggles and the oil-hauler gloves. I drained the acid into a handling pail and, trying not to spill again, gingerly walked it out of the sugarhouse to the middle of Blossom Road, where I carefully poured it out in the dirt. Back inside, I dumped baking soda into the pan, which neutralized any leftover acid, and then rinsed the hell out of it.

We hit another stretch where we were collecting and boiling almost every day, an extraordinary final run of sap across New England and as far as the Upper Midwest. Producers were blowing up social media with photos and videos of full loads of sap on the backs of their trucks and sap gushing into releasers and dumping into tanks like a levee break.

My body was beat up. Every muscle was sore. During my nightly mirror check, I noticed my arms were covered with bruises and scalds. My hands crowded with slices and cuts. My eyesight was a lens of haze from staring intently through columns of steam at monitors and gauges day after day, night after night. On the scale, my weight was up seven pounds, despite the daily calisthenics of going up Blossom Hill chasing leaks. The flab was probably the result of sampling syrup every ten minutes and stress-eating junk food the rest of the time. And my back, oy. Already compromised from years of playing football back in Mound (lineman, pulling guard), my poor spine, in protest of the constant uprightness in front of the evaporator, sent punishments to my pain receptors with the aggravating repetition of a robocall.

One day, while I was on yet another leak-checking maneuver, I reached for a lone outlier tree that stood on the edge of a jagged slate outcropping. I slipped and landed shin-first on a chunk of rock. I tried to keep going and pretend I wasn't injured but my jeans said otherwise. Blood soaked through the fabric, and my leg began to swell. Forty-five minutes later, it looked like someone had shoved a mango up my pants. It took weeks for the swelling to subside. As I write this, there's still a purplish, raised blotch on my shin about the size of a flared leech.

One Tuesday evening, we got a miserly amount of sap, just barely enough to flood the pans and boil it. "Look at this pishy ca-ca," I whined to Bert. It would be a short in and out kind of night. The syrup was darkening.

Bert and I fell into our routines. Me boiling, hauling in firewood from the woodshed; he monitoring the sap and minding the RO machine. Scrubbing the tanks as they emptied.

During a quiet moment, I brought up something that had been on my mind.

"So you know how we're always talking about wars and shit?"

He turned to look at me through the gray vapor in the room. "Yeah?"

"I think I read all those books and watch all those damn war movies because I always wonder how I'd do if it were me in all those fights," I said.

He leaned against a wall. "Hmmm."

"The older I get, the more obsessed about it I get. Like in the past six months, I think I've read six or seven books just on the Pacific Theatre alone. Hand-to-hand combat, prison camps, disease, beatings, ships sinking in shark-infested waters, flame throwers, kamikazes. Every challenge, I wonder how I'd do?"

He walked over to the filter press and started breaking it down, taking the plates out of the machine and soaking them in hot water to get the crud off them.

"Yeah, I hear ya. I do the same thing," he said. "Gen Xers of a certain age. Never been tested. Maybe the only generation in American history."

I threw some logs into the arch. "So, the only man in my family ever to fight in any war was my great-grandpa R.L.," I said. "He was in World War I in all the major battles. Poor R.L. was gassed twice. Once with mustard gas and the other with phosgene gas. *Phosgene gas.* Imagine a canister of something called phosgene gas landing in your foxhole? It messed him up pretty good, that stuff—his lungs. He still smoked unfiltered cigarettes until the day he died, though. Hand-rolled. When I was a kid, he'd come to visit from Florida and he'd let me roll 'em for him. Bugler tobacco. Came in an aqua-blue tin can. I think that's the tobacco brand they gave all the doughboys over there and he stuck with it right to the end."

"Yeah, in World War II they gave 'em Lucky Strikes," Bert said.

I checked the sight-level gauge on the side of the rig. "Grandpa had this rolling machine with a belt thingamabob and a handle that you'd *cha-schink*, and a rolled cigarette would appear in the cloth pocket. I thought it was the coolest thing in the world when I was nine. That machine went with him everywhere. He'd unpack it from his suitcase and plunk it on the kitchen counter. He lived to be eighty-something, even with those lungs."

"Man, those men then were *men*," Bert said.

The temperature gauge needled at 219. I turned the gate on the draw-off valve and dispensed a few gallons of fashioned syrup into a pail. "I would've done okay maybe?" I asked him. "Lots of beshitting of my uniform, but I'd like to think I would've stepped up."

Bert chuckled. "You mean you wouldn't be the guy in those movies who cowers in a corner and can't pull the trigger of his M16 with a German standing right in front of him?"

I nodded forcefully. "Yeah, or the sorry bastard who cringes in the foxhole while a German stabs his buddy with a bayonet," I said. "Yeah, I hope I wouldn't've been that guy."

"We'll never know."

I turned to him. "What do you think?"

"What do I think about what?"

"How do you think I'd do in a battle?" I asked.

Bert thought for a moment. "I think you'd be the guy who reports to basic with a copy of *Leaves of Grass* in your pocket," he said. "They'd maybe call you 'soft' or 'college boy' at first. But by the end, you're a badass mother-fucker who kills the most Germans in the unit."

I smiled. "And have war paint on my face with the blood of dead Nazis and shit?"

He laughed. "Hell yeah. How about me?"

"You? I think they'd make you the general," I said.

Bert laughed again. "I'd be happier as the cook."

Things were about to get down and dirty in the sugarhouse. Sap changes in its molecular makeup as the trees start budding. In these end days, sap begins to turn yellow and cloudy in the tank, and the syrup exiting the draw-off spigot becomes a stringy slime. Bascom calls it "commercial" syrup or Grade C (though I would give it an F). Sugarmakers call it "rope." Long strands of this syrup will dangle from your draw-off valve like a yo-yo string. It's a nightmare to boil. It jumps around in the pan and goes up and down in temperature. Nasty, ridiculous stuff, with a sour, awful taste to boot. Many sugarmakers persist in boiling this ooblek and then put it in a drum. And there's a market for it, too. It's mostly used for dog food or industrial lubricants. Bascom's pays seventy-five cents per pound for commercial-grade syrup. Bert and I hoped to goose our season tally by going until the very bitter end, boiling this seep. It would still count in our production tally to reach the five-pound goal.

"I say we keep going even if we start making rope," Bert said.

I agreed. "It's our only chance," I said.

I turned onto Blossom Road one April morning and saw that Truman's taps were pulled, droplines dangling from the trees and spouts snipped off. I met him as he was walking up the lane. He had a spout-pulling prybar in his hand. I rolled down the window.

"You're . . . done?" I asked.

He sighed. "Yeah, we hit rope on Saturday night," he said, and he made a raspberry. "That was that. We never make any of that garbage."

I felt a pang of shame since Bert and I were planning on doing exactly that. Truman told me their final tally for the season was 3,400 gallons, enough to fill an above-ground swimming pool.

"*Truman hit the rope*," I texted Bert.

"*Holy shit*," he replied.

I had a half-full tank of sap to boil. I started the RO and spun back around and headed back to Sherman's to get a sandwich. I stopped in on the McClellans and they were boiling.

"Yeah, we're still in here," Archie said wearily. He looked worn out and drained, his cap askew. He was drawing off syrup into a series of pails. Walter was stationed at the filter press machine.

I asked the brothers if they were going to keep hanging on.

"We're still making good syrup, but just barely," Walter said. "It's filtering hard. You gotta put the filter aid right to it."

He handed me a Dixie cup of syrup they made the night before. He was right, it was still pretty good, but I could taste just a little bit of the end of the season in it. A hint of sour.

"Tastes a little tinny, don't it?" Walter said. "You sip it and think you're drinking good syrup and then it nips you at the end of your tongue with that 'ting'."

Despite the ting, we both agreed it was still Grade A, but on the cusp.

The brothers said they had made more than 5,000 gallons for the season, breaking their old record by a lot. That would tally to about $137,000 worth of syrup at Bascom's.

I told Archie the peepers were still quiet on my end of Blossom Road. We talked about Truman shutting down. He waved a dismissive hand at me. "Yeah, we heard," Archie said. "Remember his woods face south. His season starts earlier and ends earlier because the sun hits him first."

Back at the sugarhouse that night, Bert and I boiled and filled another barrel, and it was still okay syrup. It was a dark grade on the edge of medium. We went over 340 gallons that night, making this our best season ever, but we were still a ways from five pounds per tap.

"Remember all our woods face west and north and all Truman's woods face south and east," Bert said, echoing Archie. "I say we have at least a week to go."

But it turned out to be our final boil.

At 4:53 P.M. on Tuesday, April 12, we called it a season. Everyone and everything was exhausted. I was exhausted, Bert was exhausted, the pump was exhausted, the RO was exhausted. And probably more than any of us, the trees were exhausted.

I'd been getting ready to boil again, in blind obedience to the five pounds goal despite the brackish, slimy sap oozing from the pipeline into the Fitzy, on whose cloudy surface the moths had organized a synchronized swimming competition.

In the yard, I was trying to prop up a small log against a tree stump so I could split off strips of kindling and get another fire started. But whenever I brought down the hatchet, the log would topple over. "Hold still, dammit." After three or four tries, I got fed up, flung the ax into a nearby tree, and collapsed my ass onto the stump.

I think I'm done, I said to myself.

The log that broke the camel's back.

Sometimes it's the tiniest little thing that ultimately does you in.

Just like a blown O-ring.

Bert pulled in a few minutes later. He got out of his truck and surveyed the unsplit log and the flung hatchet, which had toed into the tree. He glanced at me unfolded on the stump.

"Yo," he said, and saluted.

I saluted back, feebly bringing a hand to my forehead. "Yo," I said.

He walked around to the tank and looked in, then came back over, shaking his head.

"So, I see you sitting here on this stump, and I see that tank full of schmutz back there. But I don't see any steam coming out of the roof, so I'm thinking maybe things didn't go according to plan?"

I put my face in my hands. "I don't think I can go any further," I said. *"Ack, ack, ack.* Like the drill."

"Hmm, well, every man has a breaking point," he said.

I looked up at him. "But if we stop today, no five pounds."

He pondered that for a moment in his bureaucratic Bert way. Then he reached back into Red Beauty, grabbed a Thermos of coffee for himself, and handed me a Sprite.

"It's up to you, man," he said.

I really couldn't decide, I was so spent.

"Why the hell are we killing ourselves like this anyway?" I said, exasperated.

He slowly unscrewed the steel cap on the Thermos and poured some coffee into it.

Then he met eyes with me. "Wanna know why?" he said. "Wanna know why I—why *we*—do all this? I tell ya, it ain't for the pancakes."

I slapped at a mosquito on my neck. "Then why? Because at times like this, I really gotta wonder."

He dropped the tailgate on Red Beauty and sat down with his cup.

"Lemme tell you a story about my dad," he said. "Couple weeks ago, Dad had some branches he wanted to prune on a big apple tree in his front yard. So, does he call a tree service? Nope. Does he go out and buy a proper pruning saw, you know, like one of those telescoping kinds they sell at the Home frigging Depot? Nope. I stop over, and I find him standing on the top rung of a stepladder—eighty-five years old—and what he's done is he's duct-taped a Sawzall to a broomstick and he's on his tippy toes on the ladder pruning the branches with this contraption shoved way high in the air, about to goddamned kill himself."

We both laughed.

Bert put his hands on his knees and leaned forward. "Okay, here's the thing, so maybe we don't hit the five-pounds mark, but I think we'd both agree we tried as hard as we frigging could to get as much sap as we could. We got up on the ladder, stood on our tippy toes, and reached for that highest branch. And as a result, you and me got nine or ten barrels of some pretty goddamned good tasting maple syrup and an excuse to fart around in the woods together for three and a half months. Not a bad deal."

He sipped, then continued. "Yeah sure, we joke about the syrup, that we can buy the shit in a store. But a lot more fun making it ourselves—proving we can make it ourselves. Together. That's why we're doing this. It's the trying. Put another way, we're doing this because the *opposite* of this, is . . . well, sittin' alone in a recliner somewhere, and dying."

He let that float in the air a minute.

I outstretched my arm. "Help me up, will ya?"

Bert walked over, grasped my hand, and pulled me to my feet.

"That's some pretty heavy shit for a Tuesday," I said.

And then Mother Nature, in all her impossible-to-predict perfection, and as a coda to Bert's curtain speech, stepped in and got the final vote on whether to keep pushing or not.

From the pond across the way, the peepers, hundreds of them, the males, in their annual chorus call to attract the females, at once, gloriously, broke into a magnificent high-pitched symphony of whistling, amplified by their ballooning rubbery throats.

Spring had arrived on Blossom Road.

It was the end of the sugar rush.

Our absurd struggle was over.

EPILOGUE
OFF-SEASON 2022

On a Sunday morning in late April, I slept in—maybe the first Sunday since December I didn't have to tear ass up to the sugarhouse for one reason or another. I putzed around the house in my sock feet and robe, then cozied up at the table with a cup of coffee and the *Times*. The cat jumped in my lap, kneaded her claws into my thigh, and started to purr. She'd barely seen me in months.

Outside, spring was in full bloom. Blue jays scampered on my roof, dipping their beaks into the gutters searching for bugs in the leaf clogs left over from autumn. A few crocuses popped up through the lawn. The hydrangeas in the yard were beginning to mist green.

In the kitchen I mixed up a family pancake recipe—one cup flour, one cup whole milk, a few tablespoons of olive oil, one jumbo brown egg, a teaspoon and a half of baking powder, and a half teaspoon of baking soda, all whisked together and splashed with vanilla extract. I pan-fried a five-story stack. From the pantry, I pulled out a Mason jar of syrup from my private reserve and poured some onto the pile. The French call it the Maillard reaction—the chemical harmony of amino acids and reducing sugars that gives browned foods like maple syrup their distinctive flavor. Whatever it was, it was some amazingly good-tasting stuff. But, of course, I'm biased.

In the end, we didn't hit five pounds per tap, but came close. After we pried out and inventoried every spout and tallied the day-by-day production totals scribbled on the sugarhouse wall, we ran the calculations, and it came out to an average of about 4.4 pounds of syrup per tap. Respectable. In terms of gallons produced, it was the most Bert and I ever made in one season. Had we boiled that tankful of milky slime into rope on that last day when I collapsed on the stump, we maybe could have goosed the totals higher. But I was glad we didn't.

For the McClellans, and for the Dunns, for Kevin and Bob over at Dry Brook, and for the entire maple industry really, the trees gushed sap like never before. The 2022 U.S. maple syrup crop was the largest in history—2.2 million gallons, according to the USDA, with 340 gallons of that coming out of our sugarhouse on Blossom Road.

Uncle Bruce indeed raised his prices on field-run bulk syrup for the first time in many years, to about $2.65 per pound. Of course, some sugarmakers grumbled it should've been more. For our 340 gallons, Bert and I pocketed some $10,000 of tax-free New Hampshire cash, after we trucked our barrels over to Bascom's in the back of Red Beauty.

With the season over, I had all kinds of time to catch up on laundry, get a haircut, and return some overdue library books. I called Heather at the dermatologist's office and had her rebook my appointment to carve that piece of cancer from my back.

One morning, I drove to New York and met my son and daughter for breakfast at a favorite diner on the Upper East Side. My tanned son, who was visiting from LA, had the "Lumberjack Special" with eggs and bacon and a short stack of pancakes, but the restaurant didn't have any real maple syrup to pour over it. "We should bring some of ours next time," he said. That prompted my enterprising daughter to say, "Dad, why don't we start selling our syrup in the city?" which got my brain churning that maybe I should try my hand at bottling again. My equally enterprising son offered to bring some syrup back to the West Coast. "Yeah dad, they'd love it in California, too."

I shipped jars of syrup out to the Minnesotans: my mother, my father and stepmom, my sister and her walleye-catching husband, and another jar to my syrup-loving nephew who's in college up in North Dakota. I UPSed a final one to my childhood bestie back in Mound. Later, I drove up the street and dropped off a jar to some family friends who have a brave twelve-year-old with juvenile diabetes, so he can only eat our syrup one teaspoon at a time. (Pure maple syrup has a lower glycemic index than "pancake syrup," and it's considered by some to be better for people with diabetes.)

In May, I pulled up at the sugarhouse, and a one-ton pickup was backed in the driveway. It was a meter reader for the light company. I chatted with him for a moment, then had a sudden realization. "Any chance you were parked here in early March when the driveway was super muddy?" He chuckled. "Oh yeah, I remember," the dude said. "My truck sank right into it. I slid all over getting out of here." My suspected sap stealer. Mystery solved. I told Bert about it later.

"*See*, Mr. Paranoid?" he said.

One morning in June I ran into Truman at Sherman's Store. "Have you looked at the trees lately?" he said. "It's the best I've ever seen them look." I agreed. The maples on Blossom Hill were already lush and green, hopefully photosynthesizing like crazy, filling themselves with next season's sugar. Stepping through the underbrush one afternoon, I found a bright orange *eft*, which is a young Eastern (red-spotted) newt, known to be a reliable indicator of a healthy forest.

Bert and Faith spent much of their summer with realtors, going on tours of land parcels for sale in our area, trying to find more woods for us to tap and maybe scuttle a school bus. I bet they looked at ten different properties, but of course Bert couldn't decide on any of them.

I went back to H.N. Williams in Dorset and bought those goatskin gloves made by the Vermont Glove Company that I regretted not buying back in March. They've been worth every penny of the hundred bucks I paid, and I keep them in a Ziploc to thwart the mice.

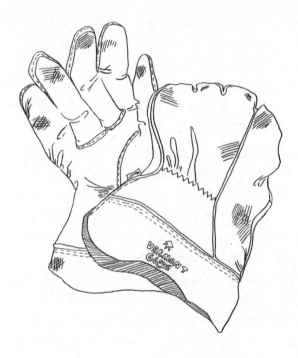

In July, my sister and brother-in-law came to visit—dyed-in-the-wool Minnesotans. "How's the fishing around here?" my brother-in-law asked. He's as handy and skilled with tools and equipment as Bert, and he's reformed my sister of her suburban naiveté much like Bert has done for me. At one point, I complained about my moody Stihl, and my sister roasted me. "Well, have you cleaned out the carburetor lately, or drained out the old gas from the winter?"

In August, I entered our syrup in the judging contest at the Washington County Fair. Incredibly, we won Best in Show with the Butter. Not bad for a couple of flatlanders. They awarded us a gigantic purple rosette.

After taking the summer off, Bert and I returned to the sugarhouse in mid-September, and over a succession of autumn Sunday mornings, as the leaves on the maples progressively vivified and fell, we hiked back into the woods to snip off the old spouts and clear branches off the lines with our chainsaws for next season. As of this writing, I still have all my limbs.

In October, I saw Shakey for the first time since maple season ended. We were gathered at a fish fry in the parking lot of Yushak's. "Got something for ya," he said, and he trotted to his truck. He dug around in the backseat and came back with a box, gift wrapped with the funny pages from the Sunday *Rutland Herald*. "I was hoping I'd see you today," he said. I gave him a WTF look. "Go ahead, open it," he said. I peeled the paper away. Inside was the red firewood lightbulb and its circuit box. He smiled. "Every time it goes off, I want you to think of me downing another Mai Tai on a beach somewheres."

In early December we got a freak Nor'easter that dumped two feet of snow, a storm they called "Sage." In West Rupert, I came upon a GMC buried in a long driveway, spinning its tires. Archie McClellan. I couldn't believe it. "*You're* stuck?" He was clearly embarrassed. "I couldn't find the edge of the damn driveway," he said. "You got that chain on ya?" I never thought I'd have an opportunity to repay a favor to Archie. "Is it opposite day?" I said, smirking a little, and he looked at me. "Yeah, yeah. Save the commentary," and he hocked some chew spit. The torquey Tundra yanked him out handily.

On a Sunday morning around Christmas, Bert and I went back to that lakeside diner for breakfast and strategized the upcoming 2023 season. Bert ordered the left side of the menu.

"I'd like to just have a nice, easy, smooth season for once," he said, and I laughed.

"C'mon, man. Don't we know by now there's no such thing in this business," I said.

Then I borrowed a ballpoint from the waitress, scribbled something on a napkin, and slid it across the table to Bert. "Five Pounders or bust!" and he rolled his eyes.

I clapped my hands together. "What the hell, let's go for it, buddy," I said. "Now that I know how to operate that damn drill properly, we just might have a chance."

ACKNOWLEDGMENTS

Grateful for the infinite counsel of my son and daughter, Bruce and Annabel, writers both, and my family back on the lake in Minnesota: Judy, Owen and Kay, Julie and Pete, and Josh Pounder up in Fargo. Deepfelt thanks to all who brought this book to print: my editor Paul Assimaco-poulos in Morningside Heights for his wizardry; my stellar agent Luba Ostashevsky and everyone at Ayesha Pande Literary; and my incredible publishing team at Pegasus Books, especially Jessica Case. And, artist Sarah Letteney in Burlington, VT, for her delightful spots. A very special thanks to the man known in these pages as Bert Jones and his wife, Faith. Shout out to the fellowship of maple people in the sugaring corridor of Hebron, NY, Salem, NY, West Rupert, VT, Sandgate, VT, Shushan, NY, Rupert, VT, Pawlet, VT, Granville, NY, and Greenwich, NY. Also, Gary and Katie Smith, Marc and Pam Kowalski, Donna, John and Rory Moore, Apple Jordan, Denny Schramek. R.I.P. Neil's Coffee Shop on 70th and Lex. where much of this book was written.